# LIGHT FROM A THOUSAND CAMPFIRES

---

## Improving Your Hiking, Backpacking and Camping Skills

FRED G. BAKER AND HANNAH PAVLIK

Bloomington, IN

authorHOUSE™

Milton Keynes, UK

*AuthorHouse™*
*1663 Liberty Drive, Suite 200*
*Bloomington, IN 47403*
*www.authorhouse.com*
*Phone: 1-800-839-8640*

*AuthorHouse™ UK Ltd.*
*500 Avebury Boulevard*
*Central Milton Keynes, MK9 2BE*
*www.authorhouse.co.uk*
*Phone: 08001974150*

*This book is a work of non-fiction. Unless otherwise noted, the author and the publisher make no explicit guarantees as to the accuracy of the information contained in this book and in some cases, names of people and places have been altered to protect their privacy.*

*First published by AuthorHouse 5/22/2006*

*ISBN: 1-4259-0867-5 (sc)*

*Library of Congress Control Number: 2006900493*

*Printed in the United States of America*
*Bloomington, Indiana*

*This book is printed on acid-free paper.*

# CONTENTS

# FOREWORD

The idea for this book came to us when we were sitting around a campfire in the wilderness of Colorado. We had returned from a day of reconnoitering the access to a peak that we wanted to climb, map and compass in hand, and had surprised a mountain goat napping in the sunshine just before lunch. While enjoying the warmth of the fire, we came to the sudden realization that we felt completely content and secure in this environment. No doubt, we thought, this was true because we had carefully planned the trip, packed all our favorite gear, knew more or less where we were going and what to expect. But why was it so easy to leave all our troubles behind, we asked? Because after years of hiking, camping and backpacking, through experience and trial and error, we had worked out a routine that made us feel completely comfortable exploring and enjoying nature. Then, while staring at the flames, we wondered how many fires we had made over the years in numerous places under various conditions and how each one varied slightly from the others. In some way, the campfires represented our net experience in outdoor living. And so the book was born. We would like to share the light from all those campfires with you, hoping that we can pass on the experiences we have learned so that you too can enjoy the outdoors as much as we do.

# CHAPTER 1       INTRODUCTION

There are many reasons why we enjoy the outdoors. Fresh air, sunlight, flowers, trees, animals, great views and secret places make it refreshing to be outside. A walk in the park, hiking a trail, camping near a lake, or climbing a mountain — all of these provide a sense of freedom and mobility that we cannot achieve indoors. People have many reasons and activities that lead them outdoors. They may be work, sports, hobbies, a sense of adventure and exploration, or just getting away from everyday life. Table 1 lists just a small sampling of the various activities we can do outdoors (Figure 1-1).

Figure 1-1. Summer backpacking is a great way to enjoy the outdoors

If you are reading this book, you might already have an interest in the outdoors and want to pursue certain activities or hobbies in nature. We will try to foster your interest by providing examples of how you can improve your basic hiking, camping and outdoor living skills. By teaching you how to walk, hike and camp safely and more efficiently, we hope that you will become more effective in your activities allowing you to enjoy them more. The sharper your outdoor skills are, the more you can accomplish, and therefore, the more predictable and pleasing your outdoor experience will become. This will reduce your worries and let you pursue your interests with increased confidence.

There are several books out on the market that cover specific sports such as skiing and hunting, but few that focus on general outdoor skills and activities. Some books written for select organizations only cover topics associated with a specific goal or type of activity, such as a merit badge or special certification. Many are so specialized that they apply only to specific seasons and geographic areas, or they tell you what equipment to buy but not why you should buy it. Some magazine articles and books present equipment comparisons but do not explain why certain features are important and others are not. Many authors tell you how they do things but not how you can select your own way of doing things or how to decide what equipment to buy.

In this book, we discuss the lost art of hiking and we explain the "how-and-why" of outdoor skills, methods and equipment. We show you how to do things and help you to make informed decisions about how and why you should consider doing them that way. Throughout the book, we try to keep the technical discussion at a reasonable level so that the text is readable.

The first four chapters of the book are reserved for general topics. Basic skills that you need for hiking are presented in Chapter 2. Included are tips on trip planning, setting goals, route selection, and the ten essential items that you should have with you on any hike. In Chapter 3 we introduce you to the art of walking and hiking, methods of efficient walking, exercise physiology and physical conditioning. The essence of camp organization and equipment needs are presented in Chapter 4, as well as common (and some uncommon) means of travel to the campsite.

Table 1. Activities people do outdoors

| | |
|---|---|
| Adventure/Exploration | Canoeing, caving, four-wheeling, hunting, kayaking, mountain climbing, orienteering, rock climbing, sailing. |
| Enjoyment/Getting Away | Enjoying nature, sightseeing, vacationing. |
| Hobbies | Animal watching, astronomy, bird watching, photography, plant collecting, rock collecting. |
| Sports | Boating, camping, cross-country skiing, downhill skiing, fishing, hiking, horseback riding, hunting, mountain bike riding, running, snowboarding, snowshoeing, swimming. |
| Work Related | Archaeology, construction, engineering, farming, geology, military, ranching, surveying, tourism, wildlife management. |

The next five chapters focus on more specialized subjects. Chapter 5 describes the construction, operation and essential features of outdoor clothing and equipment. Our objective is to teach you what to look for when you are ready to use or purchase pieces of equipment. Chapter 6 provides practical instruction on two essential outdoor skills, navigation and map reading. Chapter 7 explains how weather systems work and how to recognize changes in weather in the field. Chapter 8 introduces some basic First Aid methods for treatment of common outdoor injuries and illnesses. Lists of First Aid kits and supplies for small and large groups are also provided. Finally, Chapter 9 discusses several topics related to improving your enjoyment of the outdoors and sharing nature with other hikers and wildlife.

So why should you read this book? Because we hope that you will find it useful and informative. If you become more proficient in your outdoor activities or learn to enjoy them a little more than you did before seeing this book, then it has been worth your time reading it and our time writing it!

# CHAPTER 2                  HIKING BASICS

Walking is something that we all do to move about. Hiking is walking with a goal in mind and usually involves travel over some distance. Most people walk somewhere every day of their lives — around the house, to the store, to walk the dog, and so on. Most of these walking activities are not very demanding and we take them for granted. We don't generally have to prepare for short walking events. To prepare for longer walks or hikes, especially if we leave a paved sidewalk or roadway, we have to think about what we wear on our feet, how long we will be out walking, weather conditions and the route we will follow. If our hike takes us on a route that is new to us we might want to take a map with us and periodically check our directions. If it is a long hike, we might have to take food and drink along for lunch, and a raincoat in case the weather changes. The point is that the longer the hike, generally the more planning, time, equipment and skill go into it.

There are several factors that you should consider when you are going for a hike:

1) Goal and destination,
2) Route,
3) Weather,
4) How long it will take,
5) What to wear,
6) What to take along, and
7) Contingencies.

These form the basics of hiking because they familiarize us with the art of getting there. Although they are listed in the order in which they are generally considered, they are interdependent and a change in one often influences the others.

## 2.1    Setting Goals and Selecting Your Route

When we first decide to go for a hike we usually have some goal or destination in mind. It may be to walk to some favorite viewpoint or to look for wildflowers in the woods. It may be to hike along a stream or to reach a mountain top. It may be to get to a specific location or just to walk and enjoy the day. In all of these cases we have a general goal in mind, although a specific destination or location may not be decided on at the outset of the hike. A loosely defined goal may be acceptable for a short hike, but on longer hikes, the goal should be specifically defined at the outset so that you can plan for it and select a preferred route (Figure 2-1).

Figure 2-1. This hiking trail leads to a mountain pass

If you are hiking with other people, it is important to define the goal or destination in commonly understood terms to avoid conflicts during the hike. One person's idea of a short hike might be another's idea of a death march. Someone may want to walk at a fast pace to get exercise and another may want to go slowly to look at wildflowers. One person may want to reach a certain viewpoint and another may not really care to walk very far. All of these preferences should be briefly discussed before you set out on the hike so that some mutual goals can be established. If this is not done, some people may be disappointed because the resulting hike did not meet their goals and expectations.

It is important that you consider reasonable goals so that you have a good chance of succeeding with them. If it is early in the hiking season and you decide that you want to hike up a difficult trail to the top of a high peak, consider whether this goal is realistic for you this early in the year. You may need to be in better condition to succeed in such a venture and need more training to reach your goal. Also consider what is reasonable to expect given such factors as the weather, time of day, trail conditions and your hiking companions. Perhaps the trail conditions early in the season would make the planned hike very difficult due to deep snow or swollen streams. Under these conditions, some reconnoitering may be required before committing yourself and others to the trip goals.

Another reason to establish your goals at the outset of the hike is that you need to consider what to take with you. If you plan an all-day hike, you need to decide what clothes to wear and what extra items to carry with you. On a very short hike you may not need to be concerned with food and water, but on a long strenuous hike you will want to take water, snacks and maybe a lunch. As already mentioned, you will need to consider the weather and other factors that may potentially affect you during the hike and reduce your chances of success. You will also need to consider whether there is any chance that you may lose your way, in which case maps, compass and other pathfinding aids may be required. Depending on what resources you have available, you may need to reevaluate your goals to suit what is possible.

The upshot of all of this is that you need to establish a realistic goal for your hike, considering a number of factors before you start out to ensure a reasonable chance of success. On short hikes this may seem excessive but it is still worthwhile running through a quick mental checklist to be sure that you don't overlook something that may be important later. In many mountainous areas even a planned two-hour hike may encounter sudden changes in weather. The lack of a raincoat may turn a short outing into a miserable experience, so take the time to consider your goals and the other topics listed above.

Once a goal has been established, the next step is to select a route that allows you to achieve that goal. This sounds simple enough. If you are in a park or forest with established trails, several trails may provide acceptable routes to a given location. You need only to select a trail and after considering the remaining hiking factors, you can be on your way. In many cases, the route you take to a given point may become a part of your goal. For instance, you may decide to go to a waterfall via a trail along a river and to return by a different trail along a ridge. One goal here would be to see wildflowers in the valley and then get some nice landscape views from the ridge trail. But you may find out that there is still a lot of snow on the valley trail if you are early in the year, and that given your equipment, it may be advantageous to use the ridge route both ways. Or you may decide to proceed with the valley route but take along snowshoes and gaiters to better deal with the snow. If you don't have the right equipment, you may have to revise your choice of route (Figure 2-2).

Figure 2-2. The view is usually worth the hike

Many factors influence the choice of route:

- Familiarity with the route,
- Route difficulty or trail conditions,
- Ease of finding and following the route,
- Weather,
- Hazards such as rock fall, steep slope, water, animals, and
- Other goals along the way.

Usually the choice of route is affected to some extent by all of these factors. Having knowledge about a potential route before setting out helps you prepare for the hike with some level of confidence. Therefore, it is worthwhile to review maps, ask people that have been on the route recently, check weather reports, and read available descriptions about the route before making a final decision.

Familiarity with a route or trail eliminates much of the uncertainty about route selection. You may choose a route because you have been that way before, you know how to find it or how difficult it is. This can be a big advantage if you are hiking with others or have a limited amount of time in which to complete your hike. Knowing where the trail begins and being familiar with any branches from the trail can save you time and uncertainty about finding your way. If you are going off-trail through forest or hilly terrain, some prior knowledge about the route gives you more confidence in taking the right turns and avoiding obstacles or hazards such as cliffs, dense vegetation and difficult river crossings. It may also give you a good idea of trail conditions and what to expect in case of bad weather. In addition, familiarity may help you select some intermediate goals such as selecting a nice viewpoint as the location for your lunch break.

It is very important to have some knowledge of the difficulty of the route ahead and of trail conditions. If you are with a group of hikers of mixed abilities, this will help you to select a route that everyone in the group can be comfortable with. Making the potential difficulties of the planned route known ahead of time lets each person know what he or she will encounter, so that they can be prepared for the effort.

This is similar to making clear to the group what the goals of the hike are before setting out. Frequently, when you inform people about the expected difficulty of the route, you find out that someone in your group may not feel up to that level of difficulty. This is true of trail conditions as well. If steep snow is expected along the route you may need to verify that everyone in the group is prepared for this condition. You don't want to risk injury or have to turn back because someone is physically or psychologically unprepared for a steep snow slope. If you are leading the hike, it is your responsibility to learn as much as possible about route difficulty and trail conditions so that there are no big surprises for your fellow hikers. If the level of difficulty of the hike is too severe, you may need to revise your goals and/or select another more feasible route.

There are many ways to learn about route difficulty and trail conditions before arriving at the trailhead. If you are planning to hike trails in national parks, monuments or forests or on Bureau of Land Management (BLM) lands, you can often find useful general information on various Internet Web sites published by those federal agencies. Many state parks and some local parks also have information available online (Figure 2-3). The US Forest Service (USFS) also maintains information about forest fires on its Web site that may affect trip planning. If you have the time, you can call or write to National Park Service (NPS), BLM and USFS field offices about trails, trail maps and general information about their facilities, campgrounds and possible backcountry restrictions. Once you have identified an area or trail of interest in a park or forest, you can contact the appropriate park or field office and talk directly with a staff member there. The staffer can usually give you a good idea of the terrain, weather and/or current trail conditions in that area. We have found that NPS, BLM and USFS personnel are very helpful when we have called for information. Most agency offices have at least one person designated to answer inquires from the public. If the information officer does not know the answer to your question, he or she will often forward your call to someone familiar with the trail or area of interest. Keep in mind that these people have other duties and don't usually have lots of time to field unlimited questions. For example, we once called into an USFS office regarding conditions in an area near Gunnison, Colorado where we planned a horse-packing trip. The person we talked to was able to give us good information about how much water and grazing we could count on for our horses and general information about the pack trail that we were considering. This was very helpful in planning our route and reducing uncertainty about the trip.

A number of guidebooks provide good regional information about popular hiking and camping areas. These books are often available in libraries and general bookstores, but more complete and current selections are frequently found in stores that specialize in outdoor and camping equipment. The best coverage of local areas and trails is usually found in stores in or near the area where you plan to hike or camp. It is worth checking local stores when you are in the area of your

Figure 2-3. The NPS Web site

trip. If you are mostly interested in hiking around your home state, you should check out several likely stores to find out who has a good selection of trail guides, books and maps.

Maps are invaluable for planning hiking and camping trips. Most national and state parks and forests have trail maps available at their local offices and/or information centers. You can download some maps at no cost from Internet Web sites and print them out to carry with you. Topographic maps (maps showing roads, major trails, parking areas, topographic contours and other features) are readily available from a number of sources, such as the US Geological Survey (USGS), Trails Illustrated and a number of other map makers. Topographic maps are usually the most useful because they contain a great deal of information such as steepness of slopes and trails, locations of steep rocky areas, streams, lakes, roads and major trails (Figure 2-4). Some maps have brief trail descriptions printed on them that can be helpful for planning your hike and selecting a suitable route. Many guidebooks include small maps as figures to illustrate the routes being discussed. In many cases, this is all you will need for planning purposes and to take along with you.

Other sources of information for planning your trip include local outing or hiking clubs and guide services. Finding these organizations may require searching the Internet for their Web sites (if they have them) or perusing the local telephone book. Most colleges and universities have some form of outing club that can be helpful. Many larger metropolitan areas also have outing clubs that can provide information or at least direct you to someone who can give you relevant information. In Colorado, for example, we have several chapters of the Colorado Mountain Club throughout the state. This is true of other states as well, especially if there are outdoor recreation areas within those states. Keep an open mind about organizations that might be able to help you. Even though you may be interested in hiking, local four-wheeling and ski clubs may be potential information sources for you. Hunting and fishing guide services often have a detailed knowledge of the areas that they operate in and can also provide you with valuable information. Making one or two phone calls often pays off handily. If you are going to a mountainous area, the local climbing shop is often the best source of information. Some of these organizations even have regular meetings and slide shows where you can learn more about your area of interest.

Some organizations have established hike rating systems that can help you evaluate the difficulty of hiking routes. Usually these systems take into consideration the length of the route, steepness or elevation gain involved, and overall level of difficulty of the hike. The distance covered by a given route is obviously an important factor for judging how long a hike may take and evaluating whether it is suitable for your hiking goals. The amount of elevation gain along a given route may not be obvious from a simple trail map but can be determined from a topographic map. Elevation gain is important for planning and rating a hike because hiking uphill is more difficult than walking along a level path. Going a mile on the level is much easier than gaining 1,000 feet of elevation over a one-mile trail. Overall difficulty ratings for hiking trails also consider how rough the trail conditions are, such as whether the trail is paved with gravel, consists of a scramble over rocky terrain or whether you have to go off-trail for part of the way. Hiking guidebooks, maps and outing clubs may also provide rating lists for hikes and climbs.

There is no single, unified classification system for hiking (that we are aware of) other than the scale established by the Union Internationale des Associations d'Alpinisme (UIAA) for climbing and mountaineering (see Glossary). This classification system is used to rank the difficulty of mountaineering or climbing routes and its lower categories consider the overall hiking or traveling difficulty of routes. These include: Class I – easy walking or travel over relatively easy terrain or on a trail; Class II – travel off-trail over rough terrain where boots are needed and some bush-whacking or travel over rocky slopes is included. A third point of balance, such as a handhold, may be occasionally needed. This class often involves some scrambling. Class III is the easiest climbing category where you need to use hand placements regularly for upward movement on part of the route. Classes IV and V involve technical climbing and are beyond the scope of this book. It should be noted that

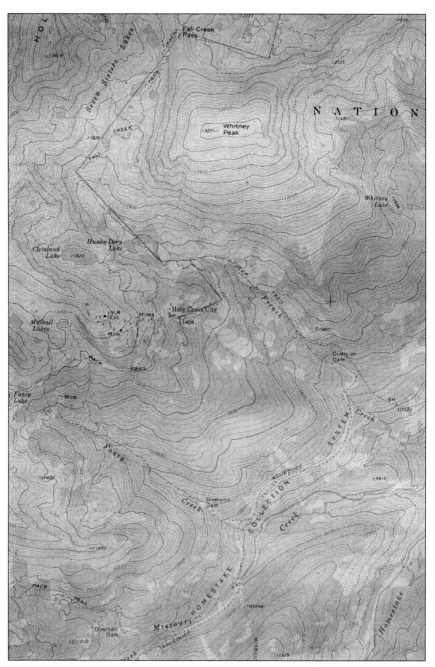

Figure 2-4. A topographic map showing hiking trails

in most climbing classification systems, including that of the UIAA, the rating reflects the most difficult part of the route and usually does not imply that the entire route is of the same difficulty. So a Class IV climb may be mostly Class III difficulty and have only a short distance of Class IV difficulty.

## 2.2   WEATHER AND TIME CONSIDERATIONS

### 2.2.1
### Weather Factors

Weather conditions at the beginning of your hike and expected weather changes throughout the day greatly influence hike planning, preparation and goals. A fine morning may give way to afternoon showers or even an unexpected storm. In either case, planning and preparation can overcome most potential difficulties. A weather forecast may cause you to reconsider the hike goals or routes to avoid weather risks. Where weather is concerned, you should prepare for a full range of expected conditions and avoid extreme storm and weather events as much as you can.

The first step in incorporating weather conditions into a hike is to obtain a weather forecast and evaluate conditions for yourself. The weather report broadcast over television or radio is adequate for general planning purposes and may warn of approaching weather fronts and storms. However, this information should be supplemented with more local information provided in local newspapers or posted in local offices of Federal or state agencies (NPS, USFS, BLM, etc.). The US National Weather Service (NWS) issues forecasts for specific regions, and often on a county-by-county basis for most of the United States (Figure 2-5). Similar detailed forecasts are available for portions for Canada, Mexico and most of Europe. Weather satellite photos are good indicators of cloud cover activity and movement of fronts into an area and they supplement the forecasts well. Many television stations post weather maps, satellite photos and multiday forecasts on their Internet Web sites and often have a link to the NWS Web site. When planning your hike, remember to supplement the information gleaned from these sources with your own observations to be sure that the weather forecast makes sense and to interpret how it may apply to the area where you plan to hike.

After learning what type of weather to expect on your hike, the next step is to prepare for the anticipated weather conditions by taking along appropriate rain gear, clothing and other essentials. This includes the clothing that you will start out wearing at the beginning of the hike and extra clothes that may be needed based on the expected conditions. If a sunny summer day is forecast, light trail shoes may be appropriate, but if rain or snow is expected, then leather hiking boots may be advisable. Other clothing and gear taken along should be suitable for hiking under the expected conditions.

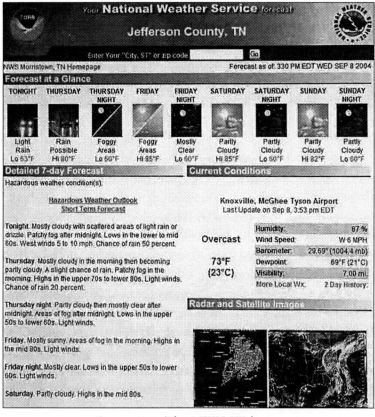

Figure 2-5. The NWS Web site

If storms or other significant changes in weather are forecast, then the hike should be reevaluated to ensure that the planned goals and routes are still feasible. A hike along an exposed ridge in the afternoon when thunderstorm activity is forecast may prove to be dangerous due to lightning strikes and strong winds. An alternate route or earlier starting time can be substituted to reduce risks. In some cases, the hike itself may have to be postponed due to severe weather. Weather considerations are especially important if you are leading a group of mixed hiking experience and ability.

## 2.2.2
## Time Constraints and Planning

Time constraints often limit what can be achieved on a day hike. By its nature, a day hike is generally six to 12 hours long and faces limitations due to available daylight. Only so much can be done in the time available. Therefore, realistic goals must be set for the hike, those that consider the distance, elevation and difficulty of the route and time needed for activities at the planned destination. Consideration must also be given to the capabilities of fellow hikers and their level of conditioning if it is early in the hiking season. The three-hour hike that you took to the lake last fall may take four or five hours on your first outing in the spring.

Plan ahead to accommodate the hiking time, rest stops, sightseeing, lunch breaks, activities at the destination of the hike and extra time for contingencies. The length of time needed to reach a given point depends on the hiking speed of your group of hikers. That speed is generally based on the sustainable hiking speed of the slowest member of the group. So even though you may be able to cruise up to the lake in three hours alone, if the slowest member of the group takes five hours, that is the hiking time you should plan for. Allow time for short breaks every hour or so and a lunch break at midday at the lake. Plan some time at the lake to enjoy being there and for sightseeing en route. If your estimate allows five hours to hike in including short breaks, two hours at the lake for lunch and general enjoyment, and five hours on the return hike; you are looking at a 12-hour day. This does not include a contingency for a sprained ankle, thunderstorm or other unexpected delay. If there is inclement weather coming, you have an airplane flight to catch or nightfall comes early, you should plan to start early so that you can finish the hike in daylight.

In many mountainous areas, it is advisable to begin your hike very early in the morning. This is necessary due to weather considerations as mountain weather often leads to afternoon rain or snowstorms. It is not unusual to begin a hike at daylight or earlier if a long hike is expected or a large elevation gain is planned.

## 2.3     What to Wear and Take Along

A hiker needs to be prepared for events and conditions that can occur during the hike. You can do this by good planning, preparation and carrying the right clothing and equipment for the trip. This means being in a position to deal with weather and trail condition changes, injury, thirst, hunger, misdirection and delay. In general, most of these contingencies can be overcome with proper knowledge, clothing and equipment.

### 2.3.1
### The Ten Essentials

There are ten essential items that all hikers should take along on any hike. These are practical things that are needed throughout the day and in case of an emergency (Figure 2-6). They include:

1) Map,
2) Compass,
3) Flashlight or head lamp,
4) Extra water and food,
5) Extra clothing,
6) Sunglasses,
7) First Aid kit,
8) Pocket knife,
9) Matches, and
10) Fire starting materials.

This particular list closely follows the essentials recommended in the book "Mountaineering: The Freedom of the Hills" by the Seattle Mountaineers (Graydon, 1997). Different organizations have somewhat different "Top Ten" lists, but include most of the same items listed above. From a true survival point of view, drinking water and extra clothing are probably the most essential of all these items. Avoiding hypothermia in cold weather is an immediate need and one cannot go without water for more than a few days. Implied in the list is a backpack or buttpack to carry the ten essential items in.

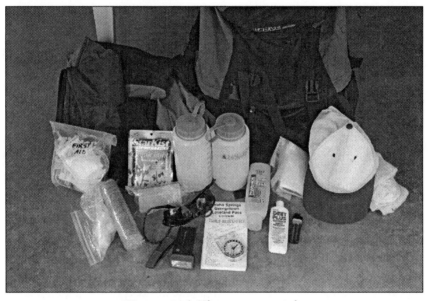

Figure 2-6. The ten essentials

The map and compass are essential tools for finding one's way and keeping on course. Whether you are on a prepared trail or rough track, it is possible to go off course and become disoriented. The map and compass will usually get you back on track if you know how to use them and have paid attention to where you have come from.

If there is any possibility that your hike may keep you out after dark, then a light source should be taken along. In most cases, a small flashlight will be sufficient for following a prepared trail after dark. A wider and more powerful beam will help when you are moving along a rough track or going cross-country. A headlamp will free up your hands and automatically point the light to where you are looking. Carry extra batteries, especially if your light source drains your batteries in less than three hours. If you are planning to hike at night or start an alpine ascent before dawn, be sure that you have enough batteries and a spare lamp or light bulb. Know where the batteries and bulb are in your pack because you will probably be in the dark when you need them.

## Hiking In Trinidad

We once spent a dark night waiting for dawn in a rain forest on the island of Trinidad when our only flashlight went dead during a night hike. We did not want to continue along the trail in the dark because of the wild animals we might encounter and possibly confront and also because we could not see well. Wild pigs, poisonous snakes, scorpions and other animals were known to frequent that particular trail and it was better to let them find us and go around us than for us to inadvertently bump into them. We always carry backup batteries or an extra light to avoid such situations now.

Water and food should be carried on all but the shortest hikes because they are necessary to sustain your energy levels, not to mention you might need them in an emergency. In hot weather, your need for water is especially high to replace losses due to perspiration and respiration. The body requires two or more quarts of water per day when resting and up to five quarts per day when working hard at high elevations or in dry air. Without water, heatstroke, exhaustion and lethargy can quickly set in. In some areas, replacement water can be found in streams or ponds but frequently surface water needs to be treated before you can safely drink it. A good rule of thumb is to carry at least one quart of water for a half-day hike on a warm day and two quarts for a full day's hike. On hot days, carry at least 50 percent more water.

Extra food should be carried even on short hikes. For a day hike, carry a lunch and/or several snacks to keep your energy levels up (Figure 2-7). When working steadily the body needs nourishment to keep going. Dried fruits, nuts, candy bars, hard candy and fresh fruit make great snacks. There is no need to overeat — a simple sandwich is adequate for lunch. In general, several small snacks during the day keep energy levels on a more even keel. Don't wait until you are completely dead on your feet before eating something and drink some water with each snack or meal. Experiment with different snacks until you identify foods that you enjoy on the trail.

Figure 2-7. A typical lunch and snacks

The clothing that you wear on a hike depends on the weather, elevation, length of hike, and your personal preference. In general, you should start the hike wearing what seems to be the most comfortable combination of clothing layers. As the hike progresses, you may need to add or shed clothing as conditions change. Conditions may change in response to the weather, elevation gain or because you are overheating or cooling down. The key is to carry several layers of clothing with you so that you can add or subtract layers as needed. The extra clothing goes in your backpack or buttpack, or in some cases, it can be carried in the pockets of your jacket.

Layering is a well-accepted concept in outdoor clothing. The underlying principle is that you need a graduation in the amount of insulation on your body at any given time, and the more combinations or choices you have, the better. Instead of wearing one or two garments that provide all the insulation you need but often make you feel either too hot or too cold, you should wear several lighter garments to use in combination. Instead of one heavy coat, carry a light outer shirt, light sweater and windproof shell jacket. With a heavy coat you may feel cold with it off and overheat with it on. With layers you have several combinations to choose from. You can wear one or all of these layers depending on how cold it is and how much heat and perspiration you generate. You should choose the layers so that they can be easily added or subtracted. For example, when hiking up a steep slope, you are working hard and generate a lot of heat. A light polypropylene or polyester shirt may be all you need in summer, but when you stop to rest, you may need to don a wind jacket to keep from cooling off too much in a windy situation. After you begin hiking again you will generate heat and can remove the jacket to stay comfortable.

Selecting the right combination of layers of clothing requires some forethought and experience to get it right. Usually you have more flexibility during a hike to change your upper body garments than those on your lower body. This is because it takes more time and effort to change your pants or long underwear on cool days. Zip-off convertible pants that allow you to change from long pants to shorts are a great help in this regard because you can convert from one to the other relatively easily. The same is true for full-zip rain and wind pants that can be pulled on or off without removing one's boots. However, it is not so easy to change in and out of long underwear. There are a number of combinations of cotton, polypropylene, nylon, synthetic fleece, Capilene® and wool available for inner and outer shirts and pullovers. Vests and insulated jackets can be made from any of these materials as well as from down and other bulkier synthetic fibers.

Because down compresses easily and therefore loses its insulating loft, it should usually be used as an outer layer or just beneath the wind- and water-resistant outer shell.

The boots and socks that you take along on your hike should be chosen on the basis of fit and function. Although you can expect to wear your boots all day, plan on having to change your socks if your feet get wet from sweat, soggy ground, snow or open water. It is highly advisable to carry extra dry socks if your feet sweat a lot or if you expect to get your feet wet along the trail. We recommend that hikers wear two pairs of socks: an inner "liner" sock and an outer heavier sock. The liner can be made from polypropylene, wool or silk. Its role is to wick moisture away from the skin to the outer sock. The outer sock is the primary insulating layer and also serves as a cushion for the foot. In general, wool is the best material for cool-weather outer socks because it provides good insulation even when wet. Wearing two sock layers reduces the stress placed on the skin of the foot and helps reduce the formation of blisters. A single sock layer can be worn for short hikes in light shoes or boots, but two layers should be worn in heavier boots and for long hikes.

A hat may be the most useful piece of clothing that you carry with you on a hike. It can keep sun off your face and neck to prevent sunburn and it can insulate your head to reduce overheating on hot days. It can also keep your head warm on cold and windy days and your head dry during a rainstorm. A cotton baseball cap is a good all-around cover for the head, especially in summer. In hot weather, a broad-brimmed hat will also cover your neck to avoid that "red-neck" look from sunburn. On a cold day, a knit cap, especially a heavy wool stocking cap provides good insulation. Pile and fleece hats can also be worn but some of these don't breathe well enough to let moisture out and as a result can get soaked from sweat. Finally, a jacket with a hood is a must for providing an extra layer of warmth and keeping your head and neck dry in wet weather.

Your hat is the most important article of clothing for providing body temperature control. Fully a third of your body's heat loss occurs from your head and neck on a cold day. Wearing a good wool cap can dramatically reduce heat loss, allowing the rest of your body to keep warm. An old saying goes like this: "If your feet feel cold, put on your hat!" Conversely, keep your head shaded on hot sunny days to help cool off your entire body.

Good quality sunglasses protect the eyes from brightness, glare and blowing dust and grit. Protection of the eyes is self-evident. Severe headaches can result from eyestrain caused by exposure to very bright sunlight and glare over several hours. On snow, the intense reflected light can completely incapacitate a hiker for days during which any exposure to light is searingly painful. Wind blown dust can get into unprotected eyes creating discomfort, and in some cases, significant eye damage. Sunglasses can also protect your eyes from unseen tree branches and other potentially damaging obstacles.

A simple First Aid kit is a necessity for any hike. At a minimum, your kit should contain Band-Aid or equivalent bandages, gauze, adhesive tape, blister-repair materials and sunscreen. Some people also include mosquito repellant.

A pocket knife serves many useful purposes on a hike and can be an important tool in an emergency. The knife can either be a folding knife or an ordinary hunting knife — the primary requirement being that it has one or two, strong, sharp blades to be used for cutting. Swiss Army knives and their equivalent may have a lot of additional "gizmos" but many of these features are of limited value on a hike, although tweezers can be handy at times.

Finally, matches and fire starting materials are useful for starting a fire when needed. The matches should be the strike-anywhere type and should be stored in a waterproof container. Starting materials can be dry paper, wood shavings, cotton wool, extra toilet paper or other dry, easily ignitable material that can get larger kindling burning. Many people carry an inexpensive cigarette lighter with them for this purpose. It is a good idea to carry both matches and a lighter as a backup.

Nearly any small backpack, rucksack or buttpack is suitable for carrying the ten essentials with you on a short hike of up to one day's length (Figure 2-8). If you plan to carry more than 10 or 12 pounds of weight on a regular basis, then it is worth investing in a good quality backpack that is comfortable to wear for long periods.

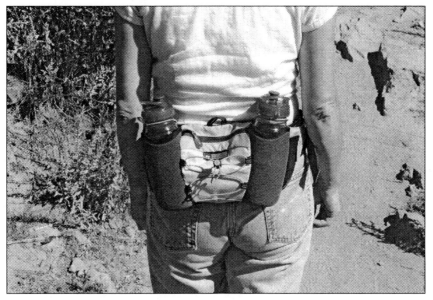

Figure 2-8. A buttpack is a good alternative for short day hikes

# CHAPTER 3 THE ART OF HIKING

Hiking is traveling to a goal on foot for an extended distance. It is essentially going for a long walk over a range of terrain or trail conditions. Factors that make hiking different from casual walking are the duration, distance and often the intensity of the travel. Yet, to most people, the difference between going for an easy walk or a hike is largely a subjective interpretation which varies from person to person.

Walking is something most of us take for granted. We generally walk on flat floors or sidewalks to go about our business or we walk for short distances to our cars or to the store. We don't usually walk far enough to become tired unless we have to walk up several flights of stairs to get home. During most short walks we don't really need to be efficient walkers or even in good physical condition. But on longer hikes, efficiency and conditioning are very important and determine the distance, speed and ultimate success of our outings (Figure 3-1).

Figure 3-1. Backpacking over a
rough mountain trail

## 3.1    How to Walk and Hike

When a person is hiking efficiently, each step is made in such a manner that the distance traveled or elevation gained by that step is completed using minimal effort. There are several elements involved in walking, such as stride, foot placement, pace, rest and recovery. Selecting the right combination of these factors for different terrain conditions leads to efficient hiking.

### 3.1.1
### *Stride and Foot Placement*

Stride refers to the length of the individual steps we make while walking. Foot placement refers to the orientation of the foot as it moves through each step. Longer strides can be made on level ground than on steep uphill slopes. This is true because the legs do more work going uphill, lifting the entire body mass up against gravity, whereas in level walking, the body remains more or less at the same elevation. When walking downhill, the upper thigh muscles work to support the weight of the body as the leg steps downward. This is why you can get out of breath and have sore legs from going down several flights of stairs. It is better to take smaller steps when going uphill so that your legs do less work on each step. A similar case can be made for taking smaller steps when going downhill. As a test, try climbing up three flights of stairs, one step at a time and again two steps at a time. Also try descending the stairs first with one step and then two steps at a time. The larger steps should cause you to breathe harder and it should temporarily seem more difficult for your muscles to perform. Another thing to note is that you generally have better balance when you move up or down with smaller steps. Now imagine carrying a backpack while taking large and small steps. The advantage of small manageable steps will be clear on long upward slopes.

When hiking on a rough trail, especially when carrying a heavy load, you should avoid taking large vertical steps up or down, such as up a high stair or onto a log or rock. This allows you to avoid injuries caused by overstressing leg muscles and tendons. Stepping down a large step can also cause your leg to buckle, throwing you off balance or even causing a fall. When confronted with a large step, look for an easier way such as taking a series of two or more smaller steps on an adjacent smaller rock or tree root. You want to avoid incidents that will weaken your legs, pull a muscle or cause a fall. Remember you still have to get back to your car.

When descending a slope, adjust your stride to absorb shock to your ankles, knees and hips. Your legs are great shock absorbers if used correctly, but too large a step can wear down even the best trained muscles and joints. The most important thing to avoid is letting your knee lock backward during a downward step. While your knee can support you in that position, it is very jarring and puts undue stress on ligaments, tendons and soft tissue that pad your joints. It is better to keep your knees slightly flexed on downward steps so that your muscles can cushion the impact of the step and act as shock absorbers (Figure 3-2). On a long descent, your flexed legs may get tired but you will avoid unnecessary injuries. It is especially important to be aware of knee flexing at the end of the day when your legs are hard to control due to fatigue.

(a)                                    (b)

Figure 3-2. Stepping down a slope with small steps and trekking poles: a) poles placed forward before the right foot advances b) right foot in the advanced position

Optimal foot placement can be used to improve the length of stride, efficiency and traction of a given step. When walking on a level surface our foot placement is generally a heel-and-toe motion. During a stride, our leg straightens, the heel touches the ground, our foot rolls forward onto the ball of the foot and we push off again with the ball and toes. That leg is then raised at the hip, flexes at the knee, swings forward and extends for the next step. Both legs alternate this motion, each taking their turn propelling the body forward. When we begin walking, we lean our center of gravity (COG) forward a bit, keep it forward as we walk and lean back to an upright position when we stop walking. While walking, most of us raise and lower our COG with each step. We can, of course, control this up-and-down motion to some extent if we think about it. This is why we can carry a cup of coffee or balance a book on our head (for at least a short distance).

What is not readily obvious is that our body sways from side to side as well as rotates with each stride. This results from our automatic need to stay in balance as we shift our weight back and forth to alternate feet. Our COG oscillates from left to right as we walk, even though the trend of the oscillations is more or less along our direction of travel (Figure 3-3). The slight rotations of our body are due to the force required to make each stride. We compensate for this naturally by swinging our arms and shoulders, twisting slightly to stabilize the motion and keep on balance. The more we oscillate or "wobble" about our general direction of travel, the more effort is required to bring our COG back into balance. Minimizing the wobble is therefore one way that we can reduce the effort required for each stride, making that energy available for forward movement and increasing our efficiency.

One way to reduce wobble and at the same time lengthen your stride is to align your feet with your direction of travel. By aligning the feet, we mean to walk without turning the toes of the foot outward during each foot placement. Imagine a line running between your big toe and the center of your heel (Figure 3-4a). When you stand with your feet together, these imaginary lines are approximately parallel. When walking, most people rotate their feet outward from parallel by 15 to 30 degrees (Figure 3-4b). Imagine now that the direction in which you

(a)                       (b)

Figure 3-3. The rear view of a hiker wobbling: a) her center of gravity shifts left b) her center of gravity shifts right

want to walk is a straight line in front of you called your central trend line of travel (CTL). When you walk, your COG oscillates from side to side of the CTL with each stride because you are wobbling.

We can display the CTL and COG graphically in the form of a "stride diagram" to illustrate what happens during walking. We will assume a person is walking on level ground to keep the concepts simple. Figure 3-5a is a diagram of how a person's tracks might look if they belong to a typical walker with their foot axis turned outward by 20 degrees. The feet and legs swing forward and backward with each stride roughly parallel to the CTL. The heel of each foot must swing past the other leg to avoid tripping, so after just clearing the leg, each heel will fall slightly to the side of the CTL, as shown in the figure. Since the COG on each step is centered approximately over the midpoint of the foot axis, the COG trend wobbles from side to side. Some people also walk with their feet spaced a few inches apart, away from the CTL, rather than close together. When they walk, their COG follows the wider

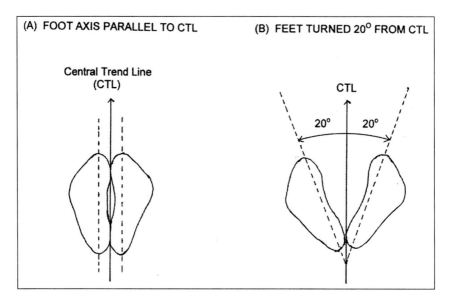

Figure 3-4. Illustrations of foot placement

stance causing them to oscillate even more, as shown in Figure 3-5b. These examples illustrate two common sources of wobble: rotation of the foot axis and widely placed strides.

Efficient walking can be achieved by walking with the foot axis nearly parallel to the CTL and striding with our feet as close to the CTL as practical. Figure 3-5c illustrates the wobble created by a person walking in this way. The COG oscillates as it shifts from foot to foot, but the oscillation is much less than in the previous two examples. This style of walking is highly efficient and actually results in a slightly longer stride. (About an inch more in the average person.) The efficiency is gained by minimizing the work the legs and feet have to do to force the COG to swing from side to side more than is absolutely necessary. This may not seem like much, but on a long hike, the energy saved on several thousand strides can be significant in terms of both energy saved and reduced muscle fatigue. In some cases, this style of walking may even reduce wear-and-tear on hips, knees and ankles. This style of walking has been called the "Indian style" because it resembles the efficient strides of Native American hunters.

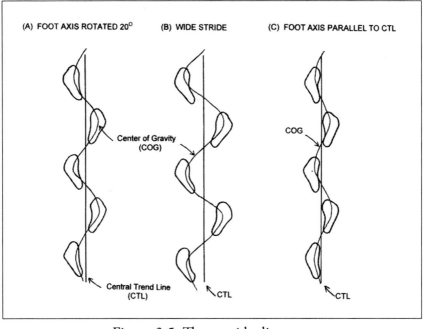

Figure 3-5. Three stride diagrams

To evaluate your own style and efficiency of walking, you can conduct a simple experiment to create your own personal COG and CTL diagram. This can be done by walking several strides along a straight line in sand or snow, on a sidewalk with wet shoes or any place where you will leave good tracks. Once you have created a set of tracks, draw in a CTL based on your tracks using chalk on hard ground or a stick in sand or snow. Then connect the center of each footprint with a series of straight lines. Now try walking as efficiently as you can while keeping your foot axes parallel to the CTL and your feet close to the CTL. Next measure the distance from the center of each footprint to the CTL for your original style of walking and for the efficient style. Most people will see a reduction in the average distance to the CTL. Try it and see how you can improve your walking efficiency! With practice, you will make it a habit to walk with greater efficiency and enhance your hiking efforts.

Another way to improve your walking efficiency is to reduce loss of traction and slippage. By this we mean reducing the amount your foot slips backward between the time you place it on the ground and the time you actually use it to move forward. The lug pattern on the bottom of your shoe or boot can, of course, make a difference. A heavily lugged boot sole will grip snow and loose soil better than the sole of a smooth shoe. The amount of slippage ultimately depends on how you place your foot on the ground surface. On a dry sidewalk, use of the heel-to-toe foot placement works well because there is a lot of friction between the sole and the pavement and the pavement does not yield. However, if you walk the same way on snow, your foot will slip backward a little bit each time you rotate your foot from heel to toe. The slippage occurs because the sole of your shoe has insufficient friction to maintain traction or because the snow cannot resist the thrust of the stride. In the first case, you simply slip over the snow surface due to low friction. In the second case, you cause the step to break out, even if you have a lugged boot sole (Figure 3-6). When walking in sand or loose soil, each stride can result in the sand/soil moving under your foot to form a more stable configuration. Anyone who has walked up a sand dune can tell you how inefficient this can be as your feet slide back dramatically with each upward step.

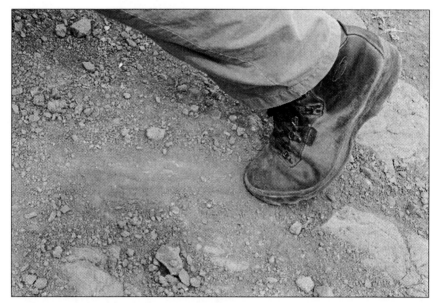

Figure 3-6. An example of step breakout showing a boot sliding on loose soil

Walking "flat-footed" can greatly reduce slippage on soft, unstable surfaces. Flat-footed walking is a method that minimizes the heel-to-toe action of the foot so that nearly all of the foot is placed on and removed from the ground simultaneously. When stepping forward, the foot is kept more or less flat on the ground and your forward motion is due to hip and knee action alone. The goal is to keep most of the foot in contact with the ground during the stride and minimize the toe thrust that pushes us forward. The result is that the foot retains more area in contact with the ground during the thrusting portion of the stride. This reduces breakout and spreads your body weight over a greater area of friction, yielding overall better traction. Flat-footed walking requires you to raise and lower your foot into place on each stride, not slide it forward by shuffling. On ice, people place their feet flat also but they usually shuffle their feet into position.

An extension of the flat-footed walking method is the "tramp step", walking with the foot pushed or tramped down onto the ground. The intent is to push the lugs of the boot sole into the soft ground to get a better grip by deforming the surface around the lugs. This is especially useful in snow, which accepts sole imprints well.

## ZANZIBAR BEACH WALK

On a recent trip to Africa, we had a chance to observe a man walking along a beach with great ease. We were on beach sand that was damp after the tide had gone out on the north shore of Zanzibar. A local fisherman walked barefoot along the beach, head up, back straight, arms swinging loosely back and forth as he made long, uniform strides. As he passed, we realized that like so many East Africans, he was an experienced and efficient walker, the result of years of walking as his chief means of transport. He left hundreds of yards of stride diagram there on the beach. As we examined his tracks, we found that they clearly matched the stride diagram of an "efficient walker". His feet remained parallel and close to the CTL as far as we could follow his tracks. In addition, the tracks showed almost no sign of slippage due to step breakout.

It is important to note that no matter how well you place your foot, you can probably cause a slip or breakout to happen if you take a sudden stride. So remember that on soft ground and slippery surfaces, move forward smoothly and without suddenly pushing off with your foot or you will slip.

The "rest step" is a technique used by mountaineers to allow leg muscles to rest briefly during each upward step. In essence, the hiker locks his knee back temporarily while he rests before taking the next step. One foot is advanced uphill and the downhill (rear) foot stays in place with the leg locked back (Figure 3-7). After a second or so (or even longer at higher elevations), the back foot is advanced, the other leg is locked and rested, and so on. The purpose behind this technique of walking is to allow the muscles of the back leg to rest briefly because they do not need to be in a high state of tension to support the leg at rest. Introducing some rest to each stride requires less energy, and therefore, increases efficiency. If you take 10,000 strides on a hike, your increased efficiency can add up to the successful completion of a climb or long uphill hike. With practice the technique can become second nature.

Figure 3-7. Legs resting during the rest step with the left leg in the back locked position

Use of a walking stick, staff, ice axe or ski/trekking poles can make hiking easier, especially if you are carrying a heavy load or are traveling on slippery ground. The primary purpose of the stick or poles is to provide an extra point of balance. This can be very helpful on snowfields, muddy tracks and gravel where one slip can throw you off balance. Most slips occur at the end of the day when you are tired and traveling downhill. Poles are especially helpful for descending loose gravel, scree and soft snow slopes because they can help you better distribute your weight and let your upper body assist with travel. Use of a walking stick or poles can also help with timing and cadence on a hike. An ice axe should be used on glaciers and hard snow or ice.

When walking with one pole or an ice axe, keep the support on the uphill side of your line of travel. The reason for this is that on a sloping surface your feet will tend to slip downhill if you slip and your weight will be shifted uphill. An uphill support will give you a wide stance for recovering your balance. If the pole is downhill you will slide toward it narrowing your stance and making it more difficult to recover your balance. Also a downward slip might kick out your pole if it is on the downhill side.

When hiking with two poles, use the poles to alternate with your feet for best balance. If you are moving fast this means you move your right foot and left pole simultaneously, then the left foot and right pole (Figure 3-8). This is the same sequence used when you are cross-country skiing. You will always have two points of contact with the ground this way. For more balance control in steep or slippery places, only move one pole or foot at a time. Move the right pole forward, then the left foot, then the left pole and finally the right foot. With practice this motion becomes second nature (Figure 3-9). If you look down at your placements, you will see that you have three points of balance on the ground forming a triangular stance at all times. It is a very stable way to move.

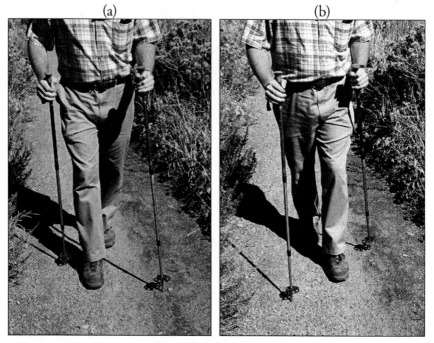

Figure 3-8. A hiker walking fast with alternating poles and feet: a) right foot forward with left pole b) left foot forward with right pole

## 3.1.2
### Setting the Pace

Your walking pace is the rate with which you make steps or strides. It is dependent on the slope of the trail, the nature of the walking surface, physical conditioning, walking style and other factors. Generally, your pace is higher on level ground than on upward slopes, due to the amount of effort required for each stride. Pace can be adjusted to provide a desired speed, which is the body's rate of movement along the CTL. Different people traveling at the same speed can be walking at different paces due to the length of their strides, weight carried, walking style and various other considerations. People can adjust the length of their stride so that they can match pace, as is done during formation marching and in parades. This creates a visual effect, and for marching bands, helps keep cadence with the music.

Figure 3-9. A hiker using poles for three points of contact: a) right pole forward b) left foot forward c) left pole forward d) right foot forward

There are several advantages to matching speed and pace on the hiking trail. If you are traveling in single-file, you need to match speed with others in your group, otherwise you will frequently have to slow down or speed up. It is also psychologically easier to match speed and pace when walking or hiking. For no sound reason, letting someone else set the pace and matching it is easier than following someone at a different pace, even if your speeds are the same. It is like a mental cruise control that frees your mind up to do other things than concentrate on matching speed. People who walk and talk together often seem to naturally match speed, pace and stride.

When leading a group and setting the pace, follow your social instinct and select a speed and pace that is comfortable for everyone in your group. This allows everyone to stay together, but also lets people keep it up for a long time. When selecting a suitable pace and overall speed, be sure to factor in an appropriate number of short breaks or rest stops at regular intervals. If you walk at a slow speed, you may not need to stop and rest very often. Periodic one or two-minute water breaks may be sufficient. But as the pace and slope of the trail become longer and more difficult, frequent rest stops may be required. Longer breaks may be needed to eat snacks, drink, take a toilet break, adjust boots and packs, or to add or subtract layers of clothing. Usually a five-minute break each half-hour or ten minutes per hour are sufficient. It is important to plan a number of breaks into the schedule and to plan your speed with these breaks in mind.

After you have been hiking for a while you will get a sense of the speed and pace that suit you best under varying conditions. Based on this knowledge, you can begin to gage how long a prospective hike should take and you can plan your hike accordingly. It may be necessary to modify your speed and pace to accommodate others hiking with you or to avoid weather problems. In either case, you will have an idea of how much faster or slower you can go than was originally planned.

## 3.2    THE PHYSIOLOGY OF HIKING

Hiking is an activity that places demands on the muscles, heart and circulatory system, and lungs. The leg muscles in particular must move the body by a repetitive series of contractions that consume nutrients and oxygen and generate excess heat and waste products. The circulatory system, powered by the heart, must collect oxygen from the lungs, carry nutrients and oxygen to the muscles, remove waste and help dissipate excess heat. If the circulation cannot keep these duties up, the muscles will have to slow down their activity or stop. The lungs transfer atmospheric oxygen to the blood stream and also help dissipate excess heat from the body. These three sets of activities must occur simultaneously and be coordinated to match the needs of the hiker's body over an extended period of time (the length of the hike). Exercise that improves these activities is called conditioning.

### 3.2.1
### The Muscles

Hiking involves the repetitive movement of the leg muscles. As you walk, your muscles contract and relax alternately to raise and lower your legs and COG. We tend to think that the major muscle groups of the leg involved in the act of walking are the calves and thighs, but we actually use many more muscles to counter the twisting and wobbling movements associated with walking and to keep us upright and balanced. Lifting the right leg requires the abdominal muscles on the right side of the body as well as the muscles in the hip and buttocks to contract. The lower back muscles counterbalance the tension created on the abdominals and the opposite (left) leg must briefly take on the full weight of the body. This also means that the COG shifts to the left foot and a plethora of other muscles in the left leg, foot, hip and abdomen have to redistribute stress to maintain an upright posture.

When we place the right foot down, stride forward and push ahead with that foot, another combination of muscle movements accommodates that action and our body weight is temporarily shifted to the right leg as the left leg is lifted up into its stride. In addition, the upper body becomes involved as we swing our arms to counter the twisting motion. This happens over and over while dozens of small muscle adjustments are made to maintain balance. Even muscles in our neck are involved to keep the head oriented properly and our chest muscles respond to the increased breathing rate. It is no wonder that walking and hiking are such good forms of exercise and overall conditioning.

Our skeletal muscles contract and then relax during each stride. Muscle contraction is powered by oxygen and nutrients, which are distributed to the muscle tissue through the blood vessels and capillaries. Oxidation of the nutrients releases the chemical energy used by the muscles in contraction and creates lactic acid, carbon dioxide and other waste products. These wastes are carried away from the muscles by the bloodstream for disposal via other organs. The carbon dioxide travels to the lungs where it is exchanged into the air. Excess heat is generated as well, representing as much as 60 percent of the energy derived from metabolism of fuels. This is partially dissipated by the blood and also radiates outward from the muscles to heat other tissues. As we exercise, more blood is routed to capillaries in the skin where excess heat radiates from the skin to the surrounding air.

Part of the fatigue that we feel during extended exercise is due to a lack of nutrients and oxygen being supplied to our muscles. Additionally, muscle pain can result from actual tears or damage to the muscle tissue, as well as the buildup of lactic acid and other waste products. Lactic acid buildup occurs when our circulatory system cannot carry away the wastes produced during exercise as quickly as they are being produced. When the lactic acid reaches moderate levels in the muscle tissue, it interferes with muscle performance. Water and salt imbalances can also occur during strenuous exercise as water vapor and salts are lost from the body due to sweating and heavy breathing. These imbalances can also cause muscle fatigue and lost efficiency.

Nutrients are supplied to the muscles in the form of glucose and fatty acids, which are released from storage. Glucose is created by breakdown of glycogen, which is stored in muscle tissue and in the liver. This is why easily digested foods, such as sugars and starches that break down into glucose, are rapidly available for muscle work. Sweet snacks eaten along the trail can supply energy for hiking relatively quickly. More complex foods such as proteins, fats and some carbohydrates may not be as easily converted for rapid use as muscle energy sources. When readily available sugars are not available from our digestive tract, then glucose is generated exclusively from the breakdown of stored energy in the form of glycogen and other sugars.

After our body has consumed all readily available glycogen and sugars, fatty acids produced from the breakdown of stored fat become a sustainable but less rapidly available energy source. We may feel a sudden decrease in energy levels when we are hiking because we are limited by the rate at which the stored fat can be aerobically converted to muscle energy. This source of energy can be sustained for a considerable period of time depending on how much fat is stored throughout the body. When people suddenly run out of glycogen-derived energy, they may feel like they have "hit a wall". In other words, it seems much harder to continue. Usually they can carry on but at a lower sustained level of effort metered out by the fatty acid energy source.

It is important to understand that the skeletal muscles are only part of the interaction of body systems that are involved in overall hiking performance. We will discuss how muscles, circulation and breathing work together in a later section, after we have introduced the other two systems in more detail.

## 3.2.2
### The Heart and Circulatory System

The circulatory system is the primary means of moving oxygen, nutrients, hormones, antigens, building materials and waste products around to various parts of the body. Its principle components are the heart, arteries, valves, capillaries and veins. The circulation process is the essential activity that keeps us alive. Within the context of hiking, it is also the limiting process that determines how fast and how long we are able to walk. No matter how big your muscles are, they can only operate as fast as they receive nutrients and oxygen from the bloodstream. No matter how large your lung capacity is, the rate at which blood supplies oxygen to the muscles determines how quickly your muscles can work.

We often forget that our heart muscles are the most important muscles in our body. In fact, they are the hardest working muscles in the body, functioning every minute of our lives without any rest beyond what they get between heartbeats. Without going into details, our heart muscles are structurally very different from our skeletal muscles and do not require periods of rest for rebuilding. They are tremendously resilient, and at a young age, seem to be able to drive the heart at remarkable rates with great endurance. As the body ages, the heart muscles lose some of their resiliency and ability to operate as quickly. Also with age, the arteries supplying blood to the heart begin to fill with plaque and become less flexible, limiting the blood supply to the heart. A heart attack occurs when the heart muscles are starved for sufficient blood flow to operate effectively, resulting in diminished circulation to the body.

All components of the circulatory system must operate well for the system to perform efficiently. Arteries and veins can enlarge with exercise to allow increased bloodflow through the system. Plaque buildup, physical damage and loss of elasticity over time reduce the rate at which blood flows through the blood vessels, increasing the work that the heart must perform to circulate blood efficiently. Small valves are located throughout the arteries and veins to check the movement of blood and reduce backflow that may occur between heartbeats. The valves are necessary to allow us to pump blood uniformly throughout the body and help to regulate and distribute blood pressure. The capillaries are extremely small-diameter blood vessels designed to facilitate the transfer of blood constituents to muscle and organ tissue. These blood vessels branch out in vast numbers, like the branches of a tree, from the small arteries that supply blood to our tissues. After passing through the tissues, the capillaries coalesce into small and then larger diameter veins for the blood's return trip to the heart.

## 3.2.3
### The Lungs and Breathing

Our lungs are the organs that allow us to transfer atmospheric oxygen to our blood for use in the body. The lungs are essentially a pair of highly evolved sacs of tissue providing a vast membrane surface that allows oxygen, water and other gases to be readily exchanged between the outside air and the capillaries in our tissues. The lung sacs fill and empty in response to the action of muscles in the chest. The lung sacs fill with air when the chest muscles contract and they empty again when the chest muscles relax.

The construction of our lungs is what makes them so effective. From a single windpipe, two bronchi branch off to deliver air to each of the two lungs. Within the lungs, air channels branch many times to reach clusters of millions of microscopic membrane sacks called "alveoli" that expand on inhalation and shrink on exhalation. It is on the surface of these membranes where exchange of atmospheric oxygen to the red blood cells takes place and also where excess carbon dioxide from the blood is exchanged to the air. The alveoli are very efficient and may represent a total exchange surface area of approximately 108,000 square inches (70 square meters) in a young adult who is in good physical condition.

Unfortunately, the alveoli are subject to degradation over time as they are exposed to contaminants in the atmosphere. Consider all the possible contaminants that you may inhale into your lungs during the course of your lifetime. Among them are tar and gases from cigarettes; particulates and fumes from auto, truck or bus exhaust; dust and smoke from fireplaces and factories; road dust; pollen; mold spores; pet dander; grain dust; gasoline vapor; chemical toxins; coal dust and even perfume. Your lungs are the unwitting collection sites for all of these contaminants, and over time, the available surface area, elasticity and efficiency of the alveoli membranes can be greatly diminished. Lifestyles that encourage smoking and occupations such as firefighting that increase your lungs' exposure to inhaled contaminants can accelerate the rate of deterioration of lung performance. In addition, certain inhaled substances can lead to the onset of lung cancer and other diseases that can greatly impact not only breathing, but life itself. It is important to safeguard your lungs against unreasonable risks caused by exposure to airborne contaminants.

The maximum volume of the adult male breath during exercise is approximately three liters. For women, the maximum volume is somewhat less due to overall smaller body size. The volume of the average resting breath may vary between 0.4 and 0.8 liter at a breathing rate of 10 to 15 breaths per minute. This can change significantly during exercise, when the breathing rate can increase from a relatively few breaths per minute to very high rates (over 60 breaths per minute). Lung volume and breathing efficiency can be improved by exercise training.

## 3.3 Conditioning – Improving Overall Performance and Endurance

The best form of training for walking and hiking is for you to actually do these activities. No combination of exercise machines can replicate all of the motions and actions that occur while walking. But they can help build up some of the principle muscle groups needed for hiking. For example, Stairmaster-type machines, which mimic the action of climbing stairs, can build up thighs, calves and gluteals. Aerobic exercises enhance the performance and efficiency of your breathing and circulation systems.

The closer your exercise routine mimics the pattern of hiking that you are training for, the more beneficial it will be. For example, climbing stairs while wearing a moderate-weight backpack is very good training for a mountain climbing trip (Figure 3-10). It allows you to exercise the appropriate muscles while you are carrying and balancing with a load. This is one reason why mountain climbers often train for a big mountain climb by climbing smaller mountains. If you need to climb with an elevation gain rate of 1,000 feet per hour, you should train at or above that vertical rate. The more exposure your body has to that rate of ascent, the better it will perform on the planned climb.

Figure 3-10. Running up stairs is good preparation for the hiking season

Improvement of our hiking performance involves optimizing our breathing, circulation and muscular activities to increase strength, speed and endurance, and therefore, enjoyment. Primarily we are interested in becoming stronger, more efficient, sure-footed and durable hikers. We are not interested in increasing our strength so that we can lift great weights, but so that we can more easily carry a heavy backpack up steep slopes and over a long distance. Increased strength and endurance often go together as a result of training, but in hiking, improved endurance is usually the goal. Improved breathing, circulation and muscular strength bring us to this goal.

The average man of age 30 breathes 10 to 15 times per minute and his heart beats 70 to 80 beats per minute when resting. The resting blood pressure for men is typically 120/80 (systolic/diastolic) and 120/74 for women of the same age (Plowman, 2001, p. 331). These rates and factors change somewhat as a function of age as wear-and-tear and common health effects accumulate.

During exercise, the body accelerates breathing and circulation to meet the demands placed on it. Breathing increases to the point of being rapid and labored in order to supply oxygen to the blood and to remove carbon monoxide, carbon dioxide and other waste products. Breathing also expels water vapor and heat as air leaves the lungs. At higher elevations, water loss associated with resting breathing rates is greater than at sea level due to the presence of drier air and lower air pressure. With moderate exercise, water loss from breathing can be significant, as much as two to three liters per day.

As you continue to exercise, the heart must increase the rate at which it pumps blood to supply the demands of the muscles and other body processes. Blood pressure increases at the same time. The range of breathing and pulse rates required for an average man who is undertaking different levels of exercise are summarized in Table 2. Even easy walking can result in a significant increase in rates compared to resting rates. Physical training for any aerobic activity can lower these breathing and pulse rates due to practice and increased efficiency. Unfortunately there is little information available on breathing and pulse rates during typical hiking activities, although walking and running data are readily available.

Table 2. Typical breathing and heart rates for a young active man during exercise

| | Percent of Maximum Work | | | | | | | | | | |
|---|---|---|---|---|---|---|---|---|---|---|---|
| | 0 | 10 | 20 | 30 | 40 | 50 | 60 | 70 | 80 | 90 | 100 |
| Breathing Rate* (breaths per minute) | 12 | 13 | 14 | 16 | 18 | 22 | 27 | 35 | 44 | 50+ | n/a |
| Heart Rate* (beats per minute) | 68 | 83 | 98 | 113 | 128 | 143 | 158 | 173 | 188 | 200 | n/a |

*Based on short term incrementally increased aerobic exercise testing. These rates were not sustained for long periods of time.*

Breathing rates can increase to 60 times per minute during heavy exercise, and become more difficult with increased elevation due to the lower oxygen content of air. The lower partial pressure of oxygen encountered at higher elevations also causes the exchange of oxygen from air to blood to be less efficient. This means more breaths are required to supply the same amount of oxygen to the bloodstream in a given time period. At high elevations, breathing is usually the process that limits how high we can go and our rate of progress when we are hiking.

The acceptable range for the pulse of an individual during exercise varies with age and presents another constraint on overall hiking performance. Studies have shown that aerobic exercise improves overall conditioning, especially cardiopulmonary performance, if the exercise pulse is kept within the range of 60 to 80 percent of maximum allowable pulse (heart rate) for a period of 20 minutes or more on a regular basis. The maximum heart rate and allowable exercise pulse rate decrease with age. Estimated maximum pulse (EMP) is generally calculated as 220 beats per minute minus your age. So for an average person of 40 years, the EMP is 180 beats per minute (220 minus 40). This is the estimated maximum for a 40-year old, and just like red-lining a car engine, if it is sustained for a length of time, it may lead to heart damage or a heart attack. The EMP formula provided above is based on the "average" person in the population and should be used with caution since in some people heart damage or heart attack may occur at a lower pulse rate than the EMP calculated for the same age. We advise everyone to calculate your own personal EMP and make sure that you never reach that level during exercise. A heart attack on a remote hillside or trail could easily be fatal.

Every hiker should calculate the pulse range that will determine his or her training and hiking target rate. This is done by calculating the EMP and then finding the 60 and 80 percent pulse rates. Taking our 40-year-old person as an example, the EMP is 180 beats per minute and the 60 and 80 percent pulse rates are 108 and 144, respectively. Our hiker now knows that he or she can reach as high as 144 beats per minute safely but should not exceed it during training. If he or she hikes with a pulse between 108 and 144 beats per minute, they will receive sufficient aerobic exercise to improve their performance over time. Below the 60 percent pulse rate, our hiker will still enjoy the outdoors and burn up calories, but he or she will probably not receive significant aerobic benefits.

Each person should discuss the recommended aerobic pulse range with his or her doctor and then select the aerobic range best for them. To avoid confusion, we will call the upper limit of the exercise range the "upper exercise pulse" or UEP. The lower limit of the aerobic range will be called the "lower exercise pulse" or LEP, and for most people, this will be equal to the 60 percent rate. High pulse rates sustained above 80 percent of EMP (above UEP) over an extended period should be avoided because they might begin to damage the heart muscles or otherwise tax the system. Keeping the pulse below the 80 percent rate also provides a reasonable buffer from the EMP itself, reducing the possible heart attack risk for most people. It should be noted that EMP, LEP and UEP are general indicators of the range of acceptable heart rates that are widely used in exercise training. Some in the medical profession consider UEP to be only a crude estimate of the safe range of heart function, but a reasonably good indicator of what the average person can rely on if they have no serious heart irregularities.

So how does a hiker implement heart rate information into everyday life and hiking? It is important for all hikers, but especially for older hikers, to monitor their pulse during exercise. You can do this by measuring your pulse at an accessible vein on the wrist and counting heartbeats over a ten-second interval (Figure 3-11). Multiplying the count by six yields the pulse in beats per minute. You need to stop hiking in order to get an accurate count, but with practice, it does not take long. Monitor your pulse several times during your hike, and especially on steep portions of the trail or when running, to observe how the rate varies under different conditions.

If you are working hard, running out of breath or sweating heavily, you should stop and monitor your pulse because these are the conditions that will push your heart rate to the upper end of your exercise range. If your heart is working too hard and your pulse exceeds your UEP, stop where you are, rest a minute or two and monitor your pulse. Your pulse

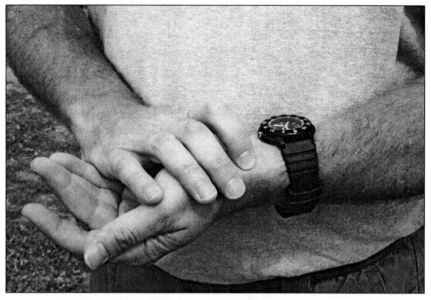

Figure 3-11. Monitor your pulse during exercise

should fall off quickly after you have stopped exercising. When your pulse decreases below the 80 percent rate, you can get going again, but try a somewhat lower pace and monitor your pulse often. If your pulse stays near the 80 percent level, then take an extended rest of 10 or 15 minutes or until your pulse falls to the 60 percent rate.

If it takes more than 30 minutes to reach the 60 percent level, you should consider this an indication that something is not right. This may indicate that you are just not up to the task on that particular day or that you are encountering a serious health constraint. In either case, it is better to retreat to the trailhead if you feel fine otherwise. If your pulse remains elevated, you feel hot, exhausted and faint or have some pains in your chest, neck or arms, or have trouble breathing, you may have overstressed your heart. Rest and call for help immediately. It is better to be overly cautious, to retreat or get help than to take a serious health risk. The trail will be waiting for you when you are ready for it.

Each person is responsible for establishing his or her own exercise pulse range and selecting a UEP. This is especially true if you do not exercise often or you are over 35 years of age. Then you must monitor your pulse frequently during exercise to establish how your body responds to physical stress. With practice and experience you will become familiar with how you feel under different conditions and how your pulse responds. When you have reached this level of experience, you may need to monitor less often, but you still need to measure your pulse when you think you might be reaching your UEP. Accept the fact that you should take a short break when you reach the UEP. With training you will become aerobically efficient and bump up against your UEP less frequently. If you are hiking with others and need a short break, just tell your group that you need a breather. Don't be afraid to stop; it is not worth risking serious health problems.

When training, you should follow the same guidance used in other aerobic sports with the following notable additions. In general, training at a level between your LEP and UEP provides aerobic benefit if sustained for at least 20 minutes. At lower pulse rates you receive the benefit of working the muscles, improving muscle tone and burning calories —all useful benefits. Short workouts involving running, fast walking or stair climbing are beneficial and contribute to overall performance. Longer workouts of a few hours, even at lower pulse rates, build overall endurance and really test the muscles. Short workouts done daily or every second day close to your UEP limit are good. Longer workouts of two hours or more at lower pulse rates but above your LEP will provide the best endurance training for those long hikes to come. Longer workouts should only be done about twice a week because your muscles need more time to recover fully after them.

# CHAPTER 4        CAMPING BASICS

A camp is simply the place where you spend the night and linger for one or more days while you pursue other outdoor goals such as fishing, hiking and backpacking. Whatever your intentions, you need to carry some basic items with you for camping and extra gear for the sport or hobby that you are going to do. You may camp in one spot for several nights or camp one night each at several campsites. Your mode of transportation (backpacking, car camping or boating) determines how much equipment and supplies you can carry with you to camp. Transportation factors will also affect what you bring to camp, how you carry it, and how much effort you put into setting up your camp. If you are backpacking, you will most likely move your camp often, and as a result, you will need light gear and an easily assembled tent. If you are car camping, weight is not a critical factor and as a result you may want to carry more gear to ensure your comfort and a more permanent setup. But regardless of how you travel and how long you remain in camp, you will still do most of the same things in any camp — eat, sleep, wash, rest and take care of other basic needs.

## 4.1    Selecting the Campsite and Getting Organized

Selecting a good campsite can make the difference between having an enjoyable camp and a miserable one. In general, you want to find a site that is relatively level, well drained and with enough room to move around in easily. In a restricted area such as a park, forest or wilderness area, be sure to follow camping rules and regulations, especially those regarding distance from trails, streams and lakes and any fire restrictions. Establish general areas where different activities will occur, such as the tent area, cooking area, food and trash storage area, resting area, washing area, and finally, the bathroom area (Figure 4-1). The amount of room you need depends on how much gear you have, how many people there are in your group and your mode of transportation.

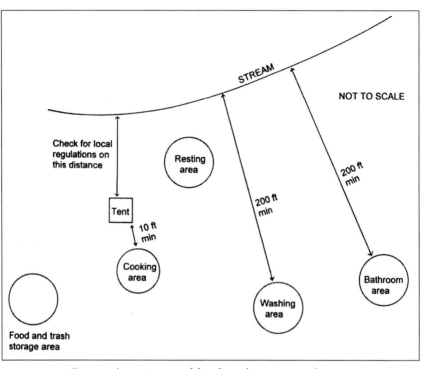

Figure 4-1. A typical backpacking camp layout

Drainage is an important consideration for establishing any campsite. Even though a site may be dry when you first find it, it may collect rainfall when there is a storm. Always try to find a somewhat convex slope for your camp and check uphill to make sure no rainfall runoff will drain onto your site. If there is no choice, you can dig a small drainage ditch around the uphill side of your tent to intercept runoff and carry it around the sides of your tent. Look for evidence that a site has been wet before, such as the presence of mud cracks in the dirt or signs of erosion. Sometimes that nice flat, soft, vegetated spot that you have selected got that way because it is located in a gentle drainageway with plenty of water to support the vegetation and build up the soil. You might want to take advantage of such a spot if you are absolutely certain that it is not going to rain, but if the weather is marginal, don't risk it. It is not worth getting your equipment wet, especially your sleeping bag.

Try to select a site that gives you room to spread out a little. Lay out your camp so that you don't have to walk by the tent all the time. This avoids tripping on tent stakes and guy lines in the dark. Prop up your pack and equipment against a tree trunk, fallen log or rock to keep it handy and clean while you work on dinner or other chores. Feel free to spread gear out for inspection during the day, but gather it together before nightfall and keep track of it carefully. It is hard to find and pack things away in the dark. Try to keep gear and supplies organized at all times and develop a consistent way of packing your items away so that you can find them easily and more predictably.

Selecting a good tent location should be your primary concern even for a one-night camp (Figure 4-2). A slight incline is acceptable but try lying on the ground before setting up your tent to decide on the best orientation. It is generally more comfortable to sleep with your head on the elevated side, even if you slide downhill slightly during the night. If the slope is very steep, you may be able to compensate somewhat by putting extra clothing under your bedroll to even out the slope a little and reduce sliding. If the ground has some gentle hollows, use these to your advantage as hip and shoulder holes to prevent sliding. Older camping guides suggest cutting pine boughs to form a cushion on which to sleep. This isn't usually very comfortable and causes unnecessary damage to trees. If you are camped on snow, you can tramp down a platform and use a shovel to level out a flat spot.

The camp cooking area should be selected with safety and convenience in mind. Keep the cooking stove 10 feet or more away from your tent. The campfire should be considerably further away than that to avoid possible damage to your shelter. During winter camping or in strong winds, it might be necessary to bring a small camp stove into your tent for cooking. If you must cook indoors, be sure to light the stove outside the tent and then bring it inside. Many people have burned themselves, their tent and their equipment when lighting stoves inside their tents. Even if you are careful while cooking, it is easy to spill food or knock over a stove with severe consequences. Remember that the heat rising above even the smallest white-gas stove is concentrated and rises straight up. It can easily melt the roof of your tent within a few minutes if it gets too close to the nylon cloth. The other hazard associated with cooking inside a tent is that carbon monoxide and carbon dioxide gases can

Figure 4-2. Enjoying a pleasant tent site

quickly build up in the enclosed space. It is necessary to provide lots of ventilation to keep healthy air in the tent while cooking. Given all these cautions, it is best to cook outside your tent.

Try to prevent spilling food, cooking oil or grease in the cooking area for two primary reasons. It is messy and inconvenient to spill food in the work area and especially in your tent. A greater concern is odor control. The smell of cooking food and any associated spills can be detected a great distance away from camp, especially in the downwind direction. These smells provide an open invitation to any hungry animal in the vicinity of the camp to come to investigate. The odor from spills and splattering oil and grease will last a long time after you leave the camp. Cooking in your tent will leave odors on the inside of the tent, on sleeping bags and other clothing and equipment. These odors will linger for days if not weeks. Keep these factors in mind when handling and cooking foods, and when you have finished, pack away all food and trash for storage away from camp.

One other note about camp odors. If you are camped in a site where others have stayed before, it is likely that the site has already acquired its share of spills and odors. This is especially true in national forest and park campgrounds where people camp on a confined camp pad and use a fixed grill or firebox. Be aware that odors build up over years of use and plan your camp accordingly. Fireplaces are often places where bacon grease and tin cans get disposed of, and are therefore, long-term odor sources.

Figure 4-3. Suspended food storage

When you are camping, it is necessary to store your food and trash in a secure area away from the immediate camp during the day and especially at night. You can do this by suspending a food bag, duffel, or plastic trash bag on a rope up a nearby tree (Figure 4-3). Try to get the bags at least 10 feet off the ground and away from other tree trunks and branches so that animals cannot climb up to raid them. Parachute cord or a nylon clothesline usually works well if you throw one end of the line over a horizontal branch, tie the bags on that end, pull them up

# GRIZZLY BEAR IN THE CANADIAN ROCKIES

My experience with a grizzly bear in the Canadian Rockies provides a good example of the importance of food handling and caching in the wild. My buddy and I were backpacking into a remote glacier that flows out from the Juneau Icefield into a 60-mile long finger lake. A floatplane dropped us off on the lakeshore and we packed in two weeks worth of gear and supplies to the toe of the glacier. We went as far as we could on the first day, set up camp and began to cook tuna casserole for dinner. We had set up our tent on a relatively flat, broad shelf on the glacial moraine, and due to strong winds, were hunched down behind the tent cooking out of the wind. When the food was ready, we stood up to get our plates. To our great surprise we found that a grizzly bear accustomed to walking along the shelf on a regular basis had wandered into our campsite from the upwind direction and found a big yellow object (our tent) in its path. While we were crouched down cooking on the downwind side, the bear had approached and stood on the upwind side sniffing our tent. When my friend and I stood up, we came face to face with the grizzly standing barely 10 feet away. We were paralyzed for a long moment, but the bear was even more shocked by the two intruders and yellow orb. It shot up the steep 200-foot slope of the moraine and was over the top in seconds, just a-tearing at the ground. We regained our composure and ate dinner, but the encounter caused us to be extra careful with our food and trash handling that day. We seared the tuna cans on our stove to burn off any oil and odor and cleaned our pots and dishes far away from our campsite. We split our food into three caches and buried them far apart in the glacial moraine, marking the sites with stone cairns. Then we moved our tent to a new site. That grizzly was a very large bear and we weren't about to take any chances.

to the appropriate height and tie off the line. This procedure not only protects the food but it also removes the source of many food odors from camp. If you are in an area with no trees, you can bury the food or build a rock cairn on top of the bags. If you are in bear country, you may want to split the food supply into two or more parcels so that if one food cache is lost you have some food left. If you are car camping, it is best to store your food and especially your cooler out of sight in the trunk of your car because many bears now associate coolers with food and they will break car windows to gain access to them.

The camp resting area is where you lounge around and enjoy the campsite. If you are backpacking, this might be a grassy knoll where you can spread out a foam pad and read a book or admire the views. If you are car camping, it is most likely where you set up a table and chairs to read or play cards. There are no set requirements for the rest area but it is the best part of any campsite.

The designated washing area for the camp is where you take care of personal hygiene (face washing, tooth brushing, etc.) and where you wash dishes. It is generally a good idea to set aside one place that will get wet and develop some odors. This area should not be right at the edge of a stream, no matter how convenient that would be. Instead, you should pick a site at least 200 feet from any open water to prevent contamination of your water supply. Dirt roads or well-drained areas with rocky or sandy soil make good choices.

The bathroom area should be located away from camp for privacy and at least 200 feet away from any stream, marsh or open water. Let everyone in camp know where the designated area is. Try to pick an area with dry soil and sparse tree roots so that digging a toilet hole is relatively easy. Use a trowel, camp shovel or ice axe to excavate a six-inch square by six-inch deep hole to contain the solids and paper. Fill the hole in when you have finished and cover it with twigs, rocks or grass to avoid an eyesore. Always bury your waste and all tissue paper, even if you have to cover it with rocks. Do not burn the paper because you could start a grass or pine needle fire. Women who pee should bury their paper or take it back to the trash bag for disposal. If you plan to camp in a remote area for a period of time, you can also construct a latrine for toilet use. This can be a simple slot trench that you straddle or a pit with a cross pole for you to lean on. Shovel in a spade full of dirt after each use and be sure to fill in the hole or trench when you leave the campsite. Afterward, try to improve the looks of the area by covering the former bathroom area with rocks, leaves or pine needles. If you are in or near a public campground, use the toilets provided.

## 4.2   WHAT YOU NEED AT CAMP

The equipment that you bring with you to camp must address your basic needs for shelter, sleeping, cooking/eating, water supply, transportation, lighting and waste management. The equipment required for each of those functions can vary from simple and inexpensive to top-of-the-line and specialized.

Shelter can be addressed in a number of ways depending on the needs and constraints of the camper. John Muir used to travel very light in the Sierra Nevada of his day with no tent much of the time. He would often crawl beneath the bowl of an evergreen tree to bed down on a layer of needles for shelter and sleep. Today's Spartan camper can build a simple lean-to or tent out of a poncho or waterproof cloth that is tied off to the branches of a tree. All that is needed is the canopy material and some nylon cord. A lean-to offers protection from rain and much of the wind but mosquitoes can still be a nuisance. Some mountaineers carry a weatherproof bivouac bag that they crawl into for the night. Such bags are generally large enough for one person to crawl in up to their chest and can be insulated to act as half sleeping bags assuming that the occupant wears a parka or jacket to cover the upper part of their body. The advantage of this approach is that a bivouac bag is light and compact and therefore eliminates the need for a tent. However, it provides no protection from insects.

Most people use a cloth tent to provide them with shelter out of doors. Tents come in a variety of sizes, shapes and materials and their weight and cost vary accordingly. Most tents have the advantage of being virtually insect proof, which can be crucial in many parts of the country during the summer. The primary function of any tent is to keep you dry and give you a place to retreat from the weather. When backpacking, you need a tent that is big enough for you and your gear but light enough to be easy to carry. On other occasions (while hunting, car camping, etc.) or in inclement weather, you may need a bigger tent that you can use for resting and other activities. The type of camping that you do ultimately determines what type of tent you will need. Many people have more than one tent — a small, light one for backpacking, and a larger, more roomy tent for family or car camping (Figure 4-4).

Figure 4-4. Car camping in autumn

Sleeping gear generally includes a sleeping bag and a foam pad or cot to lie down on. The role of the sleeping bag is to keep you warm as you sleep, when you metabolism slows down. The foam pad or cot supports you to make you more comfortable but also insulates you so that you do not lose heat to the ground. A light combination of foam pad and sleeping bag should be selected to reduce weight and bulk when backpacking. For car camping and other trips when weight is not a concern, folding cots with mattresses and bulky sleeping bags may be appropriate. The foam pad or mattress under you is often more important for your sleeping comfort than the quality of your sleeping bag. If the pad is not reasonably comfortable or you feel cold from being on the ground, you will not sleep well. This is especially true if a thin pad is used in combination with a down sleeping bag that compresses completely under your body and therefore does not provide adequate insulation between you and the ground. People often spend hundreds of dollars on top-rate sleeping bags but cheat themselves by buying inexpensive foam pads that prevent them from sleeping well. Invest in your sleeping comfort: buy a good quality pad that is thick enough to be comfortable and will not let moisture pass through. If you sleep well, you will enjoy camping.

A sleeping bag is not always necessary and one bag may not be suitable for all conditions. Some people carry lightweight sleeping bags for moderate temperatures and heavy down bags for winter camping or high altitude climbs. Others prefer to buy a medium-warmth bag and add a cloth liner to it or wear more clothes to be comfortable on cooler nights. On warm summer nights or when camping in the desert, a simple blanket may be all you need for sleeping on your pad.

When you are out camping, there is nothing like a good hot meal at night and a cup of hot coffee in the morning. The key to enjoying cooking and eating good food outdoors is having a reliable, stable, easy-to-use camp stove. A two-burner Coleman white-gas camping stove placed securely on the tailgate of our pickup truck is the most convenient and reliable cooking arrangement that we know of for car camping (Figure 4-5). But the bulky, eight-pound stove does not work well for backpacking. Fortunately, there are a wide variety of camping stoves available in a range of sizes, weights, fuel types and costs. Many are small and light enough for backpacking. Our favorite stove for backpacking is the Optimus 66, which we have used for years. It weighs about one-and-a-half pounds when full of gas, is ultimately reliable in all seasons and has never let us down. We have used it above the Arctic Circle, in the tropics and in the winter snows of Upper Michigan over a period of 30 years. What makes it a great stove is ease of use, simple construction, safety and reliability.

Whether you cook over a campfire or on a gas camp stove, the pots, pans and cooking utensils that you use must be consistent with your heat source and mode of travel. If you are cooking on an open fire, a stainless steel wire mesh secured over the fire pit will make cooking safe and efficient. Some people carry steel support rods to hold up a spit or central rod for holding pot handles. On an open fire, it is a good idea to use pots and lids with metal handles or wire "bails" that will not burn in the fire. Wooden or plastic handles will eventually burn off or melt down with use. The material that is most practical for the manufacture of camping equipment is aluminum, although other metals can also be used. Most pots and utensils are made of aluminum because of its light weight, low cost and high heat tolerance. Cast iron pans can crack if the heat is too intense on an open fire or over charcoal.

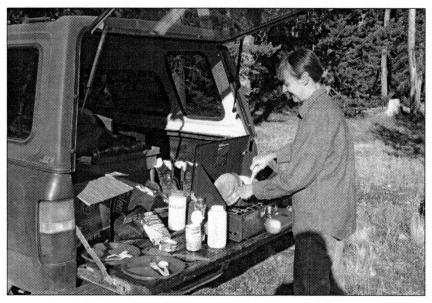

Figure 4-5. The tailgate can be your kitchen

Camping pots often come bundled together in sets offering a range of pot sizes and lids. After some experimentation, you can decide which pots you use most often and whether you want to add a pan or other item to your cook set. Generally, a lightweight frying pan and two sizes of aluminum pots with covers are all you need for backpacking. Some people carry coffeepots and Dutch ovens when weight is not too much of a concern. There are even small espresso coffee makers available for backpacking. In general, when you are concerned about reducing weight, you should eliminate specialty pots and utensils and stay with the basic, multiple use items. If you are cooking entirely freeze-dried meals, you only need one pot in which to boil water. On backcountry winter camping trips you may need a large pot to melt snow for your daily water supply.

Dishes and eating utensils should be minimal and lightweight. A wide variety of forks, spoons and knives made from plastic or Lexan are available. At a minimum, each individual should carry a cutting blade, fork, spoon, plastic cup and one medium-sized plate. Obviously, if you are car camping, you may want to have extras like glasses, bowls, chopsticks, wineglasses or whatever else you fancy. Many hikers prefer to sip their water directly from their individual water bottle, thereby reducing the need to carry extra glasses.

Cleanup after dinner is simple when you are backpacking. The washing area that you designated when setting up camp should not be within 200 feet of any open water or wetland to avoid contaminating natural waters. You need to carry a biodegradable detergent and dishrag or nylon "scrubby" with you and a water bottle as your water source. Experiment with minimizing water use when washing dishes. If you don't use excessive amounts of detergent, you will not need lots of rinse water. Let your dishes air dry. You will be surprised how little water you need to wash your dishes. Also, use purified water for this task. If you are car camping, you might consider carrying plastic wash basins for doing dishes. These are quite handy if you are traveling with a large group and can reduce overall water use. Think ahead, use some common sense and kitchen cleanup will go smoothly.

Your drinking water supply is a prime consideration when you are on the trail or in camp. Gone are the days when you could dip your tin cup into a clear mountain stream for a cool refreshing drink of water. Now we must expect to purify water for any drinking or cooking uses to ensure that it is free of biological or chemical contamination. For a day hike you can, of course, carry two or three liters of water with you and have sufficient water for a very long day. But on overnight trips, you need to plan ahead so that you can establish camp close to a water source and you are able to purify the water for potable use.

Whereas you only need limited quantities of water with you on the trail, in camp, you will generally use more water for cooking, cleanup and personal washing. All of the water that you consume for drinking, cooking, cleanup, tooth brushing and personal hygiene must be safe, purified water. This water should be free of microorganisms such as bacteria, amoebae (Giardia Lambia and others) and toxic chemicals and preferably clear of dirt, particulates, viruses, odor and foul taste. Boiling for at least 30 minutes is a tried-and-true method for eliminating bacteria, amoebae and most odor and taste problems. However, boiling will not eliminate viruses, dissolved metals or particulates. When packing for your trip, remember that boiling water takes time and requires you to bring extra fuel for your stove.

Chemical water treatments include iodine tablets and chlorine. Iodine tablets are light and very effective at eliminating bacteria and amoebae but they are not effective for treating particulates, viruses, metals, odors and taste (Figure 4-6). Some hikers and campers avoid using iodine because it gives water an acrid taste. However, secondary treatment pills are available which when added to the water take care of the iodine taste after 30 minutes. Chlorine treatments have the added advantage of being effective for most viruses, if applied for extended periods. In general, standard chemical treatments target microorganisms living in the water and do not effectively remove particulates, metals taste and odor. Specialized treatments are needed to remove these properties.

In recent years, several small, portable water filtration and purification units that are generally very effective for primary water treatment have been developed. These units are basically hand-pumped filtration systems that may or may not include secondary treatment but are ideal for outdoor applications. The filters are made from replaceable ceramic, membrane or synthetic materials that fit into a cylindrical chamber. A piston and valve system at the front of the assembly typically drives water through the filter material. On the downstream side of the filter, some units have a carbon adsorption chamber or other assembly to provide secondary treatment. A few units allow you to clean and reuse the filter material, but most require replacement of the filter cartridge when it is spent. The units generally weigh between one and two pounds

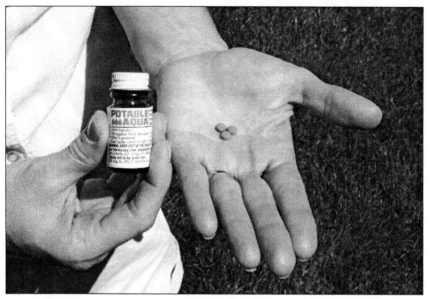

Figure 4-6. Iodine tablets are effective for treating water

and can purify several liters of water in 15 minutes when the filters are fresh. Filter life varies for different units but most will purify at least dozens of liters of water before replacements are necessary. Obviously, the dirtier the initial water, the shorter the life of the filter unit.

The primary filtration stage of a typical purification unit will remove particulates, amoebae, bacteria, and in some cases, viruses from water. A secondary chamber packed with activated carbon can remove some chemicals, odors and metals. You can count on the unit for providing safe drinking water but viruses, metals, odor and taste may still be present. Water purification units are generally safe to use in rural and wild areas of North America. If you are traveling anywhere else in the world, check on local water conditions there (especially viruses) that may require additional treatment. Proper maintenance and handling of your purification unit are necessary to ensure that your drinking water is safe. Read and follow the instructions for your individual unit (Figure 4-7).

After dark, whether you are relaxing in your camp or hiking along a trail, you may need a flashlight or other light source to see with. Most of the time you will find that a headlamp is the most convenient light source available. This is because with the light on your head, your hands are free to do other things. Also if you adjust the headlamp properly, it will direct the beam of light to where it needs to be, that is, to where you are looking. So for hiking, cooking, washing dishes or any other tasks you may want to do at night, a headlamp is just the ticket. Batteries can last up to 70 hours in some of the new, efficient headlamps so you don't need to carry pounds of batteries with you. But depending on the length of your trip and how much you use the lamp, you may need to carry extra batteries and a spare bulb or lamp. Know where you keep your spares so you can find them when things go dark and know how to replace them in the dark. It is also useful to have an extra small flashlight with you as a backup to use in emergencies.

Figure 4-7. Using a water filter pump to purify water

There are several light sources that can be used to provide general lighting and tent illumination when you are out camping. Of the many choices available, ranging from candle lamps to book lights, it is hard to beat a Coleman white-gas lantern or kerosene lamp for providing reliable camp light. But both types of lamps need to be used carefully so as not to create a fire hazard. They should definitely not be used inside your tent due to the potential fire danger and also because of the possible buildup of fumes and carbon monoxide gas. If you think that you will require better illumination inside your tent than a flashlight, consider bringing along an electric light. There are a number of electric lamps available for general and in-tent use that are safe. Be sure that you consider the battery life of your camping lights, particularly when planning longer trips. Some lights can be hooked up to the cigarette lighter or utility outlet of your car if you plan to car camp. This lets you rely on the car battery, which is easily recharged for power.

To make packing for a trip easier, we recommend that you develop an equipment check list that you can use as guide while packing for your own trips. A checklist keeps you from forgetting items that you will need. To get you started, we have provided two basic equipment lists for you to use in preparation for a typical backpacking trip and car camping trip assuming that each trip lasts three days and two nights (the average weekend). The backpacking list is provided in Table 3 and the car camping list is provided in Table 4. Obviously, you can add or delete items based on your personal preferences, including special items needed for your favorite sport or hobby. On longer trips, you might want to add some luxury items to make your camp more comfortable and enjoyable.

Table 3. Backpacking equipment list

The ten essentials (map, compass, light, extra food and water, extra clothing, sunglasses, First Aid kit, pocketknife, matches and fire starter materials)

Backpack (medium to large)

Trekking or ski poles (optional)

Tent (lightweight) and ground cloth

Sleeping pad

Sleeping bag with stuff sack

3 large, plastic garbage bags

2 to 3 water bottles

Gas stove with extra fuel bottles

2 cooking pots with lids

1 plastic cup

1 plastic dish (medium)

Plastic silverware

Biodegradable dish detergent

Water purification/filter unit or chemical treatment supplies

Food (appropriate for trip and weather conditions)

Headlamp or flashlight (or other light source)

Shell jacket with hood (windproof and waterproof)

Down vest or fleece jacket (or extra warm layers in cold weather seasons)

Rain pants

Gaiters (for snowy conditions)

Sun hat

Stocking cap

Gloves or mittens (to suit weather conditions)

Extra clothing (to suit weather conditions)

Extra socks

Extra pack straps and nylon cord

Personal hygiene supplies (toothbrush, tooth paste, biodegradable soap, wash cloth, towel, toilet paper, trowel, etc.)

Hobby and entertainment supplies (camera, film, paperback novel, pen, paper, deck of cards, field guides, etc.)

## Table 4. Car camping equipment list

The ten essentials (map, compass, light, extra food and water, extra clothing, sunglasses, First Aid kit, pocketknife, matches and fire starter materials)
Daypack (for hiking)
Trekking or ski poles (optional)
Tent and ground cloth
Sleeping pad
Sleeping bag with stuff sack
3 or more large, plastic garbage bags
2 to 3 water bottles
Large water jug or bottle (several liters in size; several gallons if you will rely on water from home)
Camp gas stove with extra fuel
Cooking pots with lids and frying pan
Plastic cup(s)
Plastic water glass(es)
Plastic dish(es)
Plastic silverware
Cooking utensils
Biodegradable dish detergent
Plastic dish pans
Dish brush scrubbing pads, etc.
Water purification filter unit or chemical treatment supplies
Food (appropriate for trip and weather conditions)
Cooler for food storage
Headlamp or flashlight
Coleman type gas lantern or a kerosene lamp for general camp lighting
Camp shovel
Wind and waterproof jacket with hood
Down vest or fleece jacket (or extra warm layers in cold weather seasons)
Rain pants
Gaiters (for snowy conditions)
Sun hat
Stocking cap
Gloves or mittens (to suit weather conditions)
Extra clothing (to suit weather conditions)
Extra socks
Extra pack straps and nylon cord
Personal hygiene supplies (toothbrush, tooth paste, biodegradable soap, wash cloth, towel, toilet paper, trowel, etc.)
Hobby and entertainment supplies (camera, film, paperback novel, pen, paper, deck of cards, field guides, etc.)

## 4.3    GETTING TO CAMP

### 4.3.1
### *Backpacking*

Backpacking is the form of travel where you hike to your campsite carrying all of your equipment and supplies with you in a backpack. It requires you to minimize the type of gear and food that you take along and to reduce bulk and weight as much as practical to allow you to carry what you need. It is up to each individual to keep the load reasonable and yet carry all the necessities and other special items that make a given trip feasible and enjoyable. Some backpackers prefer to travel very light so that they can cover more ground in a day. Others would rather carry a few more items even if it slows them down a little. Much of the preparation for backpacking trips involves trial and error until an individual develops a style that he or she is comfortable with. It also depends on the weather conditions you expect to encounter and the number of days that you will be traveling.

The backpack is the single most important piece of equipment used in backpacking. All large backpacks contain an internal or external frame constructed from either metal or plastic that provides them with their basic structure (Figure 4-8). When evaluating which pack to buy, look for one with a frame that fits your back comfortably. The fit of the pack to your back is the main factor that will allow you to carry loads for long periods of time. Some companies make two or three sizes of support frames or frames that are somewhat adjustable. Less expensive brands tend to have a one-size-fits-all approach to packs whereas more expensive brands provide adjustable frames and other helpful features such as special models designed to fit women's backs and torsos more comfortably.

Other things to look for in a pack are overall volume, compartmentalization and materials used for pack construction. The volume in cubic inches is simply a measure of how much gear you can carry in the pack. It is useful for rough comparison of backpacks but doesn't mean much until you try fitting your own food and equipment into the pack. On some trips, an outfitter might tell you to bring at least a 4,500 cubic inch pack so that you will have a good idea of what is needed.

Compartmentalization, that is the layout of the pack into compartments and pockets, is usually more important than volume alone. The number of compartments in a pack refers to how many individual packing areas are available in the main body of the pack. Look for a pack that has at least two compartments, an upper and lower, in the main body. This allows you to keep things sorted, but more important, it lets you distribute weight in the pack. Remembering our earlier discussion about the importance of COG when you are hiking, the upper and lower pack compartments let you control the COG within the pack. By loading heavier items into the upper compartment and lighter ones below, you essentially keep the COG high. You can also control weight by placing heavier items in your high outer pockets. The best backpack designs have a compartment separator or baffle that can be kept in place to maintain two compartments or can be unzipped to form a single large compartment. There are times when having one compartment is advantageous so that you can carry large or long objects. An extension sleeve at the top of the pack body also allows you to carry more in the pack. A pack should have several pockets, at least one of which should be located in the top flap providing easy access to frequently used items such as your compass and sunglasses. The number and arrangement of pockets depends on your personal preference but pockets are the easiest way to keep your smaller items organized within the backpack. Select a backpack that weighs less than three pounds when empty in the case of a medium-sized pack or seven pounds in the case of a very large pack.

The key to successful backpacking is traveling light yet still bringing everything you need with you. It takes experience to get the right balance of supplies, equipment and fuel but the backpacking equipment list provided in Table 3 should be a good guide to ensure that you have what you need. If you can assemble these items, including three days of food and two quarts of water, and the pack feels like you can carry it for a day without struggling, you are off to a good start. A medium pack should weigh in at about 30 to 35 pounds when loaded, excluding

(a)

(b)

Figure 4-8. Backpacks can have internal or external frames: a) Arc'Teryx Bora 80 Pack with an internal frame b) Kelty Long Trail Junior Pack with an external frame (Photos courtesy of Recreational Equipment Inc.)

trekking poles, food or water. This assumes that you are carrying a two-man tent, your stove and gas and not sharing these items with someone else.

In warm weather, you can probably reduce the weight to less than 25 pounds. For winter camping, your weight may increase to more than 50 pounds unless you have very light equipment. If your loads weigh more than our recommended amounts without food, water and poles, you should review each item to see where you can reduce weight. Usually the heaviest individual items are the tent (two-person backpacking) and sleeping bag. If these two items weigh more than seven pounds each for warm weather use, they should be replaced by lighter selections. Check your smaller items as well to see where you might save a few ounces here and there. It all adds up very quickly.

Efficient backpacking requires planning of equipment, supplies and daily goals. The latter point is where people are often unrealistic, expecting to travel further in a day than they can realistically hike. Plan the daily hike to be on the conservative side so that you can reach your intended campsite without having to rush or compensate with extra hours. You are out in nature to enjoy it, not to set land speed records. You also need to be realistic about speed in the event of inclement weather and other possible contingencies. Plan to get to camp early enough to find a nice spot to set up in daylight and enjoy yourself. Budget extra time in case the small meadow you planned to camp in is already occupied when you get there and you have to search out a nearby site. In short, be realistic in your planning and you will enjoy your trip.

## 4.3.2
### Traveling by Car

The most common form of travel to a campsite is by car or truck. Millions of North Americans, Europeans, Australians and other outdoor enthusiasts around the world drive to their campsites every year. People like to car camp because it is a convenient and economical way to get the family, friends and gear out so they can enjoy a brief vacation out of doors. Some environmental purists dismiss car camping as inappropriate because it relies on motorized vehicles and requires road access. But there is nothing fundamentally wrong with car camping as long as people respect nature and stay on established roadways. Many people who are getting older, are physically challenged or have limited time would not be able to enjoy nature if they could not drive into a campsite. Our philosophy on camping is all-inclusive. The outdoors should not be available to just the young and healthy but to everyone who wants to enjoy nature in an environmentally protective manner. This is called "multiple use" and has been the policy of several federal land management agencies since their establishment.

Traveling by car has many advantages. If your time is limited, you can travel to areas a reasonable distance away from home for a weekend. You can pack your necessary camping gear and other hobby, sport or luxury items without undue concern about weight and bulk. (See our suggested car camping equipment list in Table 4). You can take fresh food with you in a cooler and make homestyle foods on a grill or camp stove. For many older campers, the car camp serves as a base for day hikes, fishing and other outdoor activities. For the handicapped, a car camp can make the difference between enjoying the outdoors and missing out on the best of nature. Car camping is also an economical form of travel, one that saves the cost of motel bills when you are on vacation. No wonder it is the most popular form of camping!

Road accessibility is the main factor influencing the selection and organization of the car campsite. In addition to laying out the camp into activity zones, you must now include room for a vehicle parking area that may also serve as the kitchen or some other function (Figure 4-9). In bear country, the vehicle might be used as the sleeping area. This is especially true if you have a camper shell or pop-up camper on a pickup truck or if you have a camp trailer. In any of these cases, keeping your vehicle on an existing roadway or camp parking space is required and the location of the driving areas will largely determine camp organization. Most national parks and forests that are heavily used have permanent campgrounds set up for tents as well as for hard-wall campers.

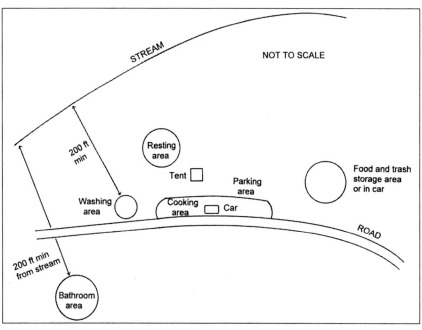

Figure 4-9. A typical car camp layout

All prospective car campers should be very clear on one point — you should not drive into a roadless area no matter how nice it looks. This is especially true if the ground is soft and/or wet because your vehicle will create ruts in the vegetation that can take years to recover. Also you may very well get stuck and nothing takes the fun out of camping like a vehicle buried up to the axles in mud! In most national forests, there are pull-outs along the side of existing roads where people have parked before and you can generally take advantage of these to park your vehicle and set up camp nearby. If an area is blocked off by boulders, posts or signs that indicate you should not park there, don't do it. There are usually a number of alternatives close by if you just look around. In most forests, the existing logging roads provide adequate access to potential campsites and you do no additional damage to the forest if you drive on these existing roads.

### 4.3.3
### *Traveling with an Animal*

In some parts of the country such as the western US, it can be very rewarding to travel to your campsite on horseback with or without the company of a packhorse or mule (Figure 4-10). Traveling with horses has some distinct advantages. Horseback riding is very enjoyable and you can experience wild areas in the way early explorers did. Because you don't have to walk, you can save some wear-and-tear on your legs and you can often cover more distance in a day than if you were walking. With a packhorse you can travel into remote areas and carry supplies for a longer stay. Horseback riding also allows many people who are not in the best of health to enjoy nature and travel greater distances than they would go under their own power.

Figure 4-10. A rider leading a packhorse

But before heading out to rent horses for a pack trip, it is worth considering some of the disadvantages of horse travel as well. First of all, you need to know how to ride well and to handle horses under a range of conditions. Your trip is going to be very different from enjoying a short ride in the park on someone's pony. You need to understand how to handle and care for large animals and anticipate how they will react in stormy weather, on steep trails and in unfamiliar situations. In addition to the normal activities associated with camping, you will be expected to perform extra horse-related duties. For instance, you will have to saddle the riding horses each morning, load up the packhorse(s), ride through various woods and meadows while leading your packhorse(s), unload the packs at the end of the day, unsaddle the horses, brush them, water them, check their feet, find them grass and keep track of them at night.

In short, traveling with horses is a lot of work and a good part of the morning and evening can be consumed by horse-related chores. Also, if you are traveling with others, you should not assume that everyone in the group has the necessary experience. Most pleasure riders deal with horses under very controlled conditions and are unprepared for the situations you may encounter on a pack trip. In fact, people who claim to know a lot about horses quite often find out that they are over their heads on a pack trip.

When you rent horses for your trip, you will quickly discover how unfamiliar you are with their training and quirks. In this case, be prepared to discover their behavior and level of ability as you go along. If you are riding your own animals, then you are familiar with their personalities and some of their quirks already. This removes some uncertainty but you will still put the animals into new situations where they may spook or falter. Be prepared to handle these difficulties. With time you will be able to anticipate and even avoid some problems as you and your horses gain experience. If available, you might consider using mules for the pack animals since they are less nervous and may adapt to packing more readily.

If you are planning to rent horses and have limited experience you should consider hiring a wrangler to go with you and take charge of the horses. The added expense may be well worthwhile on your first pack trip and it will probably make your experience more enjoyable. Some outfitters may require you to take a guide or wrangler with you anyway, to safeguard their investment in their horses.

Stowing away gear for a horse pack trip is quite different from packing for a backpacking or car camping trip. The packhorse has a special type of packsaddle that is designed to carry loads in large bags called panniers. The saddle itself is very simple (Figure 4-11) being comprised of two padded rests that sit on either side of the horse's spine to support the weight. The rests are joined by two cross-trees that the panniers hook onto. The packsaddle can support a considerable load of more than 100 pounds as long as it is packed properly. Most of the weight should be packed into the panniers to keep a low COG and lighter items such as sleeping bags and pads can be packed on top of the saddle. The panniers must be equally balanced and the load must be lashed down securely so that it will not flop around or come loose during the day.

Figure 4-11. A Pro Decker packsaddle on "Soldier of Fortune", a registered Appaloosa (Photo courtesy of Rich Tuck, Pack Saddle Shop)

The gear that you pack on the horse will essentially be inaccessible all day. If rain is possible, you should cover the load with a rubberized or cloth tarp to keep it dry. Do not use a plastic or fiberglass tarp because the crinkling noise made during handling will likely make the horse nervous if it has not heard that sound before. Keep your drinking water, lunch, ten essentials, poncho, raingear and anything else you need for the day within easy reach in the saddlebags on your riding horse.

The route and distance traveled on horseback depends on how well trained your horses are and where they can go safely. While horses are sure-footed, the rider must still select a reasonable route for them to follow. This applies to steep terrain, drop-offs and slippery trails. If the horse balks at a steep, gravelly slope or other obstacle across the trail, there is usually a good reason for it and you would be advised to seek another path. Hiking trails in forests are often not wide enough for a packhorse load. Keep in mind that a packhorse is wider than a horse carrying a rider and the panniers and other protruding items may bump into trees or rock outcrops as you ride past. Also fallen trees and other obstacles that may not be a problem when you are on foot may have to be cleared for horses to pass.

Camping with horses is similar to other forms of camping except that you need to care for your tack and provide grazing and water for the horses (Figure 4-12). A fallen log is handy to set saddles and blankets on for the night. The tack should also be covered with a tarp in case of rain. The horses need to graze and drink water after a full day's work. This means that your camp needs to be close to a stream and some grassy areas. A reliable way of controlling your horses is to tie up one or two while allowing the rest to graze freely. If your horses are trained for it, you can hobble them — tie a strap about a foot long between the front legs so they can't walk or run quickly. If horses are used to being staked out on a long lead, you can do that also, but unless they are used to this, they may get tangled up in the rope. If you have rental horses, ask the owner what works best for his horses and stick with that method for grazing and overnight control. You don't want to injure the horses or wake up to find out that they walked home during the night.

An alternate pack animal that can prove to be very useful on longer hikes across difficult terrain is the llama. Llamas are docile, gentle creatures that make good trail companions after you get familiar

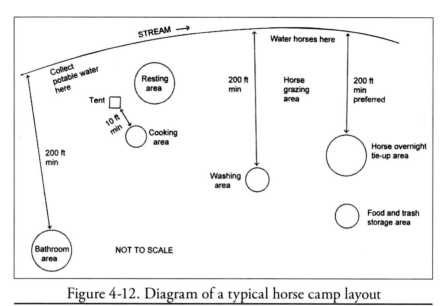

Figure 4-12. Diagram of a typical horse camp layout

with them and they can carry sizeable loads of 60 to 70 pounds per animal (Figure 4-13). The typical llama pack system consists of a smaller version of a packsaddle resembling a saddlebag or dual pannier, which is designed to spread the weight over a broad area. Llamas are strictly pack animals, not for riding. They are smaller than horses and less destructive on the trail because they do not have hard hoofs and consequently do not cut into soft, wet soil the way that horses do. They tend to have good stamina and can easily travel 8-12 miles a day with a reasonable load. Llamas can be a good choice for packing into high mountain passes and meadows similar to those found in their natural habitat in the South American Andes. They are able to eat poorer quality grasses and consume less food and water than horses do due to their superior adaptation to higher elevations and their smaller size. The only limitation to llama use is the fact that relatively few areas have them available for rent. This will undoubtedly change with time as they become more popular.

Camels and yaks are two more animals that are used for riding or pack trips in other parts of the world. In the hot, dry regions of North Africa and Asia, camels are routinely used for traveling across the desert because they are extremely well adapted to traveling great distances

Figure 4-13 Llamas with packsaddles can be great trailside companions

with little food and water in those climates. Camel safaris are a well-known tourist attraction in central Australia where the animals were originally imported as beasts of burden for the mining industry. Yaks are more common in the mountainous states of the Himalayas and the steppes of the former Soviet Union where they provide food and milk for the local population in addition to serving as pack animals. Naturally, if you are planning an exotic overseas camping trip that requires support from pack animals that you are unfamiliar with, you will need to make special arrangements to rent these animals and hire a handler to take care of them en route.

### 4.3.4
### *Traveling on Water*

Travel by boat can be an effective form of transportation in many backcountry areas of North America where roads and trails are scarce.

Sometimes a boat, raft, canoe or kayak may be the only means to reach a camp. In many parts of the upper and western US and in much of Canada, canoe travel along rivers is often the best way to get into remote forested areas. Paddling along interconnected rivers and lakes can be a very enjoyable way to get away from crowded campgrounds (Figure 4-14). If you are prepared to travel light, a kayak may be effectively used for camping travel on rivers that have too much whitewater for canoeing. Sea kayaks offer considerably more cargo space for camping expeditions and can be used in selected coastal areas. On many western rivers, rafts allow groups to carry equipment for multiday camps along the scenic river banks. Powerboats are commonly employed to access camps on larger lakes and reservoirs, although boaters usually car camp or trailer camp along the shoreline using their boats for sport and not actual camping.

Figure 4-14. Visit the wilderness by canoe

There are several camping considerations that are common to all types of watercraft that you may use for travel and camping. First of all, your equipment and supplies must be waterproof because no matter how careful you are, your gear is likely to get wet. This calls for extra planning and care to pack your gear in waterproof stuff sacks or to line the inside of your existing stuff sacks with plastic garbage bags. Some items such as gas cans and water bottles do not have to be waterproofed in any way if they are properly sealed. You also need to divide your equipment into several parcels that can be distributed around your boat to maintain an optimal weight distribution. It is best to pack heavy objects down low — below waterline is best — to keep your craft's COG low. Don't plan to stack a lot of gear above the gunwales on a canoe or kayak or you may make it tippy. Any gear that is placed in a boat should be secured so that it will not move around if you encounter rough water. If the load shifts position it can change the balance of the boat and make the boat more difficult to maneuver or cause it to take on water. Poorly secured gear that projects above the gunwales could be lost over the side.

When canoeing in whitewater, rainstorms or choppy water, a spray skirt can provide some protection from shipping water. A spray skirt is simply a waterproof sheet or tarp that can be fitted over the open areas of your boat to keep water out. The skirt fits tightly over the gunwales and is fixed to the boat by Velcro or hooks along the gunwales. It should be tight enough or supported in such a way that it will shed water to the outside of the boat. On a canoe, you may need three separate skirts (fore, middle and aft) to cover your gear and to shed rain, wave spray and the occasional wave crest. We have used spray skirts very effectively while canoe camping on long fjord-like lakes and rivers in the Yukon Territory, Canada. The skirts saw us and our gear through numerous rainstorms and some three-foot storm waves that broke over the gunwales several times. Without them, we certainly would have swamped in 40-degree water. Spray skirts are highly recommended for the open portion of any watercraft when camping.

Most of the usual rules of camping apply on lakes and along waterways and shorelines. Make sure that your watercraft is securely tied up whenever you stop and especially overnight. Changes in water levels may occur over a period of just a few hours after a thunderstorm causing your partially grounded canoe or kayak to float. Even a sudden high wind can pull a canoe off a sandbank if it is not properly secured. Overnight, it is best to move your canoe or kayak above the water line and preferably above the high tide mark before you tie it to a tree or boulder or stake it to the ground.

If you are boating and camping in a populated area where theft is a concern, you can secure your boat to a tree with a bicycle cable and lock. Be prepared for the worst. If you lose your boat, you lose your transportation and perhaps some gear as well. In the backcountry, you should bring the paddle and oars into camp to protect them from being eaten by animals. In some areas, rodents such as porcupines, beavers, marmots and squirrels find varnished wood or plastic handles especially tasty. Suspending paddles by rope in a tree is another generally safe means of overnight storage.

# CHAPTER 5    CLOTHING AND EQUIPMENT

The purpose of this chapter is to provide our readers with a basic understanding of hiking and camping gear so that you can make informed decisions when preparing for a hike or trip. We will discuss the basic principles of dressing for the outdoors, selecting materials and designs of footwear, clothing and equipment, and the functional advantages and disadvantages of different designs. Our intent is not to list and discuss every manufacturer and model of an item that is available on the market, but to inform you about what to look for when you are selecting gear. We will introduce a few specific models only by way of example and point out the features that make those models good choices. Finally, we encourage you to browse through the addresses and Internet Web sites of several manufacturers of outdoor equipment that we have compiled for you at the back of this book. You might want to contact them directly for more specific information.

## 5.1    FOOTWEAR SYSTEMS

Hiking footwear is designed to provide comfortable foot containers that (1) minimize wear-and-tear on your feet; provide (2) traction, (3) heat insulation, (4) protection and (5) support; and (6) act as a platform onto which additional equipment can be attached. On any given hike, you may favor some of these functions more than others. For example, on a hot summer day you may prefer to wear walking sandals rather than boots on a prepared trail to keep your feet cool. On a winter climbing trip, warm boots that provide insulation, ankle protection and rigid support for attached crampons might be the features you would desire in your footwear. In an ideal world, we could have a different shoe for each type of activity that we engage in. But for most hikers cost alone reduces the number of boots we can buy. Therefore, we have to compromise with respect to the functions that we need and the cost we can afford.

Footwear systems are composed of boots/shoes and socks. Boots/shoes provide the six basic functions listed above whereas socks provide additional insulation, moisture management, padding, friction control and comfort. Boots and socks work in combination to provide optimum performance on the trail.

The footwear system that you select must suit your intended activity if you want to hike efficiently and enjoy yourself. For a short walk on a sidewalk or paved trail, nearly any type of footwear will do as long as it fits and feels comfortable. For longer walks on more or less even surfaces, such as in a city park or street, a shoe designed for walking such as a Rocksport Prowalker, may be suitable. Some athletic shoes will also suffice in this application. When you get onto gravel or unmaintained trails or hillslopes, then a true hiking boot providing better foot support and traction is advised. The weight, height, materials, design and stiffness of the boot can vary depending on the duration, frequency and conditions of your hiking regimen. Generally, hiking boots can be broken down into three categories: light, medium and heavy-duty; based on the actual weight of the boots and the intensity of the hikes they were designed for.

## 5.1.1
### Boots

A boot is essentially a shoe with a tall upper that rises to cover the ankle. Hiking boots are constructed to address the six functions of footwear and their underlying construction therefore differs somewhat from ordinary shoes. Basic components of the boot are illustrated in Figure 5-1. The midsole of the boot is the platform on which the insole and the upper are built. The sole may contain a synthetic foam or leather midsole onto which a rubberized outsole and heel are attached. The lugged outsole and heel is the layer that utilizes either a ridge pattern containing lugs or a soft malleable material to provide traction. The midsole may contain a metal or synthetic shank attached along part of its length to make the sole stiff. It can also contain a stiffening layer to reduce torsion in the sole. The shank may lie above, within or below the midsole. There may also be an additional layer or plate of nylon or polyurethane within the midsole to prevent puncture of the boot sole and to provide lateral stiffness to the boot. An insole plate is usually placed on top of the midsole. The upper is glued or stitched onto the midsole by a seal called a welt. The upper itself consists of the outer layer, a layer of padding/insulation and a liner made from soft leather or cloth. On most hiking boots, the upper rises above the ankle to provide support against twisting motions of the foot. The top of the upper may be padded with what is called a "scree collar" which softens any rubbing that occurs against the skin and helps keep dirt and debris out of the boots. The closure of the boot includes a tongue, which may or may not be attached at the sides to the upper by a gusset. The upper and tongue are secured to the foot by a lacing system that can be used to stiffen the boot upper so as to enhance foot and ankle support. Additional leather or rubberized patches called counters may be added to strengthen the heel and toe of the upper and to protect them against abrasion (Figure 5-2). Finally, a removable foam footbed can be placed on the insole plate inside the boot to provide cushioning and arch support and to center the foot in the boot.

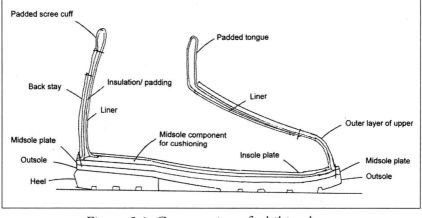

Figure 5-1. Cross-section of a hiking boot

The main feature to look for in a boot initially is support for your foot and ankle. Foot support is provided primarily by the midsole, insole and footbed. The footbed should support the arch and keep the heel centered within the rear of the boot. This is especially important when you are carrying a loaded backpack. Without proper arch support, the foot arch will have to do more work, and over time, it will flatten, weaken and lengthen the foot somewhat. So good arch support is a must. In addition to providing support, the footbed also centers the arch and heel to improve balance and distribute stress throughout the foot.

Many manufacturers supply very simple footbeds in their boots, which may be inadequate to provide your foot with support and comfort. Fortunately, such footbeds can be easily removed and replaced with more supportive inserts. Several companies manufacture replacement footbeds and supplemental insoles. If you have a particular orthopedic problem such as pronation (a common tendency for the heel to roll inward), you can have custom footbeds made for your boots or shoes to enhance support. We personally use Dr. Scholl's inserts in some of our older hiking boots, Superfeet footbeds in our newer mountaineering boots and Athletes Foot gel insoles in our running shoes. These modifications have greatly improved our arch support and general foot comfort when we are hiking.

Figure 5-2. Exterior of a hiking boot showing the rand, heel and toe counters, and lacing system

Ankle support results from the enclosure of the ankle by a padded upper and lacing system. When properly laced, the upper holds the lower leg and ankle, reducing lateral rotation of the ankle on uneven ground. This is very important on backcountry trails where a sprained ankle can be a major setback. A snug fitting boot prevents ankle sprains and foot pain by keeping the foot centered and properly oriented, even when you are walking on rocks and uneven trails.

Boots that fit properly are essential for comfort and support. Fitting should be done with one heavy sock or two lighter socks approximating the sock combination you expect to use while hiking. Each boot should be long enough in the toe so that the toes do not touch the front of the boot. For a test fit, lace the boots up tightly and kick the heel of each boot on the ground to settle your heel into the heel pocket. Then test for two things: 1) that your heel cannot move from side to side in the heel pocket and 2) that you have at least one-quarter inch of open space in front of your toes. If these conditions are met, kick the toe of each boot against a curb or step several times and see if your toes touch the front. If they touch, you need to try another half-size larger boot or change your socks to a thinner combination and try again.

Another test to see how far forward your foot has shifted when you kick the toe is to stick your finger in the boot behind your heel and see how much of a gap there is. If your foot moved forward more than one-quarter inch, it is not a good fit. Also try standing on tiptoes in the boots and feel whether your heels lift up in the heel pocket. If they move more than a quarter of an inch when you have thick socks on, this means that the boot does not fit you well enough. The best alternative is to try an equivalent model of boot made by another manufacturer and repeat the procedure until you get a good fit.

The reason why one model of boot may not fit as well as another is that each manufacturer uses slightly different foot forms (called "lasts") to build their boots around. Different lasts cause there to be differences in heel pocket width and height, foot arch, width of boot at the ball of the foot and toes and height of the top of the arch. In general, we have found that Italian boot makers carry boots that fit narrow feet and small heels better than others. When you are buying a boot, remember that different stores carry different brands, and therefore, you may have to visit two or three stores to find a wide selection of hiking boots. Don't settle for a poor fit. Once you find a boot that fits well and meets your needs, keep that brand in mind as a likely candidate for any additional boots that you might want to buy. Remember that you can change out the footbeds in nearly all boots, so you may be able to improve a boot's fit by trying another footbed in it.

Stiffness is another factor to consider in boot selection. A relatively flexible sole is preferable for light trail hiking. In winter and whenever you expect to encounter rough trail conditions, a stiffer boot is recommended from a durability and support point of view. If you plan to use crampons with your boots, then you will need to buy a relatively stiff sole so that the crampons do not loosen up as you walk. Many of the quick-release crampon bindings that are currently available on the market assume that your boot is very rigid and simply clamp onto indentations in the toe and heel of the boot sole. Stiff boots work well on snow, scree, rough ground and rocks. They also provide the extra support you need for carrying loads (Figure 5-3).

Figure 5-3. Examples of boots ranging from lightweight to heavyweight

Materials that are typically used to manufacture hiking boot uppers include leather, plastic and synthetic cloth. Leather is still the most common material used for the outer layer of the upper in all weights of boot. Leather is a flexible, permeable material that can be formed and worked easily to give a boot proper form and function. Leather from cattle can be split to yield a softer layer called "split leather" and an outer layer called "full-grain leather". The leather can be split and treated in many ways for a variety of uses. Full-grain leather has a rather smooth finish and is usually used to make the outer layer of most boot uppers. Full-grain leather is strongly recommended for most serious hiking applications because when properly sealed and cared for, it is very durable and practically waterproof. Split leather is more pliable and harder to waterproof. Consequently, it is commonly used for lightweight boots and shoes, as well as in other applications.

In recent years, manufacturers have combined Cordura nylon and other synthetic cloths with leather at key stress points to produce light hiking boots or "trail shoes" that are lighter and allow better air exchange with the exterior than full leather boots. This provides an advantage in warm weather, especially for people with sweaty feet, because the improved air exchange cools the feet and lets moisture out. The disadvantage of these boots is that they are not as easily waterproofed, frequently do not provide adequate ankle support and do not last as long as sturdier boots. Light duty boots and trail shoes can be good in dry climates, in the desert and on shorter hikes, but they don't perform well on wet trails, snow or rough terrain. In general, the fewer the seams there are in the boot upper, the better. Uppers that are made from full-grain leather cut in one piece with only one seam at the back are best for wear and waterproofing. There is usually a narrow strip of leather called a "back stay" that covers the rear seam and serves to seal and protect it.

The innermost layer of the boot upper is the liner, which forms the surface in contact with the sock. Traditionally, the liner is made of smooth, supple, finished leather. In some boots, cloth materials are used in place of leather to reduce weight and improve water resistance. Many boots have inner booties made from Gore-Tex cloth sewn and glued into them serving as liners to keep the feet dry in case the waterproofing on the outside of the boots fails. Foam rubber, Thinsolate or other pliable synthetic materials are usually placed between the liner and outer layer of the boot to provide padding, insulation and form to the inside of the boot.

Double-boots consist of a flexible, warm inner boot placed inside a heavyweight outer boot (Figure 5-4). They are designed primarily as winter boots because they are warm and waterproof. Both sets of boots usually have individual lacing systems. The inner boot can be made from a combination of felt and soft leather, heat-shaped foam or other synthetic material. It has a soft flexible sole, which allows it to slide into the outer boot. The outer boot consists of a midsole, outsole and outer portion of the upper. This acts essentially as a nearly rigid shell surrounding the inner boot. The outer boot upper can be made from heavy leather or plastic, allowing it to be very waterproof and rigid, which makes it ideal for crampon or ski attachment. Some companies have taken advantage of these properties and offer double boots for cross-country and telemark skiing applications. However, the disadvantage of heavy leather or plastic outer boots is that they generally do not "breathe" well, that is they do not allow adequate cooling or moisture exchange for your feet.

Figure 5-4. Double boots consist of an inner and outer boot

Boots made with plastic outers are much lighter than traditional leather double boots. The advantages of a double boot are the stiff, waterproof outer boot and the removable, warm, comfortable inner boot. If the inner boot becomes moist due to accumulated perspiration during a long day, it can be removed to allow it to dry overnight. The inner boot can be quite thick, providing plenty of insulation to keep the feet warm and padded. Double boots are widely used for snow and ice climbing and winter mountaineering throughout the world. Some double boots, such as the "Sorrel" type double boots and "Arctic Packs" are designed for warmth in extreme conditions but do not provide adequate foot or ankle support for general hiking use.

Once you slip your foot into a boot, a closure and lacing system seals the boot around your foot. The tongue acts to seal the gap between the two sides of the upper as the boot is closed up. The base, and in many cases the sides of the tongue, are attached to the upper with thin panels of pliable leather called a gusset or box tongue. Full-gusset uppers indicate that the leather side panels run the length of the tongue. The gusset acts to keep snow, water and dust out of the boot. With a full gusset, a hiker can step into puddles of water a few inches deep without getting wet feet, whereas the gusset-free boot will take water when the water level reaches the base of the tongue.

The lacing system is the mechanism used to close the boot, control ankle support and help control foot movement within the boot. Most boots make use of long bootlaces and a series of lace holes or hooks on either side of the upper to accomplish this. Some boots use straps to supplement the lacing system and on downhill ski boots a series of straps and buckles are employed. The lacing system can be used to adjust the fit of a boot and to stiffen it up to match the desired performance.

The welt is the feature used to attach the boot upper to the midsole. There are three basic types of welts: (1) cemented, (2) stitched or stitchdown and (3) injection molded. In a cemented welt, the bottom edges of the upper are folded under the bottom of the last and then cemented under pressure to the midsole. The result is a lightweight boot with a slightly narrower footprint compared to a stitched welt. With proper care, some glued welt boots can be resoled (with a new outsole). Stitched welt boots have the upper fitted to the last with the edges flared out around the bottom where the upper is sewn onto the insole plate. The insole plate is then glued onto the midsole (with the shank and other layers included) under great pressure. The most common stitched welt available on the market is the double-stitched Norwegian welt. Stitched welts are easily resoled and provide durable boots, although they are generally heavier and more expensive than cemented boots. The third type of welt is the injection-molded sole, which is injected into a mold placed on the bottom of the boot upper. In many injection-molded boots, a rubberized seal called a "rand" is placed around the boot at the welt to seal the seam and waterproof the boot. Most of these boots cannot be resoled.

The outsole is a rubberized layer that is glued onto the bottom of the midsole of a boot. It is in direct contact with the ground and is usually lugged to enhance traction in soil and snow. The lug pattern generally follows a traditional pattern based on the arrangement of hob nails and clinker nails used on old-style leather boot soles before rubber soles were invented. Vibram® rubber soles copy this pattern, although Vibram® and some other companies use different lug patterns as well (Figure 5-5).

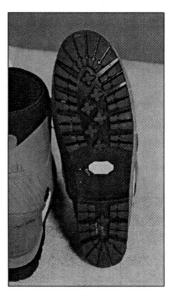

Figure 5-5. A Vibram lug pattern

When selecting a boot, you must compromise between the many factors that we have discussed above, and the cost. You should begin the process with a clear idea of what you need for the type of hiking that you do. Make a thorough comparison of boots from several manufacturers that meet your basic criteria. Try on several pairs of boots while wearing the two pairs of socks that you expect to use when hiking. Walk around the store, go up and down stairs, and conduct the fit tests described in the previous pages. Don't let the store salesperson talk you into anything, but listen and let him or her explain the advantages and disadvantages of each model. If you are lucky enough to find a knowledgeable salesperson, they can potentially help you find a boot with good value. Many but not all outdoor store personnel are quite knowledgeable about the gear that they sell. Look for good quality leather; smooth, uniform seams; a secure, well-executed welt and a sole with rubber lugs that are not too hard to grip a rock surface. Select a boot with an upper that opens up sufficiently so that you can get your foot into it even when it is cold, stiff or frozen and with a lacing system that uses hooks for the upper tie points. The main cost factors to consider are quality of leather and boot construction. You generally get what you pay for with boots, but shopping between stores and brands can get you a better value. Don't sink a lot of money into boots if you don't expect to do a lot of hiking. But remember that a good boot is the single most important piece of hiking equipment that you will own.

If you are buying your first pair of boots, buy a medium-weight pair. If you wind up hiking a lot you will likely buy other boots for other conditions: a light pair for summer or desert use and a heavier duty pair for rough travel and mountaineering. If cost is a limitation (many boots sell for over $200 a pair), consider buying a used pair of boots or lighter duty boots to get started.

Once you have purchased your boots, you will need to condition them for outdoor wear. There will be a breaking-in period during which you will work the leather, softening and stretching it while you walk. At the same time, your feet will adjust somewhat to your boots, hardening and/or callusing your skin at points of pressure with the boot liners.

This give-and-take between your feet and boots is normal. During the breaking-in period, you can gradually take longer and longer walks as your boots slowly adjust to your feet. Do not venture out on a long hike with new boots right away, or you will get sore skin or blisters at rub points. During the adjustment period, keep the boots clean and do not apply any waterproofing in case you decide that there is a serious problem with the fit. Some stores and manufacturers will take boots back to trade for a different size if there is an obvious mismatch within a few weeks. Ask about store exchange and trade-in policies at the time of purchase if you have any doubts about the fit.

> ## BOOTS
>
> My first hiking boots were a pair of Vasque lightweight, leather trail boots. I completely wore them out in three years, but by then I could afford good quality Kastinger medium-weight boots, which I bought in Austria at a very reasonable price. I applied the information that is discussed in this book to select those boots. They served as my primary hiking, mountaineering and cross-country ski boots through eight years and two re-soling attempts. Now I own two pairs of Rocksport leather walking shoes, two pairs of Brooks lightweight walking/athletic shoes, two pairs of medium-weight boots (Montrail, Riechle), one pair of heavyweight mountaineering boots (Fabiano), one pair of plastic double boots (Koflach), one pair of heavy leather double boots (Kastinger), a pair of fleece-lined heavyweight leather cross-country ski boots (Asolo) and other specialty footwear. If you hike a lot you will own several pairs too.

Once you have determined that your boots fit properly, you should complete the conditioning process. You can continue to break in your boots by wearing them on longer and longer hikes or you can accelerate the process by wet-fitting the boots. "Wet-fitting" is a time-honored method of soaking boots in water and wearing them on a long hike to break them in. The concept works well for light and medium-weight leather boots — the water softens up the leather, and while you are walking, the leather conforms to your feet at the points where the pressure is greatest, reducing pinching and rubbing at these locations. After a few hours of wear, you allow the boots to dry out and the leather will retain the new, more-conformable shape of your feet.

Wet-fitting does not work as well for heavyweight boots or boots with large rubberized heel counters. If you are going to wet-fit your boots, do so before you apply waterproofing to them so that they can dry out more easily after the fitting. After the first hour of walking, periodically change to dry socks to draw excess water out of the boots and accelerate the drying process. Keep in mind that your skin is also softer during the wet-fitting process so beware of blister formation. Some people will tell you that wet-fitting does not work, but the ones who tell you this have probably not tried it for themselves. We have wet-fitted every pair of single boots that we have owned and think it makes a significant improvement in fit. Double boots don't need it.

Boots must be properly cared for if they are to last for several seasons. Always clean the inside and outside of your boots after any serious hiking trip. Wash off mud and salt from the outers and welt with a wet sponge and let the boots dry out. When they are dry, reapply waterproofing to the leather as needed to keep them in condition for your next outing. Wipe the inside of each boot with a paper towel or rag and allow the liners to dry out. With double boots, remove each inner boot, wipe it down and let it dry outside the outer boot. If the insides of your boots are really wet, remove the insoles, clean them and let all surfaces dry out. Clean and dry your boot laces if they need it. Let boots and insoles air-dry in a dry room. Do not let the leather get very hot by putting the boots on a wood stove or next to an open fire. The leather may get very hot and can be damaged by the high temperatures. Heat-damaged leather will crack and fail more quickly than leather that is well cared for. When applying wax, silicone seals or other leather treatments, you can cautiously use a hair dryer to speed up penetration into the leather. A good guide to use is, if your hand can't take the heat, then it is too hot for the leather as well.

Most leather treatments, sealers and conditioners are either wax or silicone based. Boot manufacturers generally recommend which treatment is best for their boots based on the tanning and finish of their leather product. It is best to follow their recommendations so as to remain compatible with the leather. Once you use a given treatment on your boots, you should continue with the same treatment for the life of the boots. This means that if you start with silicone, continue with silicone; if you start using a wax-based seal, continue with wax-based seal. For convenience, it is best to use the same wax-based treatment for all of your boots that require waxing and to be equally consistent if you are treating with silicone. Using too many compounds can be expensive and confusing. Oil-based treatments can be used on some leather footwear but oil is generally not popular or recommended for most hiking and climbing boots.

## 5.1.2
## Socks

Socks are an important component of the footwear system. They provide warmth, padding for fit and comfort, moisture management and help keep your boots clean. Two pairs of socks are recommended for wear in hiking boots — a thin liner sock and a heavier outer sock. The right combination of liner and outer sock should provide a good fit to the boot, control movement of the heel, insulate and cushion the rest of the foot and provide wiggle room for the toes. Wearing a single sock does not provide the same flexibility and protection from blisters.

The materials used in liner socks are usually silk, soft wool, polypropylene or other synthetics that wick moisture away from the foot to the outer sock. The fabric content of the outer sock should be selected on the basis of warmth, low compressibility and breathability. Wool is probably the best natural material for the outer sock due to its ability to provide warmth even when wet. But other materials also work well for this purpose. People who are sensitive to ordinary sheep's wool can still wear wool outer socks as long as the liner socks are not wool. For summer hiking, where warmth is not a factor, a synthetic liner and outer sock may work well. Each person needs to experiment a little to find the combination of socks that works best for them. You may have different combinations for different weather conditions and boots. It is also prudent to carry an extra set of socks with you on a hike in case you get your feet wet in a stream or just from excessive sweating on a hot day.

Wearing two sock layers creates an extra sliding surface that reduces wear-and-tear on your feet and limits the formation of hot spots and blisters. The liner socks remove moisture from the surface of your skin and wick it outward through your outer socks while you are hiking. This helps to keep your skin drier and tougher, thereby reducing wear-and-tear on your feet. The formation of hot spots and blisters can be reduced by the action of the outer socks sliding against the liner socks. Even if your boots fit well, your feet still move around inside your boots somewhat. As your feet move around, most likely with your heels lifting up and down a little, your socks slide against your skin and the inside of your boots. If your socks move freely against the lining of your boots (particularly in leather boots), the resulting friction generates heat along the surface of the lining. Your socks also slide against your skin, generating friction and wear-and-tear on the outer layer of your skin. If your socks do not slide inside your boots because the inner boot surfaces are not smooth (which happens in some fabric lined boots), then most of the movement and friction is concentrated at the interface between your socks and your skin. This aggravates skin abrasion and enhances the formation of hot spots and blisters. The two-sock combination helps to protect your feet from abrasion by providing an additional sliding surface (outer sock sliding over the liner sock) to dissipate some of the friction that would otherwise be directed to your feet.

Here are some additional tips about socks that can make hiking more enjoyable. Carry an extra set of clean, dry socks with you and change into them whenever your feet seem sweaty or you start to feel the pinch of a hot spot. It only takes a minute to check your feet and socks for potential problems and possibly avoid sore feet. Carry your wet socks on the outside of your pack to dry them in case you need to change socks again. Do not wear cotton socks because they tend to roll instead of sliding when wet, exacerbating wear-and-tear on your skin. When you put on your socks and boots, avoid creating wrinkles. Wrinkles cause hot spots. And remember to always use the double sock system in your boots. Some people will tell you that wearing one sock is just as good, but years of experience gained from many generations indicate that two socks are better than one.

Finally, a word about cold feet. In cold weather, cold feet are usually caused by heat loss to the ground through the boot soles, wet feet or a lack of adequate blood flow to the feet. Your socks, insoles, midsoles and outsoles of your boots provide the only insulation under your feet. If you are standing on cold ground or snow, you will lose heat out of the bottom of your feet. Wearing outer socks with thick bottoms or felt insoles can help reduce heat loss to the ground. When you are buying a pair of boots that you expect to wear in cold weather, size them so that you can wear a thick sock combination in them. The boot uppers usually have some foam padding in them (except in the toe box) which helps to keep your feet warm. Wet boots will conduct heat away from your feet, so keep your boots well waterproofed and as dry as possible. Wet socks also lead to cold feet. If you lace your boots up too tightly, wear tight-fitting gaiters or socks that are too thick, you may reduce circulation to your feet and cause them to chill. People sometimes squeeze their thickest socks into their boots thinking they will keep them warm, only to find out that their feet are actually colder than if they had worn thinner socks of the same material. Keep in mind that your feet can also get cold if you lose heat from your legs. Wearing long underwear can actually keep your feet warmer by allowing warm blood to flow to your feet. And finally, about one third of the body's heat loss occurs from the head where a large fraction of bloodflow is directed to keep the brain functioning. Often, putting on a stocking cap will control your overall heat loss and direct more heat (via warm bloodflow) to the feet. To repeat the old adage: "If your feet are cold, put on your hat."

## 5.2    JACKETS AND OTHER CLOTHING

With outdoor clothing, it is better to wear several thin layers rather than one thick layer. This principle, called "layering", allows a person to adjust clothing as weather and conditions change throughout the day. For example, if you wear a heavy winter coat on the morning of a cold day and the temperature rises, you have only two choices: coat on or coat off. Wearing the coat may be uncomfortably warm; taking it off may be too cold. If instead you wore a light sweater and a light jacket on top, you would have four possible choices (Figure 5-6): both sweater and jacket off, jacket only, sweater only, and both sweater and jacket on. Obviously, four choices are better than two and you are more likely to find a comfortable combination as conditions change during the day.

Layering also allows you to utilize different materials or fabrics in each layer. For instance, you can wear a thin wicking layer next to your skin such as a long underwear top or bottom that will help remove moisture from your skin to a secondary clothing layer. Polypropylene, polyester, Patagonia Capilene, Polartec Power Dry, silk and light wool materials can be effectively used for the wicking layer. Cotton is not a good choice for the innermost layer because it retains moisture and does not transmit it away from the skin efficiently. The middle or outer layers may be made from any materials that have desirable thermal and water repellant properties. Generally these insulating layers should be warm and sufficiently breathable to ensure removal of water vapor to the surrounding air. Materials that possess these properties are wool, polyester, pile/fleece synthetics, Thinsulate, polypropylene or Capilene. The outermost layer is usually a jacket worn with or without rain/wind pants, which acts as a protective shell to keep wind and rain from penetrating to the inner layers of clothing. In very cold dry weather, a down parka and down pants may be worn as the outermost layer. Ideally, the outer layer should be windproof, waterproof and, if possible, breathable, to let body moisture out.

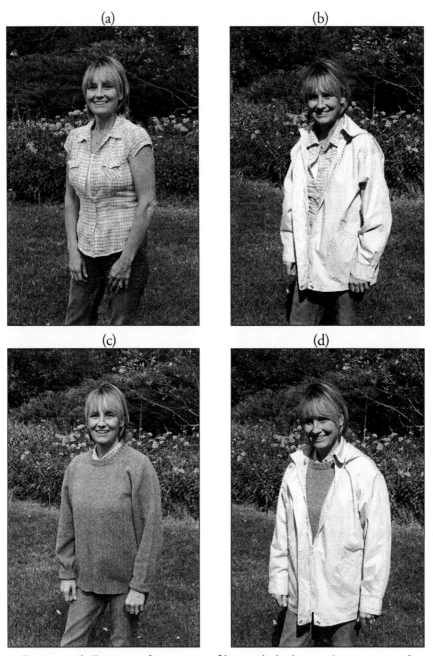

Figure 5-6. Four combinations of layered clothing: a) sweater and jacket off b) jacket only c) sweater only d) sweater and jacket on

Several natural and synthetic materials are available for the manufacture of outdoor clothing. Nearly all of them consist of textiles, pile or fleece created from threads or fibers. The air space between the fibers serves as insulation making the garments warm. In some materials, the fibers themselves are hollow providing additional insulation value. In other materials, the fibers are hydrophobic, preventing moisture from entering or clinging to the fabric. The latter materials generally provide good thermal insulation even when wet. Wool is a natural fiber that is water repellant and retains much of its insulating value when wet. Synthetic materials that have hollow fibers include Holofill˙ II, Quallofil˙, Capilene˙ and others. Materials can also be treated to make them water repellant and better insulators.

There are a number of "single-layer" or "soft-shell" garments on the market that attempt to simplify the layering system by incorporating the properties of two or more layers into a single material. This type of clothing is targeted largely toward the active sports market and activities where perspiration management is a goal. Many of these products combine the insulation layer with a water-resistant treatment to keep material as breathable as possible while making the garment water repellant but not waterproof. There are many products sold by Patagonia˙, Recreational Equipment Incorporated, Polartec˙ and other manufacturers that exhibit a range of properties in this category of garment.

The outermost clothing layer usually consists of a jacket and wind or rain pants that serve to protect the clothing underneath from the elements. The ideal jacket is both waterproof and breathable to let moisture out. There are only a few fabrics that claim to do both tasks simultaneously, generally through the use of water repellant treatments.

Gore Tex˙ is the dominant fabric on the market from which waterproof, breathable jackets and pants are made. The namesake brand consists of a Gore Tex˙ synthetic membrane laminated to a durable fabric such as nylon or polyester. The membrane allows water vapor but not liquid water to pass through the fabric. This makes the material waterproof (up to 65 pounds per square inch) but breathable. The breathability of the fabric is limited so the fabric can release water vapor as long as the wearer is not very active. However, at higher activity levels, a hiker can generate perspiration and water vapor faster than it can be transferred through the fabric, leading to moisture buildup on the inside of the material. Manufacturers have a wide variety of approaches and treatments to address this problem and provide the best of both worlds. For instance, the quality and degree of waterproofing can be varied and the outerwear can be designed to accommodate the hiker's changing ventilation needs. Some jacket designs include vents under the armpits and on the back that can be opened to allow moist air to escape.

Jacket designs vary greatly but there are a few key features that you should look for when selecting one for hiking use (Figure 5-7). A good quality, durable fabric with reinforced elbows and shoulders is necessary for long life. Waterproofing and breathability are trade-offs to be resolved by personal preference. Get a jacket that is waterproof but not water repellant — the latter has a way of soaking through in heavy rain and can get very heavy when wet. A waterproof hood is a necessity and should be stitched or zipped to the jacket collar to keep out wind and water. Detachable hoods usually let wind and rain in on the neck and should be avoided. The hood should be adjustable so that you can close it down to protect the face on windy days. Look for underarm zippered air vents for temperature and moisture control. The cuffs of the sleeves should also be adjustable so that you can open and close them easily and accommodate mittens if necessary. There should be at least one inner pocket and one large cargo pocket with Velcro° or zippered closures on each side so that you can stuff your stocking cap, mittens and other items inside. Extra pockets for maps, sunglasses and miscellaneous storage are also a plus. The jacket should have interior webbing or a light nylon liner. All exterior seams should be double-stitched and sealed. Another consideration is the weight of the jacket. Buy a jacket that is loose fitting and in which you can wear two heavy sweaters without tightness. You need to be able to add layers of warm clothes in cold weather, including a down vest or even a parka.

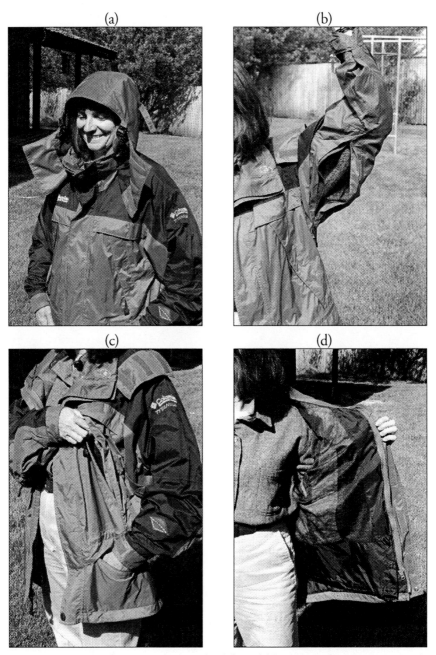

Figure 5-7. Wind/rain jacket with a) hood b) zippered armpit vents c) several pockets d) interior mesh/ nylon liner

Parkas are winter jackets that are filled with down or synthetic insulating materials. The insulation is placed loosely between cloth layers that are sewn together to form the outer portion of the jacket. Parkas are generally worn as outer garments in cold dry weather but can be worn under rain jackets if you encounter rain or sleet.

Rain and wind pants are usually made from tough nylon cloth that is flexible and durable. They should be waterproof and loose fitting to allow free leg movement. Pants with full-length zippers extending from waist to ankle along the outside of each pant leg are preferred over ones without zippers (Figure 5-8). Full-length zippers allow you to pull your pants up over everything else you are wearing without having to remove your boots. This is a big advantage in cold weather or when a sudden storm strikes. Unfortunately, fully zippered pants can be rather expensive compared to pants with partial zippers or no zippers at all.

(a)                                    (b)

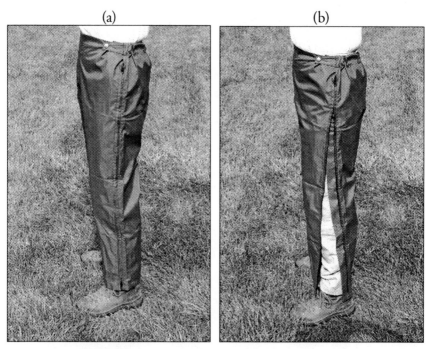

Figure 5-8. Wind/rain pants with a) legs fully zipped b) legs unzipped

Gaiters are waterproof cloth sleeves that are worn to cover your pant legs from calf to boot so that you can prevent snow and debris from entering the top of your boots. They usually come with a zipper or Velcro° seal to allow them to be easily attached and taken off with your boots in place. When buying gaiters, make sure that they are waterproof, manufactured from durable materials and large enough to fit easily over the top of your pants and boots. Neoprene straps that run under your boot insteps are typically used to keep the gaiters in place so that they do not ride up on the boots (Figure 5-9).

Figure 5-9. Gaiters protect the lower leg from snow and debris

Hats are recommended to protect your head and neck from sunburn, to shed rain and snow and to keep your head warm. A simple baseball cap is the hat most commonly used in the summer to keep the sun off the face and head. A full brim hat or baseball cap with a handkerchief draped down the back of the neck provides protection for the neck as well. Most summer hats are made from cotton and do not provide adequate insulation or keep water off the head effectively. However, hoods on rain jackets are designed for this purpose (Figure 5-10).

A wide variety of hats can be worn in cooler weather. Stocking caps can keep your head warm and dry if they are thick enough and made from suitable materials. Wool is the best natural material for stocking caps because it is a good insulator even when wet. Single or double-knit caps lined with synthetic liners on the inside may be more suitable for those who are allergic to wool or find it itchy. There are also a number of hat choices available in nylon, Gore-Tex˚, and other synthetic materials, some of which have visors and removable fleece liners. Selection is a matter of personal preference but a good hat is a necessary part of outdoor clothing in any weather. It is a good idea to pack an extra hat when you are preparing to go on a long hike in cold weather.

Figure 5-10. Choose a hat to suit the occasion

Gloves and mittens are necessary on cold-weather hikes. Mittens are generally warmer than gloves because your four fingers fit into the large compartment of the mitten and help to keep each other warm. There is a wide range of choices for gloves and mittens. When selecting a pair for winter use, remember that your hands are likely to get wet in snow. Leather gloves get wet easily and do not readily dry out, so they are not a good choice for cold weather. Boiled wool mittens of the Dachstein type work well even when wet and are recommended for winter use, especially in wet conditions. A backup pair of mittens is recommended on longer hikes. If you are desperate and find yourself without hand warmers of any type on a hiking trip, socks can be used as backup mittens.

## 5.3    Backpacks

The backpack is the equipment used for carrying clothing, gear and food on your hike or backpacking trip. A wide range of backpacks is available for standard hiking purposes. Backpacks can be relatively small for short day trips or large for multiday trips where more supplies and gear are required. Many people wear small, simple backpacks or butt packs (with waist belts) for day hikes and larger packs for longer backpacking trips. In the event of an emergency, a daypack can be improvised from a pair of pants by converting the pant legs into shoulder straps and cinching the belt loops together to make the torso of the pants into a bag. Some strap-handled duffel bags can be carried like backpacks if necessary, if you put your arms through the two strap handles.

Backpacks are usually designed with some form of support frame built into the back panel of the pack (See Figure 4-8). The frame is either internal, meaning built into the back of the pack where it contacts the body, or external, meaning the frame is plainly seen on the outside of the pack bag. The function of the frame is to stiffen the pack so that it conforms to the body and does not collapse into a formless sack. Many older models, called "rucksacks", were basically cloth bags with shoulder straps sewn onto them. They were largely formless and allowed the load in the sack to sink down and pull away from the body. The frame in the modern frame pack not only gives the pack form, but also serves as an anchor bench onto which the shoulder straps and waist belt attach. On traditional external frame packs, the frame was made from a rigid framework of aluminum tubing. The shoulder straps, belt and body of the pack were all attached to the frame by rivets. Internal frame packs usually have a flat plastic or fiberglass plate or aluminum straps fitted into a sheath of durable cloth and the shoulder straps and bag are sewn onto the sheath. Some internal frames are adjustable so that they can be fitted to match the length and contour of an individual's back. Others, while not adjustable, come in different lengths so as to fit the wearer better. When buying a backpack, especially a larger one, it is important to find a size and frame that fits your back and is comfortable. There are numerous frame and pack designs and learning about the advantages and disadvantages of each is part of the fun of selecting your backpack.

When selecting a backpack, it is important to consider several factors. Decide on the size (volume) of pack that you will need before you get too far along on your quest. A daypack of about 1,000 cubic inches is adequate for most day hikes, but if you carry extra gear for winter or hike with children, then 1,500 cubic inches may be better. For general backpacking, a pack of 3,000 to 4,000 cubic inches is more than adequate, assuming that you strap your sleeping pad onto the outside of the pack. For winter expeditions, 6,000 cubic inches or larger will be suitable. Use the volumes mentioned above as a rough guide for what you might need for your specific application. A slightly larger pack doesn't add much weight to your load as long as you don't fill up all that volume. If a slightly larger pack fits your back better or has a design that you like, by all means buy it. European manufacturers usually specify size in liters, instead of cubic inches.

Although fit is one of the most important factors for selecting a pack, also evaluate the feel and comfort of the shoulder straps and waist belt. Make sure that there is adequate padding on all of the straps as well as on the lower part of the pack where it snugs up against your back. Be wary of very soft foam rubber and narrow straps on the shoulders and belt. In general, wide sturdy straps with moderately dense foam padding are best.

Another factor to consider is the layout of compartments and pockets on the body of the pack. It is better to have two compartments in the main body of the pack so that you can control the COG of the load by placing heavier objects in the upper compartment. A removable partition between compartments is a plus because sometimes you may need to carry a long object inside the pack or to use it as a bivouac bag. You should be able to access each compartment separately from the outside of the pack. A good backpack design will have two or more pockets readily available for stowing frequently needed items such as water bottles, snacks, map, compass and gloves. Many have one or two pockets in the top flap of the pack for easy access. Most pockets have zipper closures. The arrangement of pockets on the pack is a matter of personal taste and experience, so just find a pack that you think will be convenient for your needs.

Most backpacks are made from durable, waterproof nylon cloth and have tough zippers, but you must compare these features from pack to pack. Some packs are not fully waterproof and require an extra rain cover. Generally speaking, this is a little inconvenient when you need to access your pack, but it may prove useful if you expect to hike in very rainy conditions. Many people carry extra large plastic garbage bags to put over their backpacks in case they encounter heavy rain or snow.

Whatever backpack you decide on, you should test it out in the store if you are allowed to do so. Some stores keep sandbags or bundles of newspaper available for customers to drop into packs they are interested in and the sales staff let you walk around the store wearing your prospective pack with a heavy load. This is the best way to evaluate a pack for fit and comfort.

## 5.4  TENTS AND SHELTERS

The purpose of any camping shelter, be it a lean-to, tent or bivouac sack, is to isolate you and your sleeping gear from the elements. This primarily means keeping you out of the rain, sheltering you from direct wind and protecting you from insects and small creatures. Cloth tents can do this effectively and weight little. Hardwall shelters such as camper shells and camp trailers add a higher level of protection from animals when you are car camping. There are many choices of shelters available depending on how secure you wish to be, how heavy the shelter is to transport, its size during use, materials and cost.

Lean-to shelters can be easily constructed out of doors from tree branches and plastic or cloth sheeting. The easiest shelter to build using a poncho or plastic sheeting is a simple ridgepole or nylon rope ridgeline support (Figure 5-11a). All you need is a knife or hatchet to cut the ridgepole and forked support poles and the poncho or plastic sheeting material, which should measure eight feet by 10 feet or larger. Tie nylon cord to the corners of the plastic using the grommets already attached to the poncho, or by first placing a pebble in a fold of the plastic sheet and then cinching off the pebble with cord to make a temporary tie point (Figure 5-11b). Tie down the sheet corners as shown in the figure or place large rocks to hold the corners down. A lean-to can also be constructed by running a length of cord between two trees and then under the sheet instead of using a ridgepole. We have mentioned the pebble and cord trick for tying off sheeting because you can use this technique for any number of field repairs. Readers interested in reading more about field constructed shelters and survival techniques should refer to the US Army Survival Manual (US Army, 2002).

Tents are the most common form of lightweight shelter used for camping. In this book, we will limit our discussion to cloth tents with integrated floors, vents and nylon-mesh mosquito netting. Most mesh netting nowadays is fine enough to keep out "no-see-um" insects and other small creatures. There are a wide range of recreational tent designs available, ranging from single-person ultralight tents to basecamp tents that can house ten people and are tall enough to stand up in. Pay attention and evaluate their distinguishing features, particularly the differences between three-season tents and four-season tents. A three-season tent is designed for non-winter conditions and is usually less rugged than a four-season tent. While three-season tents may have several zip-open window panels with mosquito netting, four-season tents usually have fewer windows, no zip-out panels and are built a bit sturdier. Unless you plan to do a lot of winter camping, a three-season tent will probably suit your camping needs.

Most camping tents are called "double-wall" tents because they consist of an inner tent with support poles, guylines, mesh netting, zippered windows and doors and a separate waterproof cloth rain fly that covers and surrounds the inner tent (Figure 5-12a). The rain fly that forms the second wall of these tents is separated from the inner wall by about two inches of airspace. It can easily be taken off in dry weather and added again when a storm appears. The sidewalls of the inner tent need to be tear resistant and are usually made of rip-stop nylon, taffeta nylon or

(a)

(b)

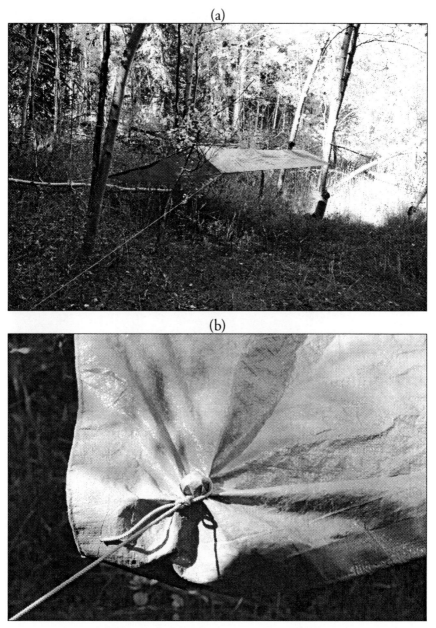

Figure 5-11. A lean-to shelter showing a) the ridgeline rope support
b) a close-up of the pebble tie point

(a)

(b)

Figure 5-12. Tent construction: a) double wall b) single wall

polyester cloth. The material is not usually waterproofed so that it can breathe and remain as light as possible. When evaluating how much a tent weighs, be sure you are looking at the combined weight of the tent, rain fly, poles, stakes and storage bag. After all, you will want to buy a light tent if you are backpacking and you need to know how many pounds you really have to carry.

There are a few tent designs available that reduce weight by eliminating the rain fly altogether and making the inner tent (now single-walled) out of a waterproof material such as Gore-Tex' (Figure 5-12b). The Bibler Tent Company and others manufacture good single wall tents. The weight of single-wall tents is dramatically lower than most double-wall tents, but they also cost significantly more due to the materials used for construction. For people who do a lot of backpacking, a single-wall tent may be worth the investment. We have a single-wall Gore-Tex' tent made by Early Winters that we purchased 20 years ago and still use for light backpacking.

There are many creative tent designs on the market to accommodate different outdoor activities. Many backpacking tents are designed to be light, easy to set up and stow into compact stuff sacks. Usually they are designed to sleep two people and are just tall enough for a person to sit up in. Lighter models can be quite small or accommodate only one person. The smallest tents fall into the ultralight category and may only weigh two-plus pounds for a single person tent and five-plus pounds for a two-person tent. Four-season tents tend to weigh more than three-season tents due to heavier construction, more durable materials and extra tent poles. Some tents are intended primarily for basecamp use, where size and comfort are desired and there are fewer setups and takedowns anticipated. There is a whole mid-range of tents with many features and special uses. For example, one tent made by Marmot Mountaineering Ltd. is designed for a single bicycle camper and has an extra large vestibule so that a bicycle can be brought in out of the rain for storage and repairs.

When selecting a tent, you must first decide what you will use your tent for because this will help you narrow the scope of your search. If you are interested in a backpacking tent, you should decide how many people will sleep in it, how much extra space you need for comfort and gear storage, whether to buy a three- or four-season tent, approximately how much you would like it to weigh and then establish a budget. Usually, you will encounter several tent models that interest you and you will have to compare features and make trade-offs before your final selection. You may find a really nice design that weighs more than you planned or that costs more than you expected. You also need to decide whether you are willing to carry an extra pound or two to provide that extra room or comfort. Crawl into the tent and stretch out to see if there is enough room for two people, two backpacks and other gear in case of rain. If you expect to camp in a rainy climate, be sure you are happy inside the tent because you may spend a lot of time in there. A bright cheery color can help your mental state if you are stormbound for any length of time.

There are several design features to look for when buying a tent. The floor of the tent should be made of waterproof, durable material such as coated nylon and the flooring should rise up the side of the tent a few inches. A "bathtub" design has the flooring sheet rising up the sides with no seams at the edge where the floor material rises into the wall. The bathtub feature avoids placement of a seam at the floor-wall edge. Instead, the seam is higher up the sidewall of the tent where the floor material joins the sidewall cloth. The benefit of this design is that it minimizes the number of seams at floor level where water can seep into the tent. Fewer seams mean fewer leaks. Extra wide tents usually have one seam across the middle of the tent floor where two sheets of the floor material are joined. The central seam is necessary because tent material comes in bolts that are approximately 60 inches wide. Regardless of their number and placement, all floor seams should be sealed with a waterproof compound or tape seal and seams in the tent floor and walls should be double-fold and double stitched for strength. Such seams are referred to as lap-felled seams (Figure 5-13). Seams in the sidewalls of the tent do not need to be sealed if they will always be protected under a rain fly.

Most tents are supported by small-diameter aluminum or fiberglass poles arranged in a pattern around the exterior of the inner tent. They usually run from one corner of the floor over the top of the tent and down to the opposite corner of the floor, acting like a bowed truss, which serves to hold up the tent. The poles may attach to the inner tent wall through a series of cloth or mesh sleeves sewn into the top of the tent, or simply hook onto the inner tent at selected points. External frame tents have a pole pattern that keeps the tent wall taut providing structure and form. Tents that utilize hooks to attach the poles directly to the walls of the inner tent are called exoskeleton tents because their frame is designed to be separate from the inner tent until it is hooked up (Figure 5-14). Exoskeleton designs are very quick to set up, a distinct advantage when a storm is approaching. In most modern tents, the pole segments are connected by an internal elastic shock cord that makes pole assembly easy. Aluminum tent poles are more durable and easier to repair in the field than fiberglass poles.

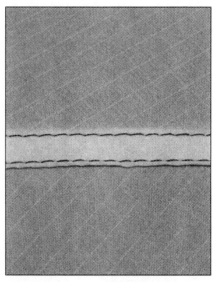

Figure 5-13. Close-up of a lap-felled tent seam

Once the frame and inner tent are set up, the rain fly fits over the top of the framing and is attached to it at selected points. The rain fly usually fits tightly around the frame but is cut to provide a vestibule or porch area over one or more entrances to the tent. This helps to keep rain out of the tent when people go in and out. The vestibule also provides shelter for backpacks and other gear that does not need to be stored inside the tent. Pay careful attention to vestibule design when you are comparing tents. Also, be sure to seal all seams on the rain fly to keep rain from coming through the needle holes. The seams can be sealed with either liquid sealant or waterproof seam tape. Several applications of liquid sealant may be needed during the camping season.

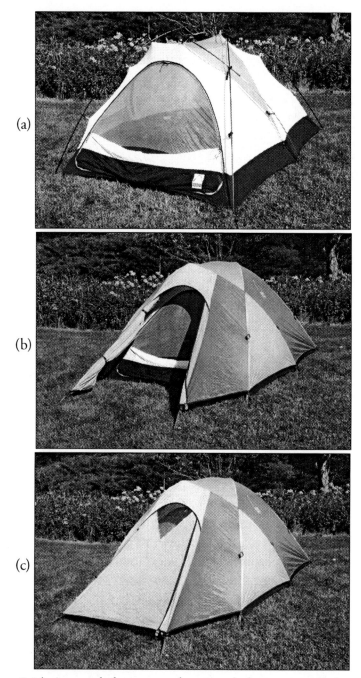

Figure 5-14. An exoskeleton tent showing a) the inner wall clipped to the exoskeleton b) the rainfly over the exoskeleton with the vestibule open c) the vestibule closed

Most tents provide two entrances for convenient access so that people don't have to crawl over each other to get in and out. The main entrance is typically a large zippered doorway complete with mesh netting and vestibule area. The secondary entrance is usually a little smaller but also has netting. When selecting a tent, try all the zippers, go in and out both doors and see if you like the vents built into the tent. For three-season use, tents often have a zip-open vent panel to let fresh air in and humid air out. Such vents are particularly handy in warmer climates where air circulation is desired.

A ground cloth is placed beneath the floor of the tent to reduce abrasion to the tent floor and to provide an additional layer of waterproofing for the tent floor. The ground cloth is cut or folded to match the shape of the tent floor with no material left sticking out beyond the tent perimeter. The ground cloth can be made of waterproof nylon cloth or two-mill plastic sheeting.

Tents are attached to the ground by stakes to keep them from blowing away in high winds and to keep them taut and well formed. There is usually a stake loop at each corner of the tent, which is also where the ends of the tent poles and rain fly fasten to the tent. The portion of the rain fly that forms the vestibule requires tie points to additional stakes. There may be additional tie points on the tent or rain fly for the attachment of guylines to keep things taut during high winds. Wire stakes work well for most ground conditions but are inadequate in loose sand and snow. Larger plastic pegs or metal blades work better under those conditions.

When buying a tent, it is important to set the tent up yourself to be sure it meets your needs. Many outdoor stores will let you set up a tent in the store to see how you like it. If the setup seems too cumbersome in the store, imagine how difficult it will be outdoors in bad weather.

There are many other forms of shelter that can be used for camping. Camper shells and campers on trucks, camp trailers and full-sized recreational vehicles can all be employed for camping in different situations. All vehicle-mounted camping options are limited by road access but they still provide a basecamp from which hiking can be enjoyed.

## 5.5   SLEEPING PADS AND BAGS

Sleeping gear commonly used by campers consists of a pad, cot or mattress to insulate the sleeper from the ground and a sleeping bag to insulate them from the cold air. Sleeping cots are typically used in fixed camps. Sleeping pads are usually made from open-cell or closed-cell foam rubber or plastic. Air mattresses can also be used but do not provide as much insulation as foam pads due to convection of air within the mattress. Air mattress/foam rubber hybrids such as ThermaRest* are gaining in popularity. These pads are warm and comfortable because the camper's body is supported on air but the foam inside the mattress prevents convection and provides insulation at the same time. Open-cell foam rubber pads are generally comfortable and insulate well but are bulky and allow water vapor to migrate through pores in the foam. Closed-cell plastic foam is much denser than foam rubber and therefore heavier, considering the same thickness of pad. It is also stiff which makes it bulky when rolled up. The advantage of closed-cell foam is that it is largely waterproof and does not transmit moisture through its pores. Personally, we have found that a thin, closed-cell foam pad is uncomfortable. We prefer either a ThermaRest-style mattress or a 1.5 inch thick, medium-density, open-cell foam pad. The foam pad by itself will eventually get dirty, but when covered with a waterproof nylon cloth sheath it will be protected for many years.

Sleeping bags are large, body-size, insulated bags open at the head end and slit by a long zippered seam for entry. They come in either rectangular or mummy shapes. Mummy bags are tapered on the foot end to eliminate extra material and conserve weight. Most mummy bags have an insulated hood at the head end, which closes down to keep the head warm. Rectangular-cut bags do not usually have hoods.

A typical sleeping bag is constructed as a double-walled bag with insulation between the walls. Some rectangular-cut and general-purpose sleeping bags have a sheet of fibrous batting insulation between two cotton fabric walls. There is stitching through the walls and insulation at regular intervals to keep the insulation from shifting inside the walls (Figure 5-15a). Usually the stitching goes all the way through the bag, pinching the insulation together at the seam and reducing its insulating value there. This design is common in less expensive sleeping bags.

A better form of construction consists of baffles of netting sewn between the two walls of the sleeping bag, holding them a fixed distance apart and forming a box-like construction (Figure 5-15b). Insulating material is placed inside the boxes. In this type of construction, there are no sewn-through seams to interfere with the uniform distribution of insulation. Nylon or other tightly woven synthetic cloths are generally used to make the walls. When down or other fine insulation materials are used as filler, a tightly woven material is required to keep the small fibers from slipping out through the weave of the cloth. In a few cases, extra layers of material are added to protect the walls or to further insulate the bag. Rarely, a second layer of boxed construction is added to reduce any possible heat loss through the box seams (Figure 5-15c).

The methods of sleeping bag construction described above are also commonly used in the manufacture of down parkas, pants and other insulated garments. In general, the more seams or boxes involved, the greater the quality of the bag or parka, and the greater the cost of the garment.

A wide variety of materials are used to insulate sleeping bags and parkas. Some synthetic, fibrous insulators that are available include Hollofil˙ II, Quallofil˙ and Polarguard˙ 3D. These are all reasonably good insulators but are heavier than down for the same warmth and are not very compressible. Other materials made with very fine synthetic fibers that are compressible and provide good loft for their weight include Thermolite˙ and Primaloft˙.

When selecting which type of insulation is best for your bag, be prepared to make a trade-off between insulating value, weight and cost. Pound for pound down is still the material that gives the best insulating value per ounce of weight. There are various qualities of down available, with the

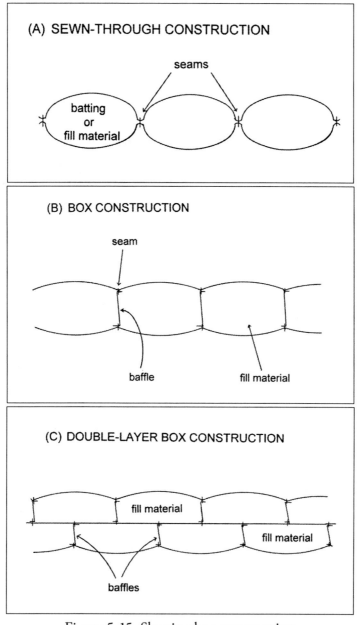

Figure 5-15. Sleeping bag construction

higher qualities being more expensive and providing better insulation. Down with an 800 "fill-power" rating will conceptually expand to fill 800 cubic inches of volume per ounce of down and is considered higher grade than down rated at 600 fill-power. The other advantage of down is that it is very compressible so that a warm sleeping bag that looks huge when fluffed up for the night also compresses into a very small parcel for transport. The disadvantage of down is that when it gets wet it mats down and loses its insulating value. Once wet, down is difficult to dry out effectively in the field. For this reason, some companies use a waterproof outer fabric to protect the down in their products from snow and water. Nevertheless, down is an excellent choice for winter camping and for camping in high mountains under relatively dry conditions. In most of the western US, down is a nearly perfect material to wear in the dry summer air and cold dry winters encountered there. However, other synthetic materials may be more appropriate for camping in wet climates such as the Pacific Northwest.

Features to look for when selecting a sleeping bag include construction methods, quality, type and volume of insulation, temperature rating and fit/comfort. You should first decide what range of temperatures you expect to encounter when using the bag. The type and amount of insulation in a bag correlate with the "comfort range" or temperature rating of the bag. Generally, the more loft there is in the insulation, the warmer the bag will be. The comfort range of the bag is a good initial indicator of the range of temperatures that you will find comfortable. These ranges provide a rough guide for the comfort of the "average" hiker. People who sleep warmer or cooler than the "average" will require less or more insulation, respectively, than the average person. Women, in general, tend to sleep cooler than men and enjoy the comfort of a little more insulation. So you should keep that in mind when selecting a bag. Remember that you can always make adjustments in camp if you need to by unzipping the bag to cool off or wearing an extra layer of clothing if you feel chilled. You can also add a liner to the sleeping bag to increase its warmth by a few degrees as well as to keep the bag clean.

There are a number of features that help make a sleeping bag more comfortable and warm. Some sleeping bags can be zipped together to form one large bag, which is pleasant for camping couples. Bags rated for low temperatures usually have insulated collars on them to prevent heat from escaping around the neck at night. Most bags have insulated flaps or tubes that fit over the inside zippers to cover the seams and retain heat. A few bags have pockets inside for stowing small personal items at night.

There is much more information available on specific designs of sleeping bags and properties of insulating materials that you should investigate before buying a bag. However, it is impossible to cover all of these details and the many new products that continuously come onto the market in this book. Therefore, we recommend that interested readers follow up with additional information available on the Internet and contact manufacturers directly about the specific properties of new insulating materials. Hopefully, the preceding discussion has provided the general reader with a basic understanding of sleeping bag construction and materials upon which to build.

## 5.6    WATER PURIFICATION

Water filtration units use a hand pump to force water through a fiberglass or ceramic filter thereby physically removing particulates and select microorganisms. Typical filters remove protozoa and most forms of bacteria but not viruses, dissolved chemicals, taste or odor. Glass-fiber filter elements are usually comprised of a pleated material containing a system of varying pore sizes that adequately capture the target microorganisms. Ceramic filters such as the series manufactured by Mountain Safety Research (MSR) utilize a compressed diatomaceous earth material that is cylindrical in shape and several millimeters thick. Pores within the ceramic material capture particulates, protozoa and most bacteria. Most ceramic filters are impregnated with chemicals that keep bacteria from growing within the filter between uses. Both types of filters eventually become clogged to one degree or another, at which time they can be partially cleaned by backflushing and physical abrasion. Ceramic filters can actually have their clogged surface layer removed by abrasion to allow freshly exposed material to continue with filtration. Most filters are constructed in the form of replaceable cartridges (Figure 5-16).

(a) (b)

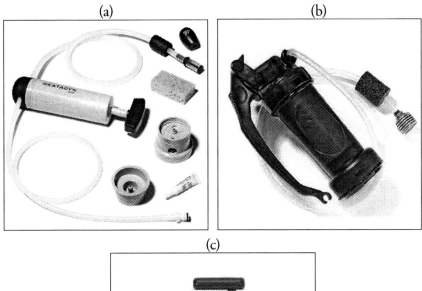

(c)

Figure 5-16. Water purification units: a) Katadyn® Guide Microfilter Pump b) MSR MiniWorks EX Filter c) Katadyn® Mini Filter (Photos courtesy of Recreational Equipment Inc.)

Filtration units that contain a secondary treatment stage are called purification units. Many filters have a secondary carbon filter integrated into the primary filter cartridge. The carbon adds another level of physical filtration but also absorbs some bacteria, viruses, dissolved chemicals, odors and taste. The carbon eventually loses its effectiveness after it has absorbed a fixed amount of contaminants. As a result, carbon cartridges must be replaced periodically in order to ensure proper performance of the purification unit.

Purification units can also contain iodized resin in combination with a physical filter to disinfect water that is being filtered. The iodized resin eliminates small bacteria as they pass through the resin. Very little iodine is released into the water during treatment so there is no resulting iodine taste. The combination filter and resin cartridge must be replaced periodically to maintain proper performance.

Most filtration and purification units are activated by pulling or pushing a hand pump that forces water through the filter. The number of pump strokes required to filter one liter of water is called the pump rate. Most pumps require 30–70 strokes to process one liter of water when the filter is clean. When the filter begins to clog up, the number of strokes per liter increases and the amount of force needed to complete each stroke goes up noticeably. This is an indication that it is time to clean off the filter or to replace the filter cartridge. A sudden increase in needed pump force can also indicate that your intake or outflow tubing is kinked, so be sure to check your lines carefully before working on the cartridge.

Factors to consider when selecting a filtration or purification unit are purification effectiveness, weight, pump rate, filter life and cost. Purification effectiveness varies from model to model and must be evaluated by reading the manufacturer's data on each unit. The maximum pore size in the filter material gives an indication of how effective the filter is for removing particulates and microorganisms. An acceptable maximum pore size is one micron, although in most common filters the largest pores are smaller, in the 0.1–1.0 micron range. The one-micron pore size is small enough to remove protozoa and most bacteria but not common viruses which can be as small as 0.004–0.1 micron. In general, the smaller the pore size, the harder it is to force water through the filter unit, leading to an increase in pumping effort. As far as weight is concerned, ceramic filter units weigh more than glass-fiber units due to the heavier weight of ceramic. However, the most accurate weight to use for comparison of filter units is the overall weight of the unit including all tubing and attachments.

"Filter life" refers to the volume of water that the filter can treat before it becomes sufficiently clogged or spent that it must be replaced. The life of a filter is usually expressed in liters or gallons of water treated. Fiber filter units can be expected to treat approximately 40–100 gallons of reasonably clear water (with low particulate load) before they require replacement. The secondary filtration materials (such as carbon and other purification stage materials) are sized to approximately match the number of gallons estimated for the life of the primary filter. Filter life is strongly affected by particulate load, as muddy water generally leads to filter clogging. If possible, relatively unclouded water should be selected for filtration, but if not, a washable prefilter should be used. It is important to follow the manufacturer's recommendations for filter replacement to ensure that your purification unit is functioning properly.

Cost is the factor that most people use to compare water filtration or purification units. Overall unit cost can be broken down into two parts: the initial cost and filter replacement costs. Initial costs can vary from $50 to $100 depending on the unit. Replacement filters can cost from 50 to 75 percent of the initial cost because most of the specialty materials are in the filter cartridges. This means that the initial cost to purify water can range from $0.50 to $1.00 per gallon (approximately $0.12 to $0.24 per liter).

## 5.7   CAMPING STOVES

A camping stove consists primarily of a fuel tank, a valve to regulate fuel flow rate, a burner unit and a mechanism to support a cooking pot or pan (Figure 5-17). The type of fuel used to fire the stove determines specifically how the stove works and whether additional components are needed to make it operate. Common fuels include propane, butane, kerosene and white gas. Propane and butane are highly volatile hydrocarbons that are liquid under pressure but readily vaporize at room temperature. When placed in a small container, these fuels create gas vapor, which can be allowed to flow to the burner element when a valve is used to control the flow rate. Propane is commonly used for gas grills and stoves in remote areas where natural gas is not available.

Because propane is highly volatile, it is generally contained in thick-walled steel tanks or bottles, which are fine for car camping but can be too heavy for backpacking. Butane is less volatile than propane and can therefore be contained in thin-walled metal bottles which are lighter. Small butane stoves can be reasonably efficient backpacking stoves although the gas may not volatilize well in cold weather. Blended butane/propane fuels and specialty fuels like isobutane are designed to overcome the cold temperature limitation of these stoves.

Kerosene and white gas fuels are liquids at normal temperatures and require a different stove construction for operation. Stoves for liquid fuel have similar fuel tanks, valves and burner units, but also require a pump or preheating pan to mobilize the fuel out of the tank. Depending on the model of gas stove used, the fuel is heated by running a fuel line through part of the flame on its way to the burner or by heating the entire valve/burner assembly. In older models, the central valve and burner assembly sits on top of the fuel tank which has a depression in it called a "spirit ring". To start these stoves, the spirit ring is filled with a few drops of alcohol or fuel that are ignited and allowed to burn off, thereby heating the central assembly and pressurizing the tank. The valve is then opened to release vapor and finely dispersed fuel out of a single-hole jet where it splashes onto the bottom of a burner plate. This jet of fuel is ignited and keeps the central assembly and tank warm and the fuel pressurized. The fine droplets of fuel burn as they mix with air in the burner making a roaring sound.

In more recent models of gas stoves, many manufacturers have replaced the single-hole jet with a different burner assembly. Instead they utilize a preheated fuel tube to vaporize the liquid fuel and a hand activated pump in the fuel tank to pressurize the system. The burner intensity of most liquid fuel stoves of this type is somewhat difficult to regulate and they often sputter when their pressure is not optimal. They are very effective for boiling water at full throttle but not very suitable for simmering soup or cooking omelets. Also, the burner jet can foul due to the accumulation of soot residue in the jetport requiring occasional unplugging with a wire cleaner.

(a)  (b)

(c)  (d)

Figure 5-17. Camping stoves: a) Brunton Optimus Crux Stove
b) Coleman Exponent Feather 442 Dual Fuel Backpacking Stove
c) MSR WhisperLite Internationale Backpacking Stove
d) Optimus Climber Svea 123R Backpacking Stove (Photos courtesy
of Recreational Equipment Inc.)

## STOVE AT BRENNER PASS

I had an interesting experience camping one morning in Brenner Pass in Austria when my butane stove failed to light. I had just woken up, dressed for the cold and stepped outside my tent. I poured water from my water bottle into a steel cooking pot and watched with great fascination as ice crystals formed immediately and visibly on the water surface. I placed the pot on my trusty Camping Gaz stove and found that my butane did not want to come out of the bottle, in fact, almost no vapor was forming. Therefore, I had no fire. I realized that I was losing ground as I watched the water continue to freeze before my very eyes. So I did the only thing practical at the moment, I detached the gas bottle and crawled back into my sleeping bag with the gas bottle between my legs to warm it up. After twenty minutes or so — Voilá — the warmed gas and stove worked fine! I then proceeded to melt the pot, which was now full of ice and boil water for tea.

When selecting a camping stove, your primary considerations should be size, weight, fuel type, reliability and performance. A compact, lightweight, single-burner stove is recommended for backpacking. The stove must also have a wide enough base and pot support to ensure stability and camp safety and to minimize food spillage. For car camping or boat travel, a two-burner stove may be more appropriate for group cooking. For basecamp, a large, high-performance, stable single burner stove can be a good choice. For three-season camping, propane/butane mixtures or white gas are suitable fuels, but liquid fuel or cold weather gas mixtures are recommended for winter camping. Try to select a stove that is easy to assemble, reliable and easy to maintain. There is a wide range of models available on the market that meets these basic requirements. The cost of a stove typically ranges from $25 to $200, depending on specific stove features.

The performance of a stove is its ability to put out heat at a sustained rate. This is often measured in British Thermal Units (BTU) which are a direct measure of the heat generated by burning fuel. A more practical measure of performance is how quickly the stove can heat a given volume of water to boiling point, which is called the "average boiling time". For example, a stove that can boil one liter of water in three minutes has a higher performance rating than one requiring four minutes to reach boiling. Another measure of performance is stove efficiency, which measures how much of the fuel burned is actually being used for heating. This is often expressed as the volume of water boiled per pint of fuel (similar to miles per gallon of car economy). Finally, the size of the fuel tank requires some consideration. No matter how compact, efficient and reliable a stove is, you do not want to buy one with an undersized fuel tank that requires constant refilling while you are trying to cook a meal.

There are many camping stove manufacturers and models available on the market. Coleman makes widely available and reliable two-burner stoves, one of which we have used for years for car camping. We also own one of their multifuel, single-burner, backpacking stoves that is simple to operate and maintain. MSR makes a variety of stoves in which the stove assembly can be attached to a standard liquid fuel bottle to eliminate the weight of an extra fuel tank. Primus, Svea, Optimus and others make a variety of stoves providing a broad range of features and costs. Take your time when selecting a stove and preferably try it out before purchase. If you choose well, it will be with you for a long time and become a welcome friend on many camping trips.

## PRIMUS STOVE HISTORY

The first kerosene "pressure stove" was invented by a Swede, Frans W. Lindquist, in 1892. He created the Primus brand of stove that has been used on expeditions all over the world. Amundsen used Primus stoves on his trek to the South Pole and Hillary used them during the first ascent of Mt. Everest.

# CHAPTER 6          FINDING YOUR WAY

Whenever you go somewhere, you navigate between a starting point and a destination. If you are walking from home to the neighborhood corner store, you probably walk along a familiar route to the end of the block. If you see a friend walking across the parking lot, you may deviate from your normal route and walk directly over to say hello using only a visual means of navigation. If you are driving to dinner at a new friend's house, you may navigate by following the verbal directions given by your host or by looking at a map to find a route to the house address. And we have all received directions like the following: "Just go north along Walnut Street for about a mile, you can't miss it!" The point is that there are many ways of navigating between two points depending on the information available. There are also a number of ways to describe a route to a given location, each relying on somewhat different types of information (Figure 6-1).

Figure 6-1. Using map and compass to find your way

The preceding examples illustrate several approaches to navigation. In the corner store example, you simply follow a known route to and from a known destination. There is no route-finding involved, just the following of a prescribed path. Navigating toward your friend in the parking lot is based on visual sighting. As long as you can see the target, you can make your way toward him around parked cars even if he is moving. As long as he is within sight and you have visual feedback about his location, you can adjust course as needed to reach him. Traveling to an unknown location for dinner relies on verbal description or your ability to read a map — you are provided with a series of directions to follow a combination of roads and set distances. The trip along Walnut Street involves following a defined path and by inference, a direction or bearing along the street to your destination. With this type of description, one needs to have a direction to follow and a distance to the goal. In summary, the main approaches to navigation are (1) following a prescribed path, (2) using visual feedback, (3) the combined prescribed path-distance approach, (4) using a map and (5) the bearing and distance method. All five route-finding approaches are based on having a point of reference and defining either a relative or absolute location.

In all examples except the one in which a map can be used for navigation, the implied point of reference is your initial location and your route is based on the location of the goal relative to the reference point. The prescribed path to the corner store is only useful when you start from home or an intermediate point along the path. Crossing the parking lot to talk to your friend is based on his position relative to your point of reference. This could occur in any parking lot as long as you can see your friend. If a fog suddenly descended cutting off your visual feedback you would no longer have a way to locate your friend by this method. The verbal directions to someone's house assume that you are coming from a defined starting point. If the directions are based on right and left turns at stop lights, you must start at the defined reference point for the directions to make sense. If the directions are given in terms of known street names, you can possibly improvise and start at a different location along the prescribed path. In the bearing and distance case, you must start at the implied reference point in order to measure off the distance in the prescribed direction. If you start at any other location, you will not reach the goal.

If you decide to consult a map before driving to dinner at your new friend's house, you are utilizing the only route-finding method based on definition of an absolute location. This is the only approach that contains sufficient information to allow us to find the house from any other reference point on the map. In this example, the address defines an absolute location that you can find on the map and the location of the goal remains accurately and independently defined no matter where you start on the map.

The different navigation approaches illustrated above rely on several implied pieces of information. They assume that you can use the starting point as a reference point and that you can then define the relative location of the goal by direction of travel. The direction of travel is defined as a series of turns, distances and prescribed paths leading to the goal. The turns may themselves be relative (right or left) or absolute (north, south, east or west). In order to interpret an absolute direction such as "east", you need to be able to orient yourself in terms of a primary reference such as north. All the information contained in a map means little if you cannot relate map directions to the real world.

The five basic navigation approaches can be applied in many different settings. In cities you may define a route by street names, give distances by counting blocks or stop lights and specify right or left turns since most streets meet at well-defined junctions. In cities we may lose track of absolute reference directions and directions of travel. But the same principles can be applied in the outdoors to trails or cross-country travel. Following a trail system is similar to finding our way along city streets except that trails seldom follow a straight line. Our direction of travel may be defined as "upstream" or "upvalley" or follow a specific compass bearing. During cross-country travel our reference points are usually natural features like mountain peaks or large trees rather than street intersections and buildings. Even with these physical differences, the underlying approaches to navigation are quite similar.

## 6.1    USING MAPS

### 6.1.1
### Recreation Maps

Learning to read maps is one of the most basic skills that you will need to navigate in the outdoors. There are several different types of maps to guide your recreational activities, each displaying a wide range of information about roads, hiking trails and natural features. Choosing the right one to meet your needs depends on the purpose of the map and the amount of information presented. The USFS publishes some of the most common and popular types of recreation maps. USFS maps, like the one reproduced in Figure 6-2, typically show the map scale, north direction and location of roads, campgrounds and trails in national forests that are managed under the agency's jurisdiction. Locational information is provided in township and range coordinates with section numbers included, as well as in coordinates of latitude and longitude. Roads, trails, streams, lakes and significant mountain peaks located within the boundaries of the forest are displayed, major features are named and land ownership is indicated by color code. Additional recreation information can also be provided, describing the facilities and assorted family activities that are available in the forest of interest.

The map shown in Figure 6-3 is a recreational trail map for Apex Park near Golden, Colorado. This map contains an additional level of information compared to the USFS map, showing hiking trails superimposed on topographic contours of the landscape. Instead of providing a map scale, the map indicates distances between fixed points on established trails. An inset highway diagram indicates which direction is north and short segments of road are labeled to orient the user to known landmarks. A legend explains the meaning of symbols used. An interesting feature of this particular map is that a table is provided containing trail names, trail descriptions and distances and elevations gained or lost along different segments of the trails. The elevation gain/loss information indicates that the trail goes up and down as you hike in a given direction. For example, the Pick N' Sledge Trail is 1.5 miles long starting at the Apex Trail junction. As you

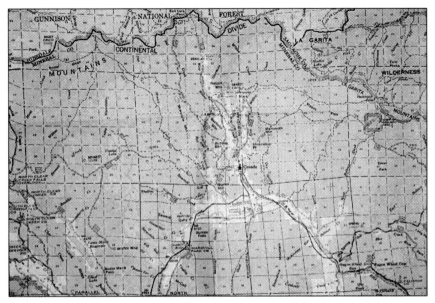

Figure 6-2. USFS topographic map, Rio Grande National Forest, Colorado

walk along the trail, you gain 878 feet and lose 202 feet in elevation due to the hilly nature of the trail. If you reverse course and go from Grubstake Trail Junction to the Apex Trail, you drop down 878 feet and rise 202 feet. This level of information is useful because on many trails the elevation gain is often listed simply as the difference between the initial and final elevation, with no indication of how much up-and-down travel is involved.

Shaded relief is often used on maps to add a sense of topography without adding all the detail of topographic contours. An example of this type of recreation map is presented in Figure 6-4, a section of the NPS map for Rocky Mountain National Park, Colorado. Shaded relief maps provide a good deal of information in compact form. In this case, the use of shading rather than contour lines to represent the rugged relief in the park leaves a lot of extra room on the map to present information on visitor centers, recreational facilities and road closures.

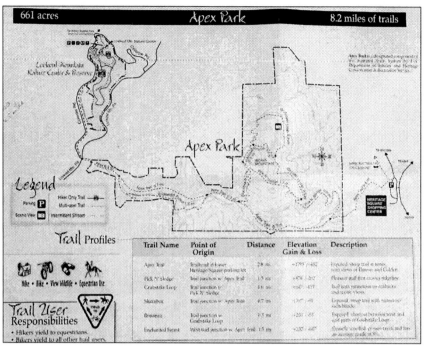

Figure 6-3. Recreational trail map with topographic contours, Apex Park, Colorado

There are various other maps available that can be very helpful for planning recreational activities. For example, maps produced for mountaineering use often display road and trail information superimposed on a photographic base. This technique is quite effective for illustrating climbing routes up a mountain slope or rock climbing routes up the face of a cliff, in which case a side view of the mountain or cliff face is generally used as the photographic base. Other mountaineering maps employ simple sketches and line drawings for the same purpose. Maps that display larger scale areas, such as watersheds and geographic basins, use aerial photographic base maps on which to display hiking trails, roads and other cultural features.

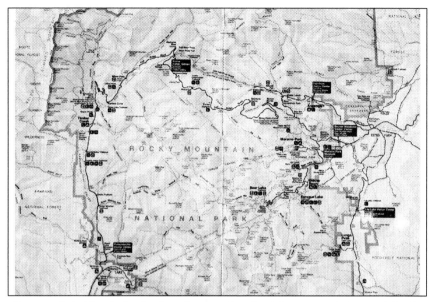

Figure 6-4. Shaded relief trail map, Rocky Mountain National Park, Colorado

## 6.1.2
### *Topographic Maps*

Topographic maps are by far the most useful types of maps for hiking and camping. They are readily available for many parts of the country in a variety of scales and usually contain a great deal of information. Topographic maps are scaled maps in which elevations on the ground surface are represented by topographic contours. Each contour line represents a line of constant elevation and the difference in elevation or spacing between adjacent contour lines is called the contour interval for the map. For example, a hillslope that rises one hundred feet can be represented by six contour lines separated by five contour intervals of 20 feet each.

Figure 6-5 depicts a three-dimensional landscape in which points of equal elevation are connected forming contour lines with 100-foot contour intervals. Each interval is presented in a different shade of gray. The mountain peaks, ridges, valleys and passes are clearly visible on the three-dimensional projection. If we look directly down onto the contoured landscape, the resulting "map view" of the contours would look like those in the plane that lies above the landscape in the figure. In this flat map view, the same geographic features can be seen represented by the topographic contours.

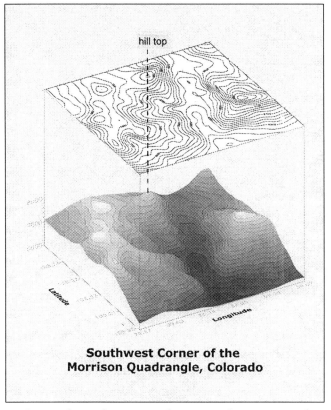

**Southwest Corner of the Morrison Quadrangle, Colorado**

Figure 6-5. A three-dimensional topographic contour drawing

On a topographic map, closer spacing of contours indicates a steep slope, whereas widely dispersed lines indicate a gentle slope. Only major elevation contours are labeled on most maps, but if you know the contour interval you can quickly figure out the elevation of any unlabeled contour line. Maps that display a wide range of elevations in a small area require larger contour intervals than ones that depict flat relief. This is because in order to represent steep, mountainous terrain, there would be too many contour lines to be readable. For example, on a map depicting elevations ranging from 5,000 to 14,000 feet, 450 contours would have to be drawn between the lowest and highest points if the contour interval was 20 feet, but only 180 would be necessary if the contour interval was 50 feet. The mapmaker has to pick a scale and contour interval that best convey the information intended.

Topographic maps contain a great deal of information about specific locations. For example, Figure 6-6 is a USGS map that is part of a four-map set covering Grand County, Colorado. It is drawn to a scale of 1 to 50,000 and is part of the USGS County Map Series. Like all USGS topographic maps, it is a scaled map showing topography, natural and man-made features and lines indicating reference location, such as township, range and section. Each map is published with the name of the map, information about the projection of the map, sources of data, date of printing and a legend explaining the various map symbols used to depict roads, trails, lakes, boundaries and other features (Figure 6-7). In this particular county map series, color is used to indicate land ownership. The map publication date is important because it reveals how recent the information displayed on the map is, which is especially important with respect to road and building locations. Some maps that have been partially updated list different dates for topographic and cultural features. If a map is more than ten years old, it may not show all current roads or trails, which would limit its use for trip planning.

All topographic maps indicate the scale at which they are published and provide distance measure bars in miles and kilometers. The contour interval for the topographic contours is also given. Frequently a map index is given to locate the map relative to other maps in the same series or with respect to USGS quadrangle maps. True north and magnetic north are indicated and the difference between the two, called "declination", is specified. Most maps include a comparative scale relating elevation in feet to elevation in meters. In Figure 6-6, the elevations of mountain peaks and other important features are given in both feet and meters. Although contour intervals on USGS maps are generally designated in feet, some use units of meters. This is important if you are trying to match maps across the US-Canadian border — Canada uses the metric system.

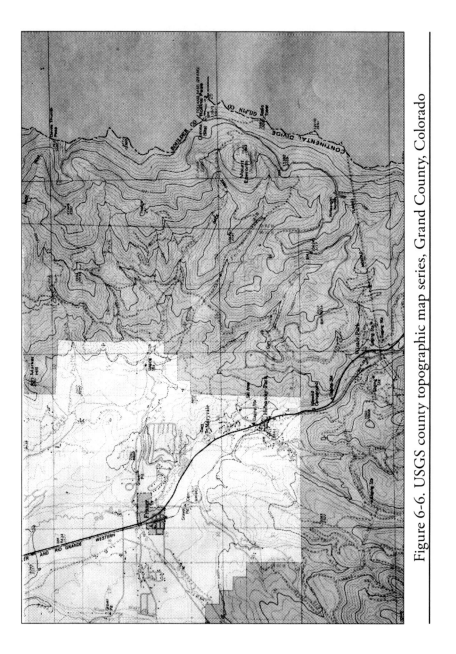

Figure 6-6. USGS county topographic map series, Grand County, Colorado

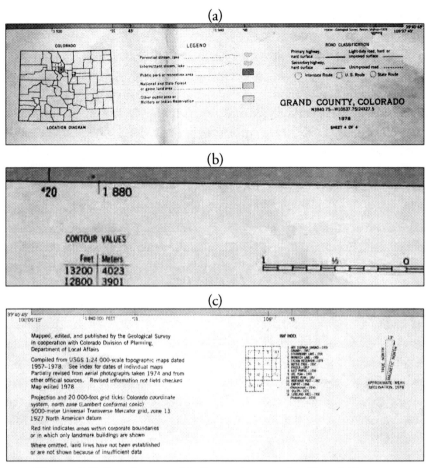

Figure 6-7. Supplemental information on the Grand County, Colorado topographic map: a) name, location and legend b) scale and contour interval c) map projection, sources and magnetic north declination

The USGS produces most of the commercially available topographic maps in the US and also makes the topographic and cultural information upon which they are based available to other mapmakers. USGS maps are published at a variety of scales in several map series that can be purchased by the public. The most useful scale and series of topographic maps for hiking and backpacking are the 7.5 and 15-minute topographic quadrangle maps. These are maps representing 7.5 x 7.5 or 15 x 15 minutes of latitude and longitude, respectively. The 7.5-

minute map series is more recent than the 15-minute series. Because it takes four 7.5-minute maps (of scale 1:24,000) to cover the same area as one 15-minute map (of scale 1:62,500, there is significantly more information shown on the newer, 7.5-minute quadrangle maps. USGS topographic quadrangle maps are sold directly by the USGS and in many sporting goods and outdoor supply stores. Independent mapmakers use USGS map information as the basis for specialty maps that they produce, sometimes adding more recent cultural or trail information.

The patterns of contours on topographic maps supply information on landscape features. For example, in Figure 6-6, contours form a v-shape along a stream course with the apex of the "v" pointing upstream or upvalley. This can be seen along the stream labeled South Fork about two and one-half miles east of Hideaway Park. In this area, the stream flows downhill from southeast to northwest, therefore the apex of each "v" points southeast with the stream outlined in the notch of the "v". Contours form closed loops around the tops of hills and mountains. This can be seen on Mount Epworth approximately five miles east of Hideaway Park. There is a drainage divide on the east side of the mountain between two small lakes. Each of the lakes forms the headwater for a small stream, one flowing southwest to form Middle Fork Creek and the other flowing northwest to form Ranch Creek. Streams and contour lines are good indicators of where the valleys lie and which direction is downhill. It should be noted that the scale at which a map is published presents a limitation on the size of object that can be displayed. Some topographic features such as cliffs, knolls, buttes, clumps of trees and ponds can be too small to show up at a given map scale.

In an effort to encourage map reading, the USGS has published a number of brochures and booklets about how to use USGS topographic maps. These publications, which are listed on the agency's Internet site, provide a good general introduction to map interpretation. Other useful references on reading maps and learning the principles of orienteering are listed for additional reading at the back of the book. The USGS also publishes free index maps for all topographic map series on a state-by-state basis. The indices depict the geographic area covered by each map series and they identify individual maps that cover specific areas that you may be interested in. The index maps are readily available by mail or telephone and can also be accessed on the USGS Internet site (www. usgs.gov or topomaps.usgs.gov).

It is worth noting that although USGS maps can be somewhat out-of-date regarding cultural features, particularly those located in fast-growing suburban areas, they are rarely incorrect. The underlying topography is generally very reliable and can be trusted even when there is a minor discrepancy in cultural features. On the other hand, we have found minor errors in maps published by independent mapmakers, usually in the form of misplaced trails and features. On one Trails Illustrated map, for example, we found a hiking trail drawn on the east side of a ridge when in fact it was about ½ mile away on the west side of the ridge. This type of error can be troubling because it can cause you to waste valuable energy looking for something that is not there.

The declination of magnetic north relative to true north gradually changes every year in a predictable manner. Magnetic north is slowly moving to the west at a rate of 6.3 minutes of arc per year or approximately one-tenth of a degree per year. This means that declination has changed somewhat since most maps were printed. Fortunately, USGS topographic maps list the year for which the declination was based allowing us to correct to the present time. For example, a declination of 13 degrees (13°) based on 1974 magnetic data will now be 30 years out of date. The correction is 13° − (30 x 0.1) = 10.0°. Note that declinations are positive in western North America and negative in eastern states and provinces.

Most maps are printed on paper sheets that gradually show wear-and-tear with use, especially if they get damp. A waterproof envelope or map tube will extend the life of paper maps. Many trail maps are produced on waterproof paper or synthetic material to improve their resistance to abrasion. The cost of waterproof maps is generally higher than paper maps but can be worthwhile if the maps are frequently used in bad weather. Topographic map data are also available on CD-ROM and can be downloaded directly over the Internet. Some mapping tools allow you to create your own maps to cover your specific area of interest.

## 6.2   Instruments of Navigation

### 6.2.1
### *Compass*

A compass is an instrument used to determine the direction of magnetic north on the earth's surface. It is composed of a magnetic needle balanced on a supporting bearing that aligns itself with the earth's magnetic field. The needle is housed in a circular, transparent, sealed chamber that is often filled with clear liquid to dampen its movement. The north end of the needle is often painted red or treated with luminous paint for night use. Even the simplest of compasses can be used to locate north and navigate in the outdoors.

Specific features are added to more advanced compass models to make them more quantitative and useful for map interpretation, orienteering and navigation. Advanced compasses typically contain a circular dial around the perimeter of the needle housing that is marked clockwise from 0 to 360 degrees in increments of degrees. This is called a bezel ring (also azimuth ring or bearing ring) and the 0 and 360 degree marks coincide with north (Figure 6-8). The transparent bottom of the needle housing on some compasses is marked with a red orienting arrow that can be rotated to indicate the degree of declination of magnetic north from true north. Supplemental lines are often provided parallel to the orienting arrow so that they can be aligned with directions on a map. On most compasses, this red arrow is marked "MN" for magnetic north and the degrees of declination are marked in an arc around it. In some cases, the azimuth ring and the MN arrow are part of the same housing and turn together as the housing is rotated. Compasses that display this feature typically have a rectangular base plate within which the needle housing rotates. The base plate is marked with centimeter and inch rulers for measuring distances on maps. It also has a direction of travel arrow (sometimes called an index line) along its long axis, which is aligned with the center of the needle housing. This line can be used to orient a map to the direction of travel. Additional features that can be incorporated into compasses to make them more useful for map interpretation are built-in magnifying lenses for reading map details and flip-up sighting mirrors for better alignment on distant landmarks.

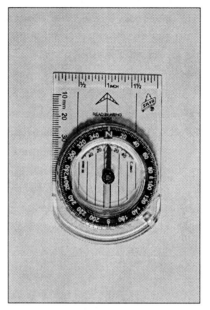

Figure 6-8. A compass with bezel ring

Some advanced compasses (like the Brunton Model 9020 and Suunto M-2D) allow you to correct for magnetic declination independently from the azimuth ring. This makes it easier to reference a map or true readings without always having to add or subtract the declination angle mentally. Compasses that include this feature cost a bit more than simpler ones but are well worth the extra cost if you travel off-trail or do much map and compass work.

Most compasses used for map interpretation are made from clear plastic materials that can easily break if you accidentally sit on them or crush them in your backpack. The most common damage that occurs is the seal on the needle chamber breaks and air bubbles form inside. The air bubbles can interfere with the compass readings by a few degrees and require careful checking to be sure the needle is accurately pointing to true north.

Many outdoor enthusiasts forget that their compasses are magnetic, therefore other magnets and metallic objects will influence them. Deviations of a few degrees are common when compasses are held next to a car, metal post, camera or even an iron-rich rock outcrop. Two compasses will interfere with each other if they are placed in close proximity to each other and batteries may also cause some interference. If you are a hiker who needs to rely on your compass for orienteering, make sure that you do not carry or store your compass near another magnet or it may lose its magnetization.

When using a compass, it is important to keep track of the type of bearing that you are talking about when giving or receiving accurate directions. The "magnetic bearing", also called the "compass bearing", is the uncorrected bearing based on zero degrees at magnetic north. This can be easily confused with the "true bearing" which is measured from true north and has already been adjusted for magnetic declination. "Azimuth" is another term indicating direction and is measured in degrees from 0 to 360° clockwise from true north where both 0° and 360° represent north.

## 6.2.2
### Altimeter

An altimeter is an instrument that indicates elevation above mean sea level (msl). It is actually a barometer calibrated to read in feet or meters of elevation rather than in units of atmospheric pressure. Altimeters operate on the principle that barometric pressure decreases with altitude because air is denser at sea level than at higher elevations. Therefore, in a perfect world, any given air pressure corresponds with a specific elevation. In practice, many factors can interfere with this assumption causing local and regional deviations from the perfect case. Weather systems containing high and low pressure gradients and changes in relative humidity are two factors that commonly cause inaccuracies in altimeter readings. Most altimeters have an adjustment screw that allows recalibration for changing local conditions. This can be used to calibrate the altimeter to a known elevation at a known landmark or known map coordinates. When you are out on an extended hiking or backpacking trip, it is best to check your altimeter calibration at the beginning of each day if possible, or more often if the weather is changing rapidly. An inaccuracy of plus or minus 100 feet, which is not significant in most hiking applications, can easily occur due to daily weather fluctuations. However, differences of up to 500 feet can occur on stormy days. All altimeter readings should be considered approximate for the above reasons, so don't be surprised if your altimeter reading is a bit different from the elevation shown on a topographic map.

## 6.2.3
### Pedometer

A pedometer is an instrument used to measure distance by counting the number of steps that you take. When attached to your belt or elsewhere on your body, the device actually counts the number of times it bounces up and down as you walk, recording each up-and-down cycle as one step. This is useful if you know what the length of your average stride is because you can multiply total number of steps times stride length to calculate the distance you have traveled. The calculation assumes that your estimate of average stride is accurate, which is often reasonable on flat, prepared trails. However on rough trails leading up and down mountain slopes, your stride may change considerably.

Hikers should be aware that pedometers perform differently for different people. A heavy walker may get an accurate count of steps but someone who is light on his feet may not get a complete count because he doesn't jar the instrument hard enough. Therefore, it is important to try wearing the pedometer on different parts of the body to get consistent and accurate readings. In addition, some models may be more sensitive to motion than others.

## 6.2.4
### Global Positioning System Receivers

The Global Positioning System (GPS) is a network of navigational satellites that orbit the earth at designated locations. Originally placed in orbit by the US Department of Defense to support the accurate navigation of military craft, they are now available for public use in selected geographic areas. Each satellite contains a very accurate clock and radio transmitter broadcasting with a specific and unique frequency. Satellites transmit signals 24 hours a day, every day of the year. A GPS receiver (Figure 6-9) can detect the signals from a satellite within its range and determine exactly how far away it is from that satellite. If the receiver can detect at least three satellites, it can triangulate its own position on the earth's surface. If more than three satellites are detected, the accuracy of the calculated position improves. Many GPS units report with an accuracy of up to 20 feet in each horizontal direction if at least four satellites are involved, but 50 to 100-foot accuracy is more common. In restricted areas, the accuracy may only be plus or minus 300 feet.

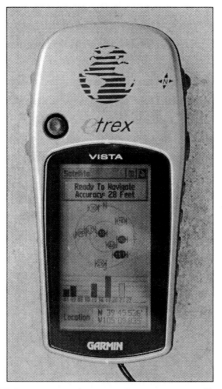

Figure 6-9. A GPS receiver showing location, satellite reception and navigation accuracy

GPS receivers report their coordinates in units of latitude and longitude. For example, as we write, we sit at N39°39.011', W106°05.165' with a reported accuracy of 19 feet based on the seven satellites that my Garmin Etrex Vista GPS receiver is picking up. This means that we are currently at 39 degrees (°) 39.011 minutes (') north of the equator and 106 degrees 5.165 minutes of arc west of the Prime Meridian at Greenwich, England (which is 0° longitude). With these coordinates, we can locate ourselves easily on a topographic map marked with latitude and longitude tick marks. On a 7.5-minute topographic quadrangle, where one minute of arc is approximately 0.8 miles or two inches on the map, this represents a precision of approximately 1/500 of an inch or approximately 20 feet in the real world. That is pretty decent triangulation! But keep in mind that even with four satellites acquired, you should not count on being more accurate than plus or minus 100 feet.

GPS receivers are not significantly affected by fog, clouds or light rainfall. All that is needed is unobstructed access to the sky to receive radio signals. Receivers work out of doors as well as inside wood-framed houses. They do not work as well in thick forests, buildings with metal frames or dense structures, metal buildings, narrow valleys, deep canyons and caves. In a narrow valley, it is best to climb to the top of the nearest ridge to get clear access to a good portion of the sky and at least three satellites. Usually the GPS unit will tell you how many satellites it can detect so you have direct feedback on the quality of signal it is receiving. Sometimes moving around on a ridge will allow you to gain access to additional satellites.

Because GPS units run on batteries, they are subject to failure when the batteries go dead. For this reason, it is important to carry a compass as a backup navigational tool at all times, even if you have a GPS unit with you. At the present time, GPS use is not widespread, chiefly because of the high price of receivers. For the most part, the technology is not something that most hikers require unless they need to have precise, absolute locations defined for making or checking maps in various resource applications. With time, the cost of the units will no doubt come down from the current hundreds of dollars to a price that more hikers can afford. Until then, a map and compass work just fine for a fraction of the cost of a GPS receiver.

## JUNEAU ICEFIELD NAVIGATION

One of the few times that I could have used a GPS receiver was in the summer of 1985 during a trip across the Juneau Icefield, in the coast ranges that separate Canada from the Alaska Panhandle. But commercial GPS units weren't available then. My climbing partner and I spent nearly two weeks hiking, camping and skiing across mountains buried to their peaks in glacial ice up to 6,000 feet thick. Several days into the trip, a blizzard blew in and laid us up in our tent for a day and a half. After the worst of the storm had passed, we found ourselves shrouded in thick fog and a low, marine cloud layer that reduced visibility to a couple hundred feet. We were able to orient ourselves on the coarse-scaled map that we had with us by occasionally sighting peaks above the clouds. But solid dead reckoning got us through.

A second storm overtook us a few days later as we were crossing a peak called Nugget Mountain where the map simply did not correspond with the terrain. Ridges ran the wrong way, summits and ridges visible on the landscape did not appear on our map and magnetic north was nowhere close to where it should be. We camped on the shoulder of the mountain that night, exhausted and confused. In the morning, we managed to feel our way through pea-soup fog down the mountain and across a glacier to another ridge where we eventually rose above cloud level. Looking back a few miles toward Nugget Mountain we sighted a few other peaks and located our position on the map again. From there we continued along our route and eventually walked down Blackerby Ridge into Juneau, Alaska a few days later.

Upon reflection, we figured out what had gone so drastically wrong with our navigation. First, the 1 to 100,000 scale map that we had with us was old, based on aerial photography that showed a pattern of snow cover and ridges quite different from what we had encountered. Second, our compass was off by nearly 90° from the expected magnetic declination because Nugget Mountain and its surrounding peaks are rich in iron, causing significant local magnetic aberrations. We learned the hard way! A GPS receiver would have been handy because it would have given us a navigational tool that was independent of magnetic north.

However, for those who want to spend the money, GPS receivers do have a number of features that are helpful in the outdoors. For instance, they can report time very accurately. Also many units allow you to upload a digital map from a computer into memory so that you can see the map on the instrument screen (Figure 6-10). These maps vary in resolution and level of detail, but are useful because they can display your location relative to local roads and trails in real time. Some receivers allow you to record your location as "waypoints" at specific time intervals or when you press a button so that you have an electronic record of your travels. This feature is very useful if you are making a trail map or want to backtrack along the same route. Some units contain an internal electronic compass that reports direction relative to true north rather than magnetic north. Others contain an altimeter capability, which is based on measuring barometric pressures. Finally, there are specialized instruments available that were developed for surveying, which can calculate accurate ground elevations directly from satellite data and are thus independent of meteorological influences.

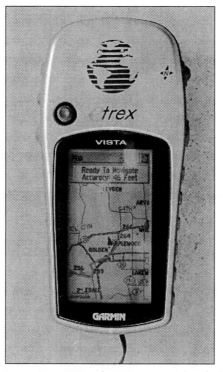

Figure 6-10. A GPS receiver showing an uploaded digital map

From the previous discussion it is clear that there are many capabilities to choose from when you are buying a GPS receiver. But keep in mind that all of these functions require the unit to be turned on and therefore reduce its battery life. In particular, operations like uploading maps and recording location waypoints require a lot of memory storage. So, if you want to be able to upload maps, be sure to buy a receiver with plenty of memory.

## 6.2.5
### Celestial Tools

When all else fails and you don't have a compass or other navigational instrument with you, it is possible to navigate using the sun, moon and stars. All that is required is some basic knowledge of astronomy, a clear sky and the realization that you may not be able to chart a very precise path because there is no scale for you to use to quantify directions.

In the Northern Hemisphere, the sun rises in the east and sets in the west during the equinoxes (March 21st and September 23rd). During the summer solstice (June 21st), the sun rises approximately in the northeast and sets in the northwest. During the winter solstice (December 21st), the sun rises roughly in the southeast and sets in the southwest. At noon Standard Time (1:00 p.m. Daylight Savings Time) the sun is nearly due south at locations in the Northern Hemisphere. The terrain will of course influence the direction of sunrise and sunset because any mountains or hills will effectively intercept the sun's path before it reaches the same angle as it would on an open plain. Nevertheless, sunrise and sunset can give you a good indication of the cardinal directions.

The moon also rises in the east and sets in the west, but it does not rotate around the earth in the same plane as the sun. The moon's orbital plane is very close to the plane of the equator and therefore its location in the sky does not change much with the seasons. In addition, the moon orbits on a different period than the sun, making it difficult for us to infer which direction is south at any specific time without additional knowledge of its movement. In other words, it will not indicate due south at midnight except on rare occasions.

The North Star (also called the Pole Star and Polaris) is a reliable indicator of true north at night because it is located in the heavens at a point almost directly in line with the earth's North Pole. At this location, it is nearly stationary as the earth spins on its axis. As a result, the rest of the sky and the earth with us on it appear to rotate slowly around the North Star. This makes the star an ideal reference point indicating true north from anywhere in the Northern Hemisphere in most seasons. The North Star is directly overhead at the North Pole.

Finding the North Star is easily done if the Big Dipper (also called the Great Bear and Ursa Major) is located first (Figure 6-11). The Big Dipper is usually very easy to find in the sky with a little practice. Once located, we can use the two stars that form the front of the Dipper to point to the North Star. The North Star is also the last star at the end of the handle of the star formation called the Little Dipper (Ursa Minor).

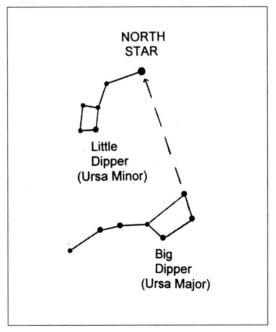

Figure 6-11. The location of the North Star relative to the Big and Little Dipper

## 6.3 PUTTING IT TOGETHER

### 6.3.1
### Finding Your Location on a Map or in the Landscape

The simplest way to find your location on a map or in a landscape is to find a sign that says "You Are Here". Since there are few of these signs in the world, you need an alternate way of defining your location by known reference location and object. The reference point may be a trailhead, road, trail intersection or other milestone that correlates where you are with a point on a map and allows you to describe your location to someone else. As long as the landscape reference point is defined on the map, you have a correlation point.

Another method of locating yourself in a landscape is to find an obvious landmark or landscape feature that is distinctive, large and unique enough to show up on a topographic map. This can be a highway bridge, large rock pinnacle, lake, junction of two streams or trails, mountain peak or mountain pass of a distinctive nature.

In order to locate yourself more accurately you can sight a bearing from your current location to any unique landscape features within your view. Figure 6-12 represents a portion of the 7.5-minute Quadrangle for Harris Park, Colorado. Suppose that we are standing on the trailhead at the junction of the Tanglewood Creek Trail and the Deer Creek gravel road shown in the figure. We can define our location as the trailhead, road-trailhead intersection or by a set of bearings that we measure to the three surrounding hilltops indicated on the map. In this case, we will read azimuth angles referenced to true north on the map (solid lines). The 11,495-foot peak is at azimuth 25°, which can also be defined as a bearing of N25°E, or 25° east of north. Our second directional reference is a peak just under 10,200 feet in elevation at azimuth 223° or bearing S33°W. Finally, Bandit Peak is at azimuth 304° (bearing N56°W). Note again that these relative positions are all given with respect to true north.

If we were determining our relative location using our compass, we would actually be measuring the azimuth with our compass to triangulate our location. In this case, we could sight in the three hills in azimuth angles with respect to magnetic north and then convert them to true north to locate ourselves on the map (Figure 6-13). The magnetic declination for the Harris Peak area is corrected to be +10°. When we sight in the azimuth angles, we get 15°m (N15°Em), 213°m (S23°Wm) and 294°m (N66°Wm) for the three peaks. Note that we can indicate magnetic bearings by adding a small "m" behind the reading to avoid confusion with bearings referenced to true north. If you add 10° to each azimuth and bearing measurement to correct for the declination, you obtain the same true north azimuth and bearings that we had in Figure 6-12.

It is important to note that up to this point, we have made a clear distinction between azimuth and bearings. In most literature, the terms azimuth and bearing are used interchangeably although there is a difference in definition between the two. Be aware that when you encounter a "bearing" given in terms of an angle alone, it is really an azimuth angle. Bearings such as N30°E always include additional directional references to north, south, east or west.

To actually plot our location on the map, we can take our sightings (in azimuth) and find our location by plotting "back bearings" from the three peaks to intersect at our location. A "back bearing" is simply the opposite direction from the azimuth, or the azimuth plus or minus 180°. So plotting from the 11,495-foot peak, we would draw a line at an azimuth of 180° + 25° = 205° (Figure 6-12). The back bearing from the 10,200-foot hill is 230° − 180° = 33° and the back bearing from Bandit Peak is 304° − 180° = 124°. If we draw lines from each of these peaks at the calculated back bearing, the three lines intersect at the location of our trailhead.

So far we have defined our position in the landscape relative to known map locations. However, in order to find our location at the trailhead, a person would have to know where the trailhead is or which peaks we referenced. A more direct approach is to define our location in absolute terms using map information based on latitude and longitude or Universal Transverse Mercator (UTM) coordinates. This can only be done if you have a topographic quadrangle with latitude/longitude.

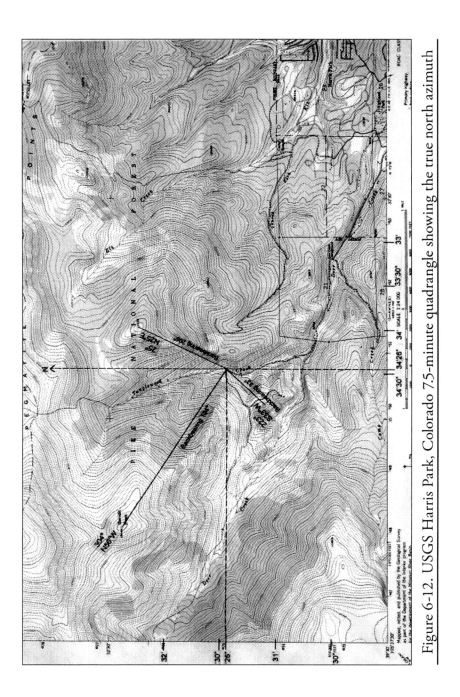

Figure 6-12. USGS Harris Park, Colorado 7.5-minute quadrangle showing the true north azimuth

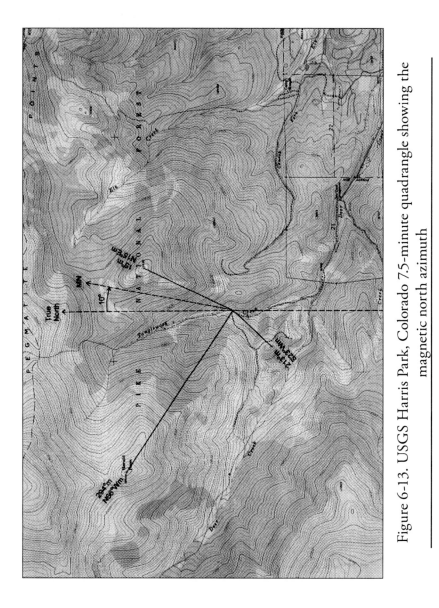

Figure 6-13. USGS Harris Park, Colorado 7.5-minute quadrangle showing the magnetic north azimuth

or UTM ticks marked around the margin of the map. To define our location in absolute coordinates on the Harris Park Quadrangle, we can start by drawing dashed lines parallel to true north and true west through our trailhead location to the edge of the map (Figure 6-12). We also need to draw in additional tick marks along the map edges. So we can place four more ticks between 32'30" and 35' along the bottom margin of the map using a ruler, representing equally spaced divisions of one-half minute. Similarly on the left margin of the map, we can add four equally spaced tick marks between 30' and 32'30". We can then read the coordinates of the trailhead from our map in latitude/longitude as North 39°31'26", West 105°34'26". This is a unique location that does not require any visual sighting of landscape features or prior knowledge about the location of the trailhead. In any emergency, be it during bad weather, day or night, the latitude and longitude coordinates define our location in absolute terms and a search team with a GPS unit will be able to find us

A similar procedure can be used to define our location using the UTM grid coordinates marked along the side of Figure 6-12 to yield another unique coordinate location. In this case, the trailhead is located at Northing 4374950, Easting 45640. Note that on USGS Quadrangles, the UTM tick marks are given in thousands of meters. For example, the Northing tick mark of 4375 actually means 4,375,000 meters north. Many people prefer to use UTM coordinates because they are part of a rectangular grid with cells measuring 1km by 1km which requires less interpolation than latitude/longitude coordinates.

## 6.3.2
### Tracking Your Position Along a Trail

When traveling along a well-defined trail it is useful to keep track of your location at various points along the way. This can help you assess your progress and eliminate possible confusion at trail intersections or other uncertain points along the way. The easiest way to track your progress if you have a trail map is to note where you encounter trail intersections, crossroads, bridges, streams and other unique landforms or aspects of the trail. Make a mark on your map when you reach a distinctive point, note the time and write down any unique characteristics of that spot. In some cases, it may also be useful to take bearings along a straight stretch of the trail to compare with the map or to take bearings and back bearings on significant landmarks along the way. It is helpful to periodically look back along the trail in the direction you came from to record a mental image of what the landscape looks like. The trail may look very different from one direction than it does from the other. This is particularly important at trail intersections because if one trail is less traveled, you might walk right past it on your return because you don't recognize the turnoff.

It is generally considered good orienteering practice to keep track of the distance traveled along a trail. A rough estimate is usually adequate if the distance traveled is within a range that you can judge reasonably well. Check the estimated distance traveled against your map at obvious waypoints like stream crossings and trail intersections, and mark them on the map. If you start to notice that map distances do not seem to match up with what you estimate on the trail, something may have gone wrong. It is common when hiking back along a trail that you walked on hours or days before, that you may miss a turnoff. If you cross a stream and your turnoff is a mile away, you will realize that you missed the trail when you have gone one and a half miles and the trail looks unfamiliar. In this case you are not lost, you are just misplaced one-half mile from where you wanted to turn off the trail.

### 6.3.3
### Tracking Your Position Cross-Country

The same methods that we recommended for tracking your position along established trails also apply when you are traveling cross-country. Off-trail hiking requires that you make more careful and frequent observations of landscape position, direction of travel, distance traveled, elevation and location. Keep track of landforms that you can see from a distance such as easily recognized mountain peaks, big trees, ridges or stream valleys. These features will help you maintain a general sense of orientation and help you locate yourself on a map. Sometimes when selecting a route over open country it is helpful to follow a stream or ridgeline as long as it goes in the direction of interest. From a ridge, you will have a good view of the landscape and landmarks. Also, take forward and back bearings at key waypoints so that you can find your way back later. Take occasional bearings on landmarks or peaks so that you can triangulate your position if necessary. Note this information on your map or in a notebook and plot your position on the map. You can even plot your route as you go. Finally and perhaps most importantly, when traveling off-trail, remember to look back in the direction you came from as well as in the direction you are traveling.

If you are not sure that you will find your way back along a given track, you can always place a marker to guide you on your return. In rocky areas such as along roads and streambeds or above tree line, you can stack rocks to form a cairn. This is easy to do and the rocks can be scattered again when you no longer need the marker. Piles of sticks, a broken tree branch and marks in the dirt can serve as additional markers on the trail. Cutting tree blazes in the bark of trees is not recommended except in emergencies because they cause tree damage and mar the forest. Sometimes people arrange small stones into an obvious sign or arrow on the ground as a marker. People have even taken to dropping handfuls of colored sand on the trail like breadcrumbs to mark their passing. Colored surveyor flagging material can be used effectively in wooded areas or even in tall grass and brush as long as it is biodegradable or collected on your way back. Keep in mind that markers that are clearly visible on your way up the trail may not necessarily stand out in rain, fog or darkness. So use your compass as a backup to fix your location if you anticipate any trouble on the way back.

## 6.3.4
### Following a Bearing

Sometimes it is desirable to define a route by using either a fixed bearing or a series of sequential bearings. To do so, you need to define the direction of travel and follow that bearing for a specified distance. An example of this is shown in Figure 6-14, where a cross-country course is laid out in three segments that define a route from the Tanglewood

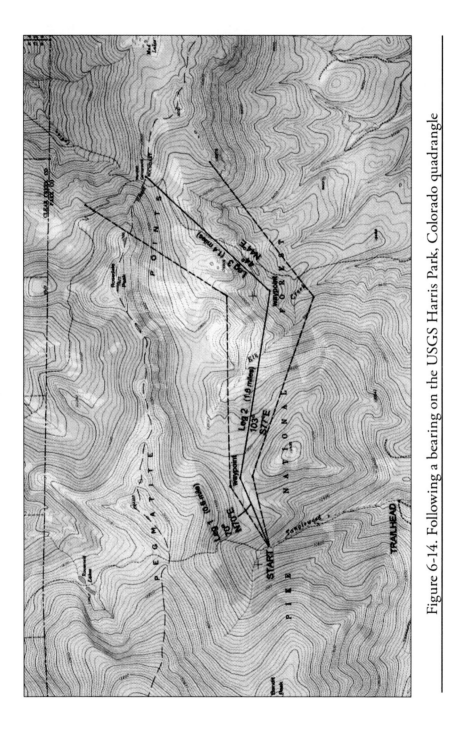

Figure 6-14. Following a bearing on the USGS Harris Park, Colorado quadrangle

Creek Trail to the Meridian Campground. The course begins at the point where the trail crosses the stream approximately 1.2 miles from the trailhead. The first segment follows a bearing of N70°E (70°) for a distance of 0.6 mile into the saddle above the trail. From that point, the second segment runs along bearing S77°E (103°) for 1.6 miles to a knob above Elk Creek. The third segment extends 1.4 miles along bearing N44°E (44°) to the campground. Note that all of these bearings are given relative to true north.

To follow this course in the field you can use a compass that has already been corrected for magnetic declination (10° east of north for the Harris Park Quadrangle) or you can use an uncorrected compass and mentally subtract 10° from each bearing. Figure 6-15 illustrates what a Suunto M-2D compass would look like after being corrected for declination and set to the first bearing. To correct the compass for magnetic declination, turn the compass declination set screw to 10° east of north. When you are ready to plot your course, place the compass on the map over your starting point and orient the map and compass in such a way as to align the compass needle with the magnetic north arrow on the compass. Setting the declination in advance allows the map and compass to automatically line up on true north by centering the magnetic needle within the magnetic north arrow. Once properly oriented, the bearing of the first segment of your course can be read directly from the compass azimuth scale in degrees. To follow that bearing, rotate the compass so that the direction of travel arrow is set at 70°, hold the compass at waist height in front of you and rotate yourself until the needle is within the MN arrow. When the needle lines up, you will be facing in the direction of bearing N70°E (70°). Sight a distant point on the saddle straight in front of you and begin walking. Check that you stay on course occasionally by using the same method and you will follow the proper bearing to the saddle.

A somewhat different approach is necessary if you are using an uncorrected compass, such as the Silva illustrated in Figure 6-16. In this case, the magnetic north arrow is not independent of the azimuth scale, so all bearing measurements are relative to magnetic north. When the needle is aligned with the MN arrow, the azimuth scale

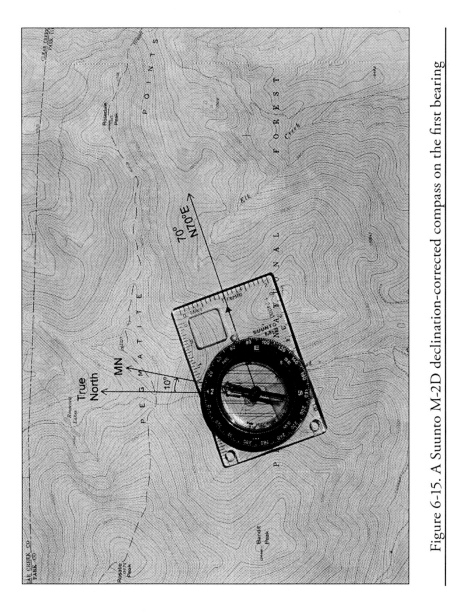

Figure 6-15. A Suunto M-2D declination-corrected compass on the first bearing

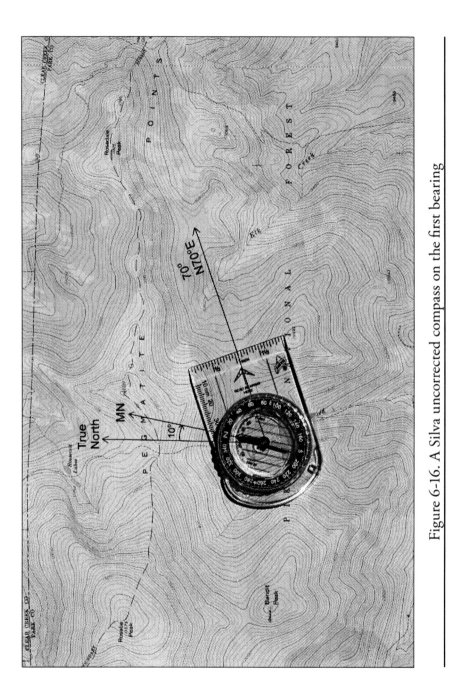

Figure 6-16. A Silva uncorrected compass on the first bearing

will read a magnetic bearing of N60°Em (60°m). In other words, the magnetic bearing is 10° less than the true bearing. When you hold the compass out in front of you, rotate the direction of travel arrow to 60° and align the needle and MN arrow, you will follow a N60°Em (60°m) bearing to the saddle waypoint. It is clear from the above example that a declination-correcting compass is far easier to use than one that cannot be corrected and it is well worth the few dollars in extra cost.

When you are sighting, following or communicating bearings to other people it is crucial that you specify whether you are talking with respect to true north or magnetic north. Otherwise you will find out the hard way that something is wrong when you do not arrive at the expected rendezvous point. Figure 6-14 illustrates what can happen if bearings are given or interpreted incorrectly. The two dashed lines in the figure represent the route that would be taken if a hiker made a 10° error in bearing at each waypoint on the three-segment course. The result is an error of more that one-half mile in location over a distance of only 3.6 miles traveled. This is a significant deviation that would cause the hiker to miss the campground entirely if no other information was available to verify his or her location.

Some publications are very lax in their explanation of how to apply compasses and locational information, never really explaining whether they are talking about true or magnetic bearings. Beware of the publication or trail description that does not specify the reference for the bearings that are given — it can get you into a lot of trouble. Some publications even assume that all bearings are magnetic bearings, which can lead to confusion and poor map and compass technique.

Sometimes on a stormy day, at night, or in foggy weather when it is impossible to rely on visual cues to define your route you will be forced to navigate by "dead reckoning". Dead reckoning is the practice of following a course using only bearing and distance information. This becomes necessary whenever you are caught in unfamiliar terrain and visibility is poor. Travel by dead reckoning should usually be avoided, but it is a good idea to practice map and compass technique in preparation for an unplanned need on some stormy night when you cannot see familiar landmarks or use other navigational aids.

## 6.4 What to Do If You Are Lost

If you follow the advice provided in this chapter, that is, stay alert in your surroundings and track your movements on a map or notebook, it is unlikely that you will ever become truly "lost". However, you may find yourself temporarily misplaced — not exactly where you expected to be — but not in a situation where you truly do not know where you are. This is because, if you frequently check your location in comparison to landmarks and/or a map, you will not be very far from your last known waypoint. By carefully backtracking a short distance, you can reach that last known point and you will then be able to reconstruct where you are. So finding the right way again is relatively easy, if you pay attention and keep track of your route.

Most people get "lost" when they travel a long distance without paying attention along the way. This happens most frequently to people traveling by snowmobile, motorbike or car who focus on the thrill of speeding through turns or forks in the route rather than on the landscape around them. Hikers are less likely to get lost because they travel at relatively slow speeds and don't cover as much ground without looking around as they go.

The best thing to do if you think you may be lost is to stop and think about your situation. Do not run blindly along a trail hoping to see something familiar. If darkness or weather limits your visibility, you should probably stay put until visibility returns. Your immediate goals should be to avoid getting more lost than you already are and to logically figure out how to get to a familiar location. You also need to make sure that you can survive long enough to get out of the situation.

There are two basic approaches to get out of your predicament: one is to stay put and wait to be found by others and the other is to move with a logic that will either get you to an area you recognize or to a place where there are people. The best approach to follow depends on your specific situation. For example, if no one knows that you are missing, then a search party is not likely to appear until someone discovers an abandoned car in the trailhead parking lot or you are discovered by accident. Ways to avoid being caught out alone include signing in on the trailhead logbook, notifying the forest ranger if you will be gone for several days and letting someone at home know where you are going and how long you expect to be gone. If the odds are low that anyone will come looking for you, then sitting in one spot and waiting for help is not likely to be successful. A more active response must be taken.

Luckily in today's world, the odds of being rescued are good. Cellular telephones provide a line of communication that significantly reduces the time you have to wait before someone notices that you are missing. You may have to hike to the top of the closest ridge to get cellular coverage in your area, but once you get a signal, you can call the nearest Forest Service Station, home or 911 for help. Keep in mind that cellular coverage is very spotty in remote areas of the US and even less available in other parts of the world. But on top of a mountain peak you may pick up a cellular receiver that is dozens of miles away. A cell phone is a good companion when you are hiking alone or in an unfamiliar area. You can use it if you are lost or injured. A Citizens Band (CB) radio or even a three-watt personal walkie-talkie, two-way radio can also be used in case of emergency in many parts of North America.

The best approach to finding your way if you become lost is to stop moving and backtrack to your last known position. Place a stone cairn or other marker to designate the location where you first realized that you were lost. Think of this as your "Lost Point". Stay calm and try to find yourself on your map and in the landscape. Even if you have not been actively recording your movements for the last few hours, like most people, you will eventually recognize some landmarks or site features that will allow you to get back to familiar ground. But as you backtrack you should pay attention to your route, note important features and mark your path with cairns or broken branches so that you can find your way back to the Lost Point if you need to. Now by carefully reversing your route and checking your position either in the landscape or on the map, you should be able to get back to your last known location.

If it is late in the day, try to establish your location and prepare to spend the night at the Lost Point or very close to it. You will not be able to navigate effectively at night and risk getting more confused, so stay put until morning. If fog or rain restrict your visibility, it is best to stay put until conditions clear before backtracking. If you have brought along the ten essentials, you should be able to weather a night in a bivouac camp. Don't panic, stay logical and you can work your way out of any bad situation.

Many experienced outdoorsmen recommend that if you are lost you should look for a stream and follow it down its course because it will eventually lead you to human habitation. This is reasonable advice if you are in a very remote area where there are no trails, roads or other features and you have no idea which direction to take. Following any continuous feature such as a ridge, stream, trail, or road is generally a good course of action. But for most situations where you have become displaced from your last known location, you are better off to logically work your way back to a familiar location.

One last point to mention about getting lost is that search-and-rescue operations cost real money and require many human resources. If you get lost and must be rescued, many people will work hard to find you, go without sleep, and in some cases, put themselves at risk of injury, to retrieve you. Generally, the cost of search-and-rescue operations is borne by city, county or agency budgets. But if your actions are found to be negligent, you may find yourself footing the bill for the recovery operation. This is just another reason to keep track of your location and avoid getting lost in the first place.

# CHAPTER 7  READING THE WEATHER

As the earth rotates, so does the atmosphere around it. If there were no sources of energy input to the atmosphere, the earth would have a layer of air around it that was thicker at the equator than at the poles due to the greater rotational velocity present at the equator. To a person standing anywhere on the earth under these conditions, the air would appear to be still because he or she would move at the same velocity as the atmosphere. However, the real world is not so simple. Solar radiation, heat from the earth's interior, radioactive decay of elements in the earth's crust and other natural processes serve to warm both the atmosphere and the earth surface causing variations in heat distribution.

Meteorology is the science of the atmosphere, its changes and phenomena, including climate and weather. Climate and weather result from the nonuniform distribution of heat on the earth's surface and atmosphere. Nonuniform heating causes air masses to warm up in some places and cool down in others, leading to the development of high and low air pressure systems with their associated winds. "Weather" describes the relatively short-term (hourly, daily, weekly) changes in atmospheric conditions. "Climate" describes the long term (seasonal, multiyear) changes in atmospheric conditions, which are typically associated with large scale and seasonal changes in solar radiation affecting the earth.

## 7.1    Weather Systems and Fronts

Radiation from the sun is generally quite uniform as a function of time, with the exception of occasional solar events that may cause temporary fluctuations. As the earth rotates around the sun, its distance from the sun varies a few percent above and below the average of 93 million miles, which has a slight influence on the amount of solar radiation that reaches earth. But the 23.5-degree tilt of the earth's axis as it revolves around the sun has a much more significant influence on the distribution of radiation on the earth and atmosphere. On the equinoxes (March 21 and September 23) when the sun lies directly over the equator, solar radiation is delivered to the equator with maximum intensity. At higher latitudes on the same dates, solar radiation strikes the upper atmosphere at a much lower angle and is therefore less intense. On June 21, the northern Summer Solstice, the sun is directly overhead at the Tropic of Cancer (23.5 degrees north latitude) and solar radiation strikes locations in the Northern Hemisphere at a steeper angle than at any other time of year. This results in the delivery of maximum solar radiation for the year at these latitudes. Similarly, on January 21, the northern Winter Solstice and southern Summer Solstice, the sun is directly overhead at the Tropic of Capricorn (23.5 degrees south latitude). At this time, the southern latitudes receive their greatest input of solar radiation for the year and the northern latitudes receive their lowest.

When solar radiation strikes the earth, it is partly absorbed and partly reflected from whatever objects it strikes. Most of the radiation is in or near the visible range of wavelengths that we perceive as daylight. How much radiation is absorbed depends on the composition of the object that it hits. If incoming radiation encounters thick clouds in the upper atmosphere as much as 95 percent may be reflected back into space. If radiation that reaches the earth surface strikes open water, 90 percent of it will be absorbed to heat the water. The fraction of incident radiation that is reflected from the surface of a material is called its "albedo". The albedo of fresh snow is high, 75 to 95 percent of incident radiation is reflected, while dense forest, grass and sand have albedos of approximately 3–10, 10–30 and 15–45 percent, respectively.

The fraction of solar radiation that is absorbed warms up the air, water or ground surface that it strikes. Because different materials absorb variable amounts of radiation, they warm up at different rates, causing the surrounding air to also warm up at different rates. Intense solar radiation causes some geographical areas such as tropical seas and dry deserts to warm up very large air masses.

The earth is continuously losing heat from its landmass, oceans, lakes and atmosphere. Most of the heat lost is in the form of infrared radiation, which is dissipated through the upper atmosphere to the cold reaches of space. A global heat balance exists between the heat gained from solar radiation and the heat lost to space. Locally, heat gained one day may be lost on the same day or at a later date when the heat gained from radiation is low, such as during a cloudy period. During the winter, snow cover imparts a high albedo on land and sea ice ensuring that most solar input is reflected off the earth's surface and little heat is absorbed. Heat lost from storage in the ground or water can still occur, cooling both land and sea. As a result, air over these surfaces cools down forming cold air masses that are denser than warm air and tend to sink into low-lying areas.

In general, large air masses form in the tropics or at the poles. They may be either continental (located over a continental landmass) or maritime (located over the oceans). In the Northern Hemisphere, cold continental polar air masses form over Alaska, western Canada, Greenland and Siberia in winter. These air masses can easily attain temperatures of below –20 °F or even –40 °F. Polar maritime air masses can also form over the northern oceans in winter but they are not usually as frigid as continental air masses. In contrast, maritime tropical air masses are warm, developing over portions of the tropical oceans due to the absorption of solar radiation by seawater. Continental tropical air masses form over dry tropical portions of the continents, such as northern Mexico in the summer.

Continental and maritime air masses serve as sources of warm or cold air in different seasons, and under certain conditions, can provide mobile air masses that migrate north or south from their points of origin. An example of this occurs over the US in winter when the jet stream and continental polar air mass (also called "arctic air" or "Canadian air mass") moves south for a few days. Air masses often mix in the middle latitudes (30–60° zone of latitude) where westerly winds (moving from west to east) predominate, forming most of the significant weather fronts that affect the Northern Hemisphere.

The barometric pressure of the atmosphere varies across the earth's surface due to the irregular heating and cooling of land and sea and the convergence or divergence of air due to upper air movement.

Areas where the pressure is relatively higher than normal develop into "highs" and those that are lower than normal form "lows". In general, air flows from areas of high pressure to areas of low pressure. The path followed is not along a straight line but semicircular due to the Coriolis effect, which causes air to flow clockwise around areas of high pressure and counter clockwise around areas of low pressure in the Northern Hemisphere. The situation is reversed in the Southern Hemisphere, where airflow is counter clockwise around highs and clockwise around lows. The Coriolis effect is illustrated in Figure 7-1.

The presence of high and low-pressure areas in the atmosphere determines the relative pressure near the earth's surface. In areas of surface heating, air near the ground or over water is warmed up and rises into the atmosphere. The upward movement lowers the air pressure near the ground forming a local low-pressure area and causing an influx of air to replace the air that has risen. In the Northern Hemisphere, air flows inward toward the low in a counter clockwise vortex (Figure 7-1). The rising air carries moisture upward until it condenses at a higher level in the atmosphere forming clouds. Under extreme conditions, the rising air can also develop a spin causing a strong cyclonic flow to develop, which depending on the scale and intensity of the flow, may result in the formation of a hurricane or tornado.

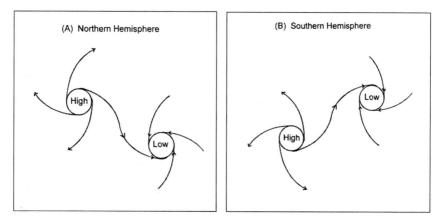

Figure 7-1. Wind direction around low- and high-pressure centers as influenced by Coriolis force

In areas where there is surface cooling, air descends from the upper levels of the atmosphere increasing the air pressure near the ground surface and causing air to move outward from the high-pressure area. Air flowing outward from the high-pressure cell moves in a clockwise direction in the Northern Hemisphere. The descending air absorbs moisture as it descends and moves outward leading to the dissolution of clouds. Some air masses pick up enough water near the earth's surface that they dry out the land below forming semiarid zones or deserts.

The distribution of winds in the atmosphere is determined by the location and movement of high and low pressure cells. Winds move warm and cold air masses away from source areas in which they form and bring them into contact along fronts. As one air mass encounters and displaces another, the interaction between them causes unsettled weather or storms. The movement of air masses and fronts is usually linked to the movement of low-pressure systems. Air masses generally move around migrating lows. If warm air overrides cold air, the boundary is called a "warm front"; if cold air displaces warm air, the boundary is called a "cold front". In some cases, air masses come in contact but neither mass is displaced, resulting in a "stationary front".

The juxtaposition of two contrasting air masses along a front provides the energy for mixing and formation of turbulent convecting air, conditions leading to cloud formation and precipitation. A cold front is usually defined by a relatively sharp or well-defined boundary as cold air pushes warm air out of the way. Strong turbulence at the boundary of the cold front causes vertical clouds to develop accompanied by thunderstorms and heavy rainfall. A warm front is characterized by a more gradual displacement of cold air as the lighter, warm air advances and displaces cold air at the air mass boundary. As it rises, warm air condenses to form clouds over a broad area and different types of clouds form at different elevations along the slope of the front. Precipitation associated with a warm front is less dramatic than that produced by a cold front due to the gradual rise of warm moist air over the cold air mass. A stationary front represents a relatively well-defined boundary where there is limited mixing and release of energy. Therefore, only limited precipitation is associated with clouds that form along these fronts.

When storm systems are depicted on weather maps, they are frequently represented by simple diagrams such as the one depicted in Figure 7-2. The low-pressure area is indicated by "L" and the cold and warm fronts radiate outward from the low. As the low moves eastward, the fronts move with it. The fronts usually travel with the same velocity but sometimes the cold front overtakes the warm front and becomes occluded. The storm track usually depends on the path followed by the low-pressure center, which is determined by the jet stream and other upper air wind patterns. These patterns are generally bounded by the locations of the major warm and cold air masses.

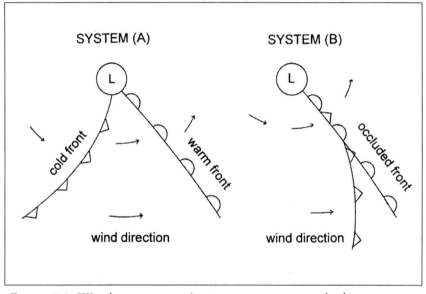

Figure 7-2. Weather systems: a) air movement around a low-pressure center b) air movement associated with an occluded front

Not all storms are caused by the migration of large-scale low-pressure systems. Localized storms of one to several hours in duration may develop due to the diurnal heating of the earth's surface by the sun. Solar heating causes evaporation and convection of warm, wet air into the atmosphere. Many summer afternoon showers and thunderstorms in North America are caused by the daily heating of moist air that rises and forms turbulent clouds. The rising moisture condenses to form raindrops that may rise and fall several times within a turbulent cell before falling to the ground as rain. As the air cools down at night, the storms subside. In mountainous areas, the rise of moist air up west-facing mountain slopes can supplement this process on a daily basis. In some areas of the western US, the formation of thunderstorms is so predictable that you can plan your activities around the expected rainfall.

## 7.2  CLOUDS AND WIND AS INDICATORS OF UPCOMING WEATHER

When you are outdoors, you can gain valuable insight into the upcoming weather by observing the types of clouds that appear in the sky and the direction and nature of the wind. Clouds provide clues about winds present at high altitudes, the moisture content of the air and atmospheric turbulence. Wind direction and wind speed are good indicators of an approaching storm system. Simple observations combined with general knowledge about the movement of air masses can provide you with the basis for a generalized weather forecast.

There are four general categories of clouds based on their general shape and character: cirrus, stratus, cumulus and nimbus. Cirrus clouds (Latin for "curl of hair") are high, wispy, thin clouds formed from fine ice crystals at high altitude (Figure 7-3a). These high-level clouds generally occur above 20,000 feet (6,000 meters). Cumulus clouds (derived from the Latin for "heap") generally have fluffy or rounded tops and somewhat flattened bottoms. They develop at low (below 6,500 feet) to high (above 20,000 feet) elevations and are composed of water droplets (Figures 7-3b and c). Stratus clouds (Latin for "layer") form at low to middle elevations and are characterized by flat tops and bottoms (Figure 7-3d). Finally, the term "nimbus" (Latin for "rain") or the prefix "nimbo" is used to indicate the presence of a variety of clouds that are thick with moisture and rain-forming (Figures 7-3e and f). Nimbus clouds are the dark, thick, gray clouds that we generally think of as "rain clouds". They exhibit vertical development due to convection and are associated with thunderstorms. Another common prefix for cloud names is "alto", meaning "of high elevation". An altocumulus cloud is formed at mid-elevations, greater than 6,500 feet (2,000 meters) but less than 20,000 feet (Figure 7-3b).

(a)

(b)

(c)

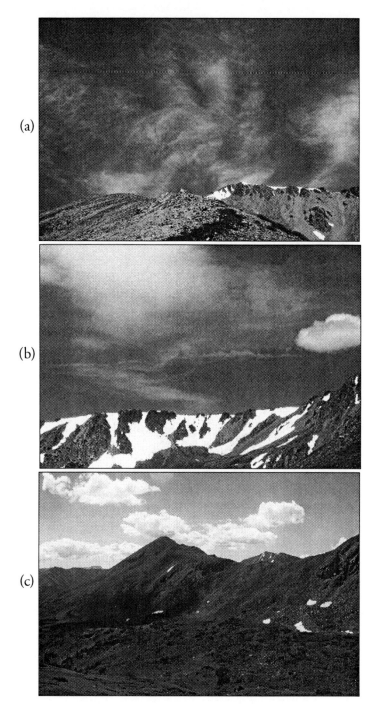

Figure 7-3. Cloud types: a) cirrus b) altocumulus c) fair weather cumulus d) altostratus e) cumulonimbus f) nimbostratus

Some cloud types are found at specific locations along fronts and in advance of weather systems. The high, leading edge of a warm front is usually heralded by the arrival of cirrus clouds in an otherwise clear sky (Figure 7-4a). These develop where high, warm air makes contact with cold air and the warm air condenses to form ice crystals. Cirrus clouds indicate that an approaching warm front is one to two days away. Altostratus clouds follow the cirrus clouds as the warm air contacts cold air at mid-elevations, leading to possible light showers as the warm front approaches. Stratus and nimbostratus clouds approach ahead of the warm front, producing light to moderate rainfall.

The clouds associated with an approaching cold front are concentrated near the front itself and do not provide significant warning of the oncoming storm (Figure 7-4b). Along the margin of a cold front, cold air displaces warm air forming cumulostratus and cumulonimbus clouds as the moist, warm air rises upward. Condensation provides the energy for additional turbulence and convection and the developing clouds may rise to significant heights if there is a large contrast in temperature across the front. Because cloud formation is relatively abrupt near a cold front, it is not usually possible to detect an approaching cold front very far in advance by cloud observations. An exception to this occurs in mountainous areas where high rain clouds may be visible from miles away on mountain peaks and ridges. This may provide sufficient time for hikers to retreat from exposed areas and prepare for the coming rain and cool weather.

Winds are useful indicators of approaching inclement weather. The velocity and direction of airflow on a regional scale are caused by the pressure gradient that develops between high and low-pressure areas. The closer the high and low are together and the greater their pressure difference, the higher is the velocity of the wind blowing from high to low pressure. As a low-pressure center approaches a given area, the relative direction of the wind changes. In North America, this means that winds moving counter clockwise around a low will appear to change direction as the low moves past your location. If the low passes to the north of your location (Figures 7-5a, b, c), winds will first blow in from the south or southwest when the low is west of you, from the west when

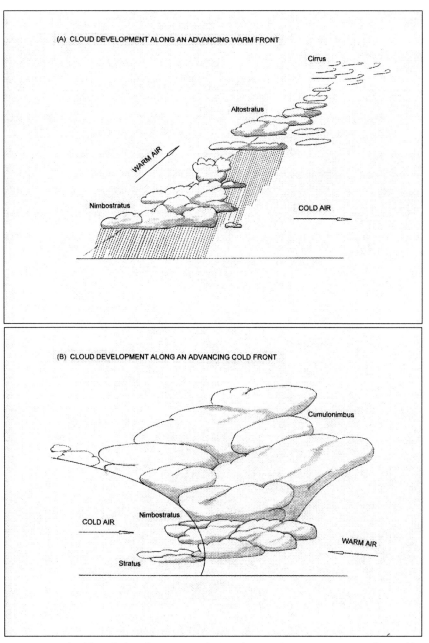

Figure 7-4. Cloud development along a) an advancing warm front b) an advancing cold front

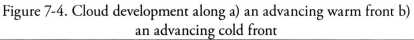

the low is north of you, and from the north or northeast when the low is east of you. Similarly, if the low passes to the south of your location (Figures 7-5d, e, f), the wind will initially blow in from the south or southeast when the low is west of you, from the east when the low is south of you, and from the north or northeast when the low is east of you. The wind directions that you observe are based on airflow in the upper atmosphere. Surface winds blowing at lower elevations or on the ground surface may be redirected by topography and local effects such as buildings, mountains or other large-scale features. The direction and movement of low to mid-level clouds are better indicators of wind direction because they are relatively undisturbed by surface features.

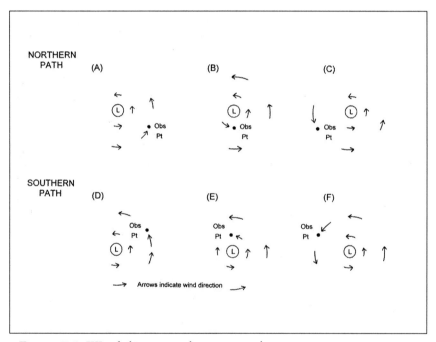

Figure 7-5. Wind direction changes as a low-pressure system passes along a northern path (a, b, c) and a southern path (d, e, f)

An altimeter can be a useful weather forecasting tool on a camping trip. As mentioned previously, an altimeter is basically a barometer with a modified scale but it can also be used to measure changes in barometric pressure. For example, if at night your altimeter reads 6,500 feet and next morning it reads 6,800 feet, the change tells you that the air pressure decreased overnight and a low-pressure system is most likely approaching. (Your camp did not rise 300 feet on its own!) Depending on your location and the season of the year, you can expect a storm of some kind to blow in within a day or two. If the barometric pressure holds steady overnight (at a relatively high pressure), this generally indicates that fair weather will continue for the next day or so.

## MUMMY RANGE WEATHER

During a spring backpacking trip across the Mummy Range in northern Colorado, we had the opportunity to observe the passage of a low-pressure system first hand. The first day out we snowshoed in clear weather up three mountain peaks on the south side of the range, accompanied by mild westerly winds. The next morning brought stratus clouds and a shift in winds to the south as a low approached us from the southwest, carrying light snow late in the day. The next morning we found several inches of light snow on our tent as the winds shifted from south to southeast. We pushed onward crossing a second mountain pass, dropping into a deep stream valley and fording a stream. At this point, the welt on my old Kastinger hiking boots blew out, causing us to pitch camp for the night in a heavy, wet snowfall. During the night, the winds shifted again, this time blowing from the east, and heavy snow began piling up on the rainfly of the tent. This caused the walls of our tent to push in to such a degree that we had to dig snow off the tent twice during the night. The easterly winds confirmed that the low had moved south of us creating a classic "upslope" airflow drawing warm, moist air from the Gulf of Mexico and delivering it directly to Colorado's mountains. The storm lasted all day and resulted in over three feet of new snow falling in our little valley. We lay low in our tent and let the storm spin out. On the fifth and final morning, low on food, we plowed over Mummy Pass on snowshoes. From there, we dropped down the north side of the range along a steep and treacherous gully to avoid near-certain avalanche conditions along the normal route which crosses a moderately steep, open slope. By now the sky had cleared and cool winds were blowing from the north.

Putting meteorological information together on an outdoor trip requires some thought and experience with weather conditions in your area. If you see cirrus clouds in a blue sky or a halo around the moon at night, expect a warm front and some rain in a day or two. If you see altostratus clouds approaching, then a warm front is advancing and you can expect light rain in several hours. If you notice that the barometric pressure is slowly falling under any of the above conditions, this confirms the approach of a warm front.

If there is a sudden drop in pressure, expect potentially strong winds and a rapid change in weather conditions. An approaching cold front generally causes a decrease in air pressure and an increase in wind velocity. Changes in wind direction give you an idea of the location of the low-pressure center that is driving the storm. A gradual shift in wind direction can mean that the low is moving slowly or that you are far away from the center of the low-pressure cell. A rapid shift in wind direction suggests rapid movement of the low or that you are closer to its center.

## 7.3    CHECKING LOCAL WEATHER FORECASTS

There are many sources of weather information available for trip planning purposes. Most newspapers provide general weather forecasts that are reasonably accurate in metropolitan and suburban areas but less useful in rural areas. Some local newspapers publish more localized forecasts for their readership and are therefore worth checking before you start out on an extended camping trip. Television and newscasts are often of limited use because they tend to focus on a short-term, four to five-day temperature and rainfall prediction that is again geared toward metropolitan areas and provides little insight into approaching weather systems. Most radio broadcasts suffer from the same limitations.

The best forecasts are those that can provide a regional overview of existing and developing weather systems yet are detailed enough that you can refine them to address your local area of interest. For these, you need to check your cable television and the Internet. The Weather Channel on cable television gives reasonable predictions of weather on a regional basis as well as for specific localities, but you may have to wait a while to get the information you need because of the presentation format. The Internet is an excellent source of weather information when you are planning a trip. The NWS maintains a Web site that gives current conditions at nearby weather stations and provides a seven-day forecast (www.srh.noaa.gov/data/forecasts/). It also publishes satellite and radar images that give a regional overview of current weather conditions. An example of a weather forecast issued for Kanab, Utah on September 8, 2004 is provided in Figure 7-6. Most state and national parks, forests and monuments maintain Web sites with weather information available online for various locations. Radio stations maintained by the NWS can provide current conditions in many parts of the country if you can pick them up on a portable radio. Weather Band radios are particularly useful for this purpose.

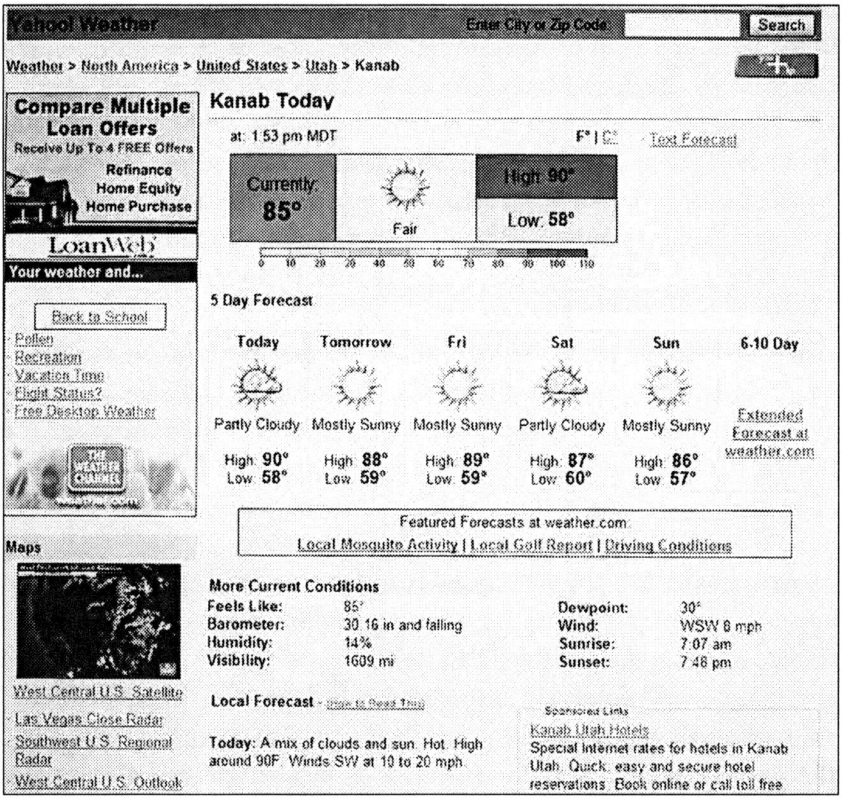

Figure 7-6. A weather information Web page for Kanab, Utah on September 8, 2004

## 7.4 WEATHER DANGERS

### 7.4.1
### Lightning

Lightning is the second leading weather-related killer in the US, killing an average of 73 people per year and injuring hundreds. Lightning is associated with thunderstorms in which severe air turbulence causes a buildup of static charge in clouds and on the ground surface. During a typical thunderstorm, a strong negative charge builds up in the clouds and the ground surface develops a corresponding positive charge. Discharge occurs when a lower resistance path between the cloud and ground allows positive charge to rise up into the cloud thereby partially neutralizing the charge imbalance between the two. The discharge is in the form of a flash or strike of lightning followed by thunder, which is formed by the disruption of the air as the electrical discharge occurs. Discharge commonly occurs directly beneath the cloud that generates the turbulence and static charge. But discharge can also be directed to adjacent clouds or to a point some distance away from the main center of turbulence. Lightning strikes to ground have been recorded in some storms up to a few miles away from the turbulence center.

Discharge usually occurs at high points on the ground such as towers, wet trees or hilltops where electrical currents can be launched into the air. Hikers should avoid being the highest point or standing near the highest point in a landscape during a lightning storm. Common victims of lightning are wet golfers standing out in the open or those who huddle under an isolated, wet tree during a storm. In both cases, the humans or the tree provide a good launch point for electrical discharge upward. If you happen to be standing under a tree in a dense forest during a storm, the odds are that lightning will strike some other tree and not the one you are sheltering under. But there is still a chance that your tree will be the luckless recipient of an electrifying experience. If lightning occurs or is imminent, it is best to get down from any exposed location such as a peak, ridge, and convex or open slope.

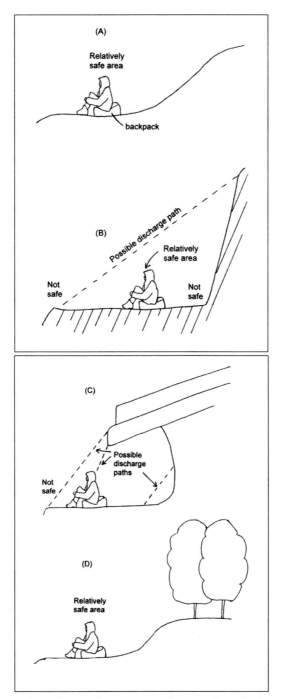

Figure 7-7. Safe and unsafe positions for avoiding lightning strikes

Ground currents that develop around the point of discharge and in areas where charge passes along the ground surface can also be dangerous. Avoid being the short circuit for a ground discharge by insulating yourself from the ground by sitting on your backpack or rope and curling up into a tight ball to minimize the distance between your points of contact with the ground (Figure 7-7a). Place any metal objects such as trekking poles, ice axes and metal snowshoes away from you so that they do not act as conduits for electrical discharge. Stay low and do not bridge gaps in what might become a ground current circuit (Figures 7-7b, c, d).

## 7.4.2
### Floods

Floods can pose great danger to hikers and campers caught outdoors after a heavy rainstorm or day of intense snowmelt. Heavy rain accumulation can quickly cause a stream or river that drains a valley or canyon to rise above its normal flow levels. In the southwestern deserts of the US and northern Mexico, the danger of flash flooding is very real during spring and late summer when monsoon airflow leads to sudden and very heavy rainfall. Desert areas subject to frequent flooding often contain bedrock outcrops with the exposed rock carved into narrow channels that restrict runoff. In addition, sparse vegetation and thin soils cause much of the rainfall to run off into gullies and gulches, thereby accentuating the flood hazard.

Low-lying areas near a stream channel are the first to become flooded during a thunderstorm. Sudden flooding is usually not a serious hazard during the daytime because you can keep an eye out for coming storms. However, if you have decided to spend the day in a slot canyon with a limited view of the sky, a storm can arrive without warning and your retreat from the canyon may take hours. If you plan to hike or camp in narrow canyons in the desert southwest, make sure that you check the local weather forecast before you start out, as many people before you have been caught unaware during sudden storms and drowned.

Sudden storms that sweep in overnight can be hazardous if you are unprepared. Selection of a safe campsite and consideration of the following tips are paramount for avoiding flooding hazards. Look for high ground and pay attention to the lay of the land to avoid anything that remotely resembles a drainage way or flood plain. Check the weather before turning in at night for signs of an approaching storm. Organize your gear before dark so that you have it together and handy in case a sudden move is required in the dark. Finally, in the event that you are caught in a sudden flood in the middle of the night, pack up and make a quick exit to safety on higher ground.

Flooding can represent an additional hazard if the trail to your campsite crosses a river or stream. The stream that you easily waded across on your way in may be difficult or impossible to cross during flood stage. Footbridges may also be flooded after major storm events, requiring a change of route or a long wait for the water levels to recede. Glacial streams represent a special case because early in the morning when melting of snow and ice is minimal, they can usually be easily forded. But late in the day, after hours of melting in sunlight, the same streams may have significantly higher flows than they had earlier in the day.

## 7.4.3
### Snowstorms and Avalanches

Snowstorms can be quite enjoyable to the well-prepared hiker but they can represent a serious hazard for the unsuspecting or unprepared. Most light snowstorms add a touch of color to a winter forest and muffle sounds so that the landscape seems a remote and almost private experience. If you have prepared for a light to moderate snowfall, the snow becomes a pleasant inconvenience. But if you are unprepared for snow, then hiking and camping become wet, cold and unpleasant experiences characterized by slow travel, much delay and extra work. Depending on the time of year, intensity of the storm and the terrain being traveled, you may also have serious concerns about orienteering through the storm and the adequacy of your outdoor equipment.

Many people who are caught in an unexpected snow storm get nervous because hiking becomes more difficult, finding your way may be confusing, and your clothing can quickly get wet and cold. One immediate concern is the possibility that you will become lost. Everything looks different under even a light snow cover and marker cairns may be hard to find. In addition, falling snow reduces visibility making it difficult to orient according to landscape markers that were previously clearly visible.

If you have been diligent in observing and recording your travels, there should be no major problem with staying on track. If the snowstorm is intense, way-finding is confusing or travel becomes either difficult or dangerous, then it is best to camp for the night, particularly if you are still a significant distance away from the trailhead or other shelter. It is better to wait until visibility returns and conditions improve before continuing. If you are uncertain of the way, you may inadvertently wander over a cliff or below an avalanche slope and risk personal injury. If you do not have camping gear along, but you can keep relatively dry and warm, consider a bivouac for the night. If you need to move to keep warm, run in place just long enough to stay warm and wait out the worst of the storm. Do not try to press on in a storm at night unless you really know the trail like the back of your hand. Otherwise you will just get lost, wear yourself out or encounter an otherwise avoidable hazard. It is always better to wait until you have more favorable conditions.

If you are caught in a significant snowstorm, you did not have a clue that it was coming and you do not have the right gear to survive a night in reasonable comfort, you missed something in earlier sections of this book. In that case, you should re-read the preceding chapters and take notes this time! Always be prepared for a potential storm and carry the appropriate gear and clothing with you!

In deep snow there are a number of hazards that may not be apparent to you. Be aware that heavy snow tends to bridge and drift over objects like holes in the ground, small boulders, tree branches, cracks in bedrock, tree stumps and fallen trees. If the snow is windblown and crusted, you can easily sink in up to your waist with little or no warning. Also beware of marshes and streams that disappear under the snow cover leading to wet clothes and feet. A fall under any of these conditions can severely endanger any hiker causing injury, possible incapacitation and even hypothermia. Steep slopes and rocky ledges can be treacherous and require finding a safer route.

One of the common hazards of winter travel in mountainous terrain is avalanche. Even light snowfall can trigger an avalanche if the conditions are right. Prime avalanche conditions are created when a moderate to heavy snowfall occurs after a few warm or sunny days. During the warm spell significant melting of existing snow takes place, imparting the old snow with a smooth and icy surface that can serve as the perfect sliding plane. When the next snowfall occurs, the new snow will not bond to the slippery surface. Instead it builds up until the slope cannot support the mass of accumulated snow and the fresh snow suddenly slides off. This can occur during the snowstorm or days later when the sliding surface is further lubricated by melting snow. In the latter case, tons of snow may be released to slide downslope.

Another cause of avalanche is the weakening of the structure of old snow on mountain slopes during relatively warm days. Under these conditions, a layer of snow deep within the snow pack melts into poorly connected snow crystals called "depth hoar" or "sugar snow". When a new load of fresh snow is placed on the old snow, the old snow collapses at the crystalline layer and the entire overlying snow pack slides downslope in the form of slabs of icy, heavy, hardened snow. Slab avalanches can be devastating in scale and intensity and they are rarely survivable if you happen to be caught in one.

Finally, an avalanche can be triggered when snow builds up on any steep slope. Powder snow avalanches usually occur on slopes and rock faces with angles that are steeper than 60 degrees. These are often smaller, powdery sloughs that occur frequently throughout the winter season because the falling snow cannot stick to and accumulate on the steep surfaces. Powder snow avalanches can be dangerous if you are in a couloir or under a cliff, because they tend to concentrate in these areas and you can be swept away in snow carrying a large fraction of rocks and debris.

Most avalanches occur on slopes that are between 25 and 60 degrees steep (Figure 7-8). Slopes that are less than 25 degrees usually have insufficient energy to move snow downward in avalanches. Slopes steeper than 60 degrees slough snow off frequently enough that they do not allow a snow pack of significant depth to accumulate. It is the intermediate slopes in the 25 to 60 degree range that are able to accumulate substantial depths of snow cover and have the energy to sustain snow slides. So beware of intermediate slopes in winter.

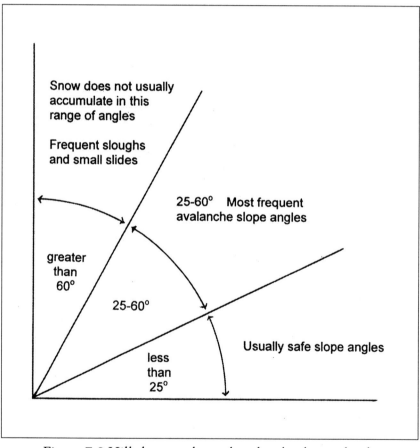

Figure 7-8 Hill slope angles and avalanche danger levels

Several additional factors determine whether snow will be released as an avalanche or not. These include the presence of vegetation, slope aspect, wind and humans. The first snow of the winter season or snow in windblown areas is typically not very deep and may be "grounded" by vegetation or rocks. Such snow is generally quite stable and does not pose an avalanche hazard. This is why mountain climbers often climb up windswept ridges on snowclad peaks to avoid peril. Later in the year, a snow slope that is grounded on grass or soft vegetation may become unstable as the vegetation forms a sliding surface on which an avalanche can occur.

The absence of snow on an exposed slope below treeline is something that is worth careful consideration. Areas that avalanche frequently, called "avalanche chutes", are clear of mature trees because frequent avalanches clear away the tree cover faster than it can revegetate the slopes (Figure 7-9). Skiers and snowboarders beware! Avoid the bases of avalanche chutes in winter as avalanches can start high up on the mountain above and race down through the chutes with little or no warning.

The aspect of the snow slope is also an important factor for evaluating the avalanche hazard because aspect determines the amount of sun the slope receives. In the Northern Hemisphere, south-facing slopes receive the most sun and, therefore, are more strongly subject to melting and restructuring of the snowpack. In contrast, north-facing slopes receive little solar energy to recrystallize or glaze snow, but on these slopes, the snow may not consolidate and develop a stable structure.

Wind can cause drifting of snow onto leeward slopes accentuating the loading effect of new snow. The resulting "wind slabs" can significantly increase the likelihood of an avalanche. Wind can also create huge steep-sided drifts called "cornices" on the leeward side of ridges. Some cornices creep outward forming significant cliff overhangs that eventually collapse from the load and topple onto the snowfields below, triggering one or more avalanches.

Figure 7-9. Slopes that avalanche frequently have few trees

One of the most common causes of avalanche release today is the weight of hikers, skiers or snowmobilers crossing snow slopes that are either too steep or unstable. The best way to avoid an avalanche is to stay off suspicious snow slopes that are 25 to 60 degrees steep, especially after dramatic changes in weather or new snowfall. If there is any doubt about how steep the slope is, you can measure the angle with an inclinometer (which is built into some compasses).

## 7.4.4
### Wind Chill and Apparent Temperature

Wind chill is a measure of how cold the air feels on bare skin when there is a breeze blowing. It is the temperature at which heat lost from the skin in still air feels equivalent to the temperature and heat loss of air passing over the skin at some velocity. The wind chill factor only applies to humans and animals that rely on internal heat generation to regulate their body temperature.

When you are in a cool environment, heat radiates from your skin and warms up a thin layer of air adjacent to the skin. When there is no breeze, the warm layer acts as insulation and reduces heat loss from your body. However when there is a breeze, the warm air is blown away and replaced by a layer of cooler air that settles next to the surface of the skin. Your skin then has to reheat the layer of new cool air. The result is that valuable heat is lost and there is no insulating benefit to you. High velocity winds have a greater cooling effect than gentle breezes.

The wind chill effect is summarized in Table 5 where wind chill temperatures corresponding to several measured air temperatures and various wind speeds are provided. For instance, the exposed skin of a person standing outside on a 30 °F day with a steady breeze of 10 mph will feel as if it were 21 °F on a day with no wind. Because a person's skin that is exposed to wind cools faster than it would in still air, putting on a windbreaker can make a significant difference on a cool windy day. The wind chill effect is applicable to animals as well as humans. It is important for dog owners to note that a dog riding in the back of a pickup truck doing 65 miles an hour on a 40 °F day is really being subjected to a wind chill of about 22 °F!

The "heat index" (or "apparent temperature effect") is a measure of the apparent temperature of humid air on a warm day. Relative humidity has a direct effect on your ability to cool your body through evaporation of moisture from the surface of your skin. Humidity controls the rate at which perspiration evaporates from the surface of your skin. As the moisture evaporates, the surface of your skin is cooled. When the relative humidity of the ambient air is high, your body cannot cool itself as well as it would if the air was dry. Therefore, the evaporative cooling effect is less effective. If your skin can't cool well, then your body temperature will rise to possibly excessive, even dangerous levels.

Table 5. The wind chill index

| Wind Speed (miles per hour) | Thermometer Reading (degrees F) | | | | | | | | | | | | | | | | |
|---|---|---|---|---|---|---|---|---|---|---|---|---|---|---|---|---|---|
| | 40 | 35 | 30 | 25 | 20 | 15 | 10 | 5 | 0 | -5 | -10 | -15 | -20 | -25 | -30 | -35 | -40 |
| 5 | 36 | 31 | 25 | 19 | 13 | 7 | 1 | -5 | -11 | -16 | -22 | -28 | -34 | -40 | -46 | -52 | -57 |
| 10 | 34 | 27 | 21 | 15 | 9 | 3 | -4 | -10 | -16 | -22 | -28 | -35 | -41 | -47 | -53 | -59 | -66 |
| 15 | 32 | 25 | 19 | 13 | 6 | 0 | -7 | -13 | -19 | -26 | -32 | -39 | -45 | -51 | -58 | -64 | -71 |
| 20 | 30 | 24 | 17 | 11 | 4 | -2 | -9 | -15 | -22 | -29 | -35 | -42 | -48 | -55 | -61 | -68 | -74 |
| 25 | 29 | 23 | 16 | 9 | 3 | -4 | -11 | -17 | -24 | -31 | -37 | -44 | -51 | -58 | -64 | -71 | -78 |
| 30 | 28 | 22 | 15 | 8 | 1 | -5 | -12 | -19 | -26 | -33 | -39 | -46 | -53 | -60 | -67 | -73 | -80 |
| 35 | 28 | 21 | 14 | 7 | 0 | -7 | -14 | -21 | -27 | -34 | -41 | -48 | -55 | -62 | -69 | -76 | -82 |
| 40 | 27 | 20 | 13 | 6 | -1 | -8 | -15 | -22 | -29 | -36 | -43 | -50 | -57 | -64 | -71 | -78 | -84 |
| 45 | 26 | 19 | 12 | 5 | -2 | -9 | -16 | -23 | -30 | -37 | -44 | -51 | -58 | -65 | -72 | -79 | -86 |
| | Low Risk | | | | | | | Moderate Risk | | | | | | High Risk | | | |

Low Risk: Use discretion; there is little danger if you are properly clothed.

Moderate Risk: Postpone exercise if possible. Proper clothing is essential. Individuals at risk should take added precautions against overexposure.

High Risk: There is great danger from cold exposure.

(After Plowman and Smith, 1998, p. 415.)

The heat index is summarized in Figure 7-10, which presents a graph of air temperature plotted with respect to relative humidity. The figure is based on information provided by the NWS for a variety of conditions ranging from very warm to extremely hot. The graph shows that a person exposed to a temperature of 90 °F with 90 percent humidity can "feel" as hot as if it was 120 °F with 20 percent humidity. This is why westerners living in states like Arizona and New Mexico say that dry heat is easier to tolerate than the warm, humid summer air that is typical of the Midwest and East. It also explains why adding water to coals in a dry sauna can suddenly cause the room to seem unbearably hot as the relative humidity rises. It is also why runners perform better on cool, dry days than on warm, humid days —the less effort expended on cooling the body means that more capacity is available for motion.

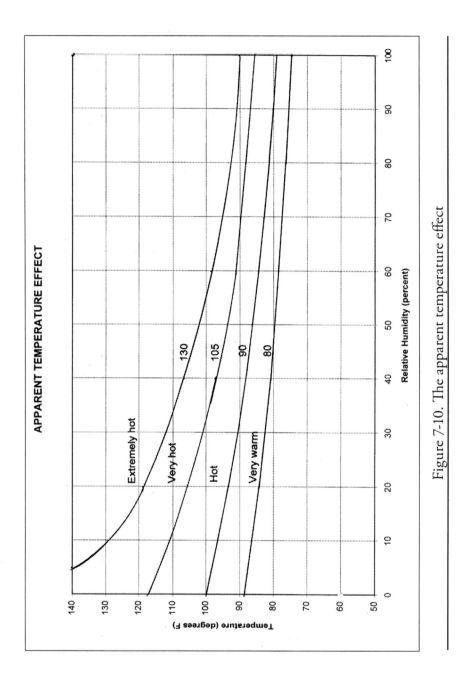

Figure 7-10. The apparent temperature effect

# CHAPTER 8     FIRST AID YOU NEED TO KNOW

First Aid is the immediate care given to a person who has been injured or has been suddenly taken ill (American National Red Cross, 1993). Accidents or injuries occur on the trail no matter how well prepared you are. In this chapter, we will present some basic First Aid treatments for injuries that you might encounter when you are outdoors. We will also discuss some common causes of outdoor health problems that are "controllable" and some over which you have little or no control. Weather conditions, altitude and lack of preparedness are the primary causes of controllable health problems. "Uncontrollable" health effects are usually caused by accidents or unforeseen systemic problems that can occur due to a variety of factors.

Injuries sustained during an outdoor accident frequently include cuts or punctures of the skin; bruises, sprains or strains in muscles, tendons or ligaments; and broken bones. Most common cuts and bruises can be treated in the field with First Aid and require little follow-up care. Strains and sprains usually heal in a few days even though they may be inconvenient and painful at the time of injury. Even a simple bone fracture can be treated outdoors assuming that there is appropriate follow-up care. However, serious sprains and broken bones in the legs, feet, back or head can immediately put an end to a hike or backpacking trip and require timely professional medical care. In some situations caused by an accident or physical exertion, such as during a heart attack or after a lightning strike, a victim's heart and breathing may stop. Under these conditions, you may be required to administer First Aid by restoring the patient's heartbeat and breathing until his autonomous nervous system recovers. Cardiopulmonary resuscitation (CPR) is the method that you will need to know in order to get the heart and lungs operating again. Even in the case of serious injuries, basic First Aid care can save life or dramatically improve a patient's chances for a quick and full recovery while you wait for professional medical assistance.

To be prepared for medical emergencies, everyone whether you are a hiker or not, should take a formal First Aid course including CPR from the American Red Cross, your local college or other professional organization. During your lifetime you will encounter any number of situations where First Aid might be needed, and if you are properly trained, you can make a significant contribution to the health and well being of another person. In particular, anyone involved in long hiking, mountaineering or camping trips should get First Aid training for your own protection as well as for the safety of your fellow hikers. If you want to read up on specific First Aid treatments or simply brush up on your basic knowledge, there are several very understandable books available from the American Red Cross.

Several advanced First Aid topics that hikers should know have been purposely omitted from our discussion because they are outside the scope of this book. Included among them are First Aid responses to serious injuries such as cuts to blood vessels, sprains, broken bones and CPR. The American Red Cross is generally considered the best source for this type of information.

## 8.1    CUTS, ABRASIONS, BURNS AND BLISTERS

Simple cuts and abrasions to the skin are potentially dangerous because they can lead to bleeding and possible infection. If you are injured, it is important to stop the bleeding quickly and at the same time cover the wound to protect it from infection. Shallow cuts usually involve the severing of capillaries or very small veins below the surface of the skin. Abrasions typically consist of a series of scrapes and bruises caused by a fall, impact or scrape against a rough surface. Falls and impacts can cause dirt, grit or other foreign matter to be introduced into abrasions. Puncture wounds are also possible if the victim falls onto a sharp rock or is caught in a rock fall.

In the case of all accidental skin injuries, proper First Aid treatment includes cleaning the wound, stopping bleeding and covering the wound with a sterile bandage. Be sure to use only potable water to clean a wound so as to avoid infection. Application of antibacterial soap or other sterile treatments such as iodine, antibiotic cream, dilute hydrogen peroxide or ointment may be useful depending on the type of wound sustained. Cuts that are longer than one-half inch may leave small scars if they are not closed up properly. For these cuts, use a butterfly bandage or a series of bandages to pull the wound closed (Figure 8-1).

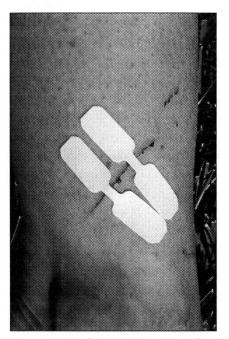

Figure 8-1. Closure of a cut with butterfly bandages

Minor burns and blisters are other injuries that commonly occur on hikes and camping trips. While such injuries usually do not result in bleeding wounds, the possibility of infection remains high. Minor burns should be cleaned, treated with a light application of antibiotic ointment and the wounds covered with one or more sterile gauze bandages.

Blisters are caused by constant rubbing and frictional heating of the skin at points of increased pressure or abrasion. The result is separation of the outer layer of skin from deeper tissue and inflammation of the underlying tissue. Once the outer layer of skin separates, the void between the skin layers may fill with watery fluid or the outer skin may tear loose opening a sensitive wound. If cared for quickly, the size of the blister and any associated damage can be minimized. Left unattended, the blister will become more painful and possibly infected.

The best treatment for blisters on the foot is to prevent them in the first place. For this reason it is best to wear clean socks and comfortable boots that have been broken in and are the right size. It is important to pay attention to any early signs of pain or hot spot development on your feet as you walk. At the first sign of pain or if you get sand or gravel in your boots, stop and take off your boots and socks and check for any problems. If you only have a hot spot or the beginnings of a small, dry blister, you can cover it with a large strip of one to two-inch wide, waterproof, adhesive tape. The tape will act as a protective layer over the skin. You can also cover the sensitive area with a liquid bandage product (such as New-Skin˚) to achieve the same effect. Put on dry socks and continue walking, but check your feet often for further developments.

If you have a larger or fluid-filled blister that is becoming painful, a different approach to treatment is required. Initially clean the wound area. Cut a patch of Moleskin˚ foam about three times the dimensions of the blister, remove the center of the patch and place it on your foot in such a way that the moleskin foam surrounds the blister but does not touch it (Figure 8-2). The Moleskin˚ foam will cushion and relieve some of the pressure on the blister when you put your socks and boots on again. If the blister is filled with fluid, it is painful or very large, you may have to drain the fluid and create a Moleskin˚ cushion around it before putting on your socks and boots. You can drain the blister by puncturing it near the edge of the separated skin with a sterile needle or the sterile tip of a small penknife blade. Put on clean dry socks after treating the blister to minimize the risk of infection.

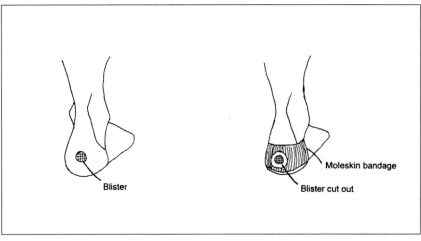

Figure 8-2. Treating a blister on the heel

If you are traveling to a remote area for an extended period of time, you might consider taking a course of broad-spectrum antibiotic with you in case blisters, cuts and other unforeseen wounds become infected. Consult your doctor for specific recommendations on the type and dose of antibiotic that is best for your situation.

## 8.2 Temperature Control – Heatstroke, Hypothermia and Frostbite

The human body is able to tolerate a wide range of temperatures when it is properly clothed and cared for. The body maintains a balance between its heat generating capability which keeps it warm, and its surface cooling capability which prevents it from overheating. Under a normal range of environmental conditions, the heating and cooling processes are held at equilibrium to keep the core body temperature at about 98.6 °F in the average person. When the body does extra work such as walking, running or other exercise, it generates waste heat that tends to raise the body temperature. When this happens, the body's cooling processes radiate heat through the skin and generate perspiration to provide evaporative cooling, both of which serve to dispose of the excess heat.

Cooling is effective as long as there is liquid to evaporate from the skin and relatively dry air to make evaporation possible. However, the cooling process breaks down if a person dehydrates by not taking in enough water to replace perspiration loss. When there is insufficient water to allow the body to generate perspiration, body temperatures can rapidly soar. The same may occur if a person is wearing clothing that limits evaporation or if the relative humidity of the ambient air is high. In either case, perspiration pumped to the skin surface cannot evaporate and therefore cannot cool the body.

The best treatment for overheating is to enhance body cooling. You can begin by adjusting your clothing to match the level of work that the body is doing. In general, this means wearing light, breathable clothes when you are exercising heavily so that your perspiration can evaporate. A pair of shorts and a T-shirt are ideal for running on a hot summer day whereas pile pants and a fleece or wool sweater are more suitable for rapid hiking on a sunny, winter outing. Plan to drink two to three liters of water a day when you are hiking in the summertime and somewhat less in winter. Keep hydrated, and if you are sweating, make sure that your perspiration can evaporate effectively. Under normal conditions, drinking some water is sufficient to replace your perspiration loss. But if you find yourself working so hard that you are sweating profusely, then you might consider drinking a salt-balanced sports drink to replenish electrolytes as well as water loss. It is generally wise to avoid salt tablets and salty snacks such as potato chips or pretzels before heavy exercise because these can cause a salt imbalance when your body is dehydrated.

Overheating can lead to heat cramps, heat exhaustion and heat stroke. Heat cramps, muscle spasms that occur in leg and abdominal muscles, are early indicators of overheating. Resting in the shade or in a cool room and drinking fluids (water or sports drinks) are usually all that is needed for the cramps to dissipate and the body to cool (Figure 8-3).

Heat exhaustion is a serious condition in which the body overheats because of excessive physical exertion and its cooling processes are unable to keep up with the heat load. The condition is commonly associated with activities in which clothing that is too heavy is worn or when the ambient relative humidity is high, both of which inhibit effective evaporation. The symptoms of heat exhaustion are wet, cool, pale or flushed skin, dizziness, weakness, exhaustion, headache and nausea. First Aid treatment consists of getting the victim to a cool place out of the sun, removing or loosening his clothing to allow better surface cooling, placing cool wet cloths on the skin to reduce skin temperatures and allowing him to drink cool water slowly at a rate of about four ounces (one-half cup) every 15 minutes. The victim should then be encouraged to rest, gradually rehydrate and avoid physical exertion for the next several hours.

Figure 8-3. Take advantage of shade to cool off along the trail

Heat stroke is a severe condition in which the body's cooling system appears to shut down, overwhelmed by the heat load placed upon it. It usually results from a failure on the part of the victim to recognize the symptoms of heat exhaustion. During heat stroke, the body temperature climbs rapidly, skin becomes dry, red and hot to the touch, pulse becomes rapid and weak, breathing becomes shallow and rapid and the victim may lose consciousness. Treatment for heat stroke is the same as for heat exhaustion, but the condition is more severe and the need for cooling is more immediate. At the onset of the condition, lie the victim down and place ice packs (ziplock bags filled with snow are suitable) over the major veins of the body (armpits, groin, side of thighs) to facilitate body cooling. Carefully watch for a change in symptoms as well as for potential breathing problems. If the victim cannot drink or keep water down, or if he begins to lose consciousness, then he is getting worse. If this happens, get medical attention immediately because the victim's condition may be life threatening.

Hypothermia results from the body's inability to maintain its core temperature above 95 °F. It results from excessive heat loss from the body due to exposure to cold air or water and a lack of sufficient insulation. Severe chilling of the body can occur when a winter fisherman or snowmobiler falls through ice on a lake, taking an unexpected cold water bath and suddenly losing most of the body's insulation when his clothes become soaked. Even after he gets out of the lake, the wet clothes insulate poorly and his body continues to lose heat rapidly. Another common cause of hypothermia is loss of heat in cool weather over an extended period. If a person is caught out in a rainstorm unprepared on a cool day, wet clothing allows continuous heat loss to occur. If a person cannot replace the lost heat by working the muscles or he cannot change to dry clothing, his core body temperature is likely to decrease further.

Indicators of hypothermia include shivering, loss of feeling, stiffness, stumbling, loss of attention or interest, weak pulse or loss of consciousness. Shivering is the body's early attempt to generate heat through the involuntary contraction of muscles when the core temperature is between approximately 90 and 95 °F. As the body cools further, shivering stops. Blood flow to the skin and extremities is reduced dramatically as the body tries to keep the core temperature up. Lack of motor coordination, mental confusion and lack of focus occur in more advanced stages of hypothermia.

Treatment of hypothermia requires that you move the victim to a warm dry place, replace his wet clothing and dry his skin to restore insulation, and slowly warm up his body to a normal temperature range. An effective method of raising the body temperature in a mild case of hypothermia is to place the newly dried and clothed victim into a sleeping bag on a foam pad in a warm room. In more severe cases or if the victim is unable to warm up on his own, direct contact with another warm body will accelerate the warming process. Warm water bottles or heating pads placed in the armpits, groin, inside of the thighs and neck can help warm the blood more quickly.

If a hypothermia victim is conscious, he should drink warm fluids gradually to avoid dehydration. Hot drinks are not necessary. Observe the victim carefully for signs of recovery or further complications. Encourage the person to rest until his temperature returns to normal and then allow him to stabilize for several hours or longer if the hypothermia was more severe.

In cases of mild hypothermia (shivering) the treatment procedure described above is usually sufficient to affect recovery. However, if the hypothermia is more severe and you observe intense shivering or advanced symptoms, the victim's temperature should be stabilized and he should be taken to a hospital for supervised rewarming. Professional medical treatment is recommended because shock and other complications can occur during the rewarming process if the core temperature has been below 95 °F for some time. In fact, some people with core temperatures below 90 °F have not recovered from hypothermia.

It is important to recognize the early signs of hypothermia so that it can be addressed before body temperature falls substantially. Often the person undergoing hypothermia is unaware what is happening to him. He may shiver for a while and not notice any other symptoms. Hikers should always observe their fellow travelers looking for signs of trouble on cool, wet days. Apparent shivering, a glassy stare, stumbling or other motor coordination difficulties can be signs that another hiker is hypothermic and may be in trouble. Early treatment is the best remedy.

## ANNAPURNA FROSTBITE

Maurice Herzog describes just how nasty things can get on a mountain when the effects of altitude, hypothermia and frostbite are compounded. In "Annapurna" (Herzog, 1952) he documents the harrowing exploits of the 1950 French Expedition to climb Annapurna, the first of the 8,000 meter peaks in Nepal to be climbed. On the descent from the summit (26,545 feet) he stopped to get something from his backpack and removed his gloves. Somehow the gloves slid downslope away from him and he continued his descent with bare hands on a bitterly cold and windy day. His climbing partner Louis Lachenal was already far below him at the time and did not realize there was a problem. Due to the effects of altitude, Herzog did not realize that he had an extra pair of wool socks in his pack that he could have put on to protect his hands from frostbite. After several hours of descending through swirling mists he arrived at Camp 5 with no feeling at all in his fingers which had turned "violet and white and hard as wood". Lachenal and Herzog both suffered severe frostbite on their feet and hands, Herzog's hands being by far the most damaged. Fortunately, two other climbers from their expedition were at Camp 5 and were able to help them get down to a doctor at Camp 2 after two days of travel through storms, mist and avalanche. Over the ensuing weeks, Herzog and Lachenal were carried from the mountain and down the Krishna Gandaki River on stretchers. During this period, they had joints removed from their fingers and toes one at a time as gangrene crept into the frostbitten and necrotic tissue. Herzog gradually recovered from his ordeal after spending three years in hospital and eventually returned to easier climbing in the Alps.

Frostbite occurs when parts of the body, usually extremities such as fingers and toes or exposed skin on cheeks, noses and ears, freeze. Cells that are exposed to extreme cold actually freeze solid, blood flow is reduced or stops and damage to cells and tissue occurs. In severe cases, the frozen tissue may not recover from the damage, as many mountaineers and outdoorsmen who have lost toes, fingers, feet, hands, legs and arms to severe frostbite can attest.

Conditions that cause frostbite are exposure to extreme cold, with or without wind for an extended period of time. Heat loss from the affected body part is the driving risk factor. The most common cause of frostbite is exposure of bare skin to the air on a cold windy day, which leads to rapid heat loss due to the wind chill effect, freezing and eventually tissue damage. Evaporative cooling of water or other liquids from the skin can also chill the skin rapidly. This can occur if you are wearing wet clothes while exposed to a cold wind or even if you are filling a camp stove with white gas on a cold day.

Early symptoms of frostbite are loss of feeling in the affected area, skin that is cold to the touch, waxy or discolored in appearance (white, blue, or yellow). The frostbitten tissue is hard when frozen, but as it warms up it will become soft again. This poses a problem because our natural tendency is to rub the frostbitten area when it thaws out. In fact, rubbing or rough handling can easily damage frostbitten tissue, so try to treat the area gently to avoid causing additional damage. The old mountain climbers' remedy of rubbing the frostbitten area to restore circulation is false — it can actually cause great harm.

The best treatment for frostbite is to get the victim to a medical facility quickly. If this is not practical, immerse the affected body part in water no warmer than 105 °F. Before proceeding, test the water temperature with a thermometer or adjust it by feel. Keep the frostbitten tissue submerged until it feels warm and looks pink or reddish. Bandage the area with dry, sterile gauze separating toes and fingers with small gauze pads to prevent them from rubbing or sticking together. If you see blisters forming, do not break them so as to avoid potential infection. Finally, seek professional medical help as soon as possible.

## 8.3    Problems At Altitude – Acute Mountain Sickness, Pulmonary and Cerebral Edema

Acute mountain sickness (AMS) refers to a number of health effects caused by a rapid increase in elevation and the lower air pressure and decreased oxygen content associated with air at high altitude. The effects of AMS are most noticeable during the first two or three days at higher elevations and gradually decrease over time as the body acclimates to the new environment. The lower oxygen content of air at high elevations causes the lungs to compensate by breathing more rapidly and deeply in an attempt to supply sufficient oxygen to the bloodstream. In response, the heart rate increases to supply less oxygenated blood to tissues and organs.

If the altitude gain is gradual, the compensatory functions become more efficient with time, but at very high elevations, the body suffers from having insufficient oxygen available and long-term physical deterioration can result. In most people AMS occurs at elevations above 8,000 feet, but in some it can set in below 7,000 feet. While humans can adjust to elevations of up to 18,000 feet, people living higher than that for days or weeks suffer subacute health effects that the body cannot adapt to. This is why there are no permanent human settlements above 18,000 feet anywhere in the world.

Initial symptoms of AMS include shortness of breath, weakness, lack of energy, drowsiness and sensitivity to temperature. In addition, some people experience headaches, dizziness, loss of appetite, pale skin color, sleepiness and nausea. One of the most widely noted effects of AMS is sleeplessness, especially during the first few nights at elevation. Breathing patterns can change and become more erratic, with alternating series of deep breaths followed by shallow breaths. Most symptoms are greatly reduced after a few days but some people are affected more strongly than others and there is no clear way to determine ahead of time how severe the problem will be. While some medications may assist with certain symptoms, there is no one medicine to prevent AMS. If a person is adversely affected, the best remedy is to descend to lower elevation for a few days to recover.

High altitude pulmonary edema (HAPE) is characterized by the accumulation of fluid in the alveoli of the lungs, reducing the surface area available for gas exchange. Left untreated, a victim of HAPE can literally suffocate as built-up fluid reduces his lung function. HAPE typically occurs after a rapid rise to high elevation (generally over

9,000 feet). Early indications of HAPE occur shortly after arrival at high elevation. These include shortness of breath, coughing, general weakness and commonly a tight feeling in the chest. Coughing becomes frequent and produces pink, white or frothy sputum, sometimes streaked with blood. Nail beds often turn pale or blue in color indicating lack of sufficient oxygen. Pulse and breathing become rapid (120 to 160 beats per minute and 20 to 40 breaths per minute, respectively) as the cardiopulmonary system attempts to respond to the low oxygen content of the blood due to insufficient lung function. Finally, popping or bubbling sounds can be heard in the chest. At this stage, HAPE is a serious life threatening illness and can lead to pneumonia, unconsciousness and death.

Treatment for HAPE consists of immediately removing the victim to a lower elevation, supplying him with a continuous supply of oxygen, and allowing him to rest and recover for at least two days or until all symptoms disappear. Recovery generally begins as soon as the person is taken to the lower elevation — sometimes a decrease of 3,000 feet is sufficient to ease the symptoms. Many people rebound from HAPE relatively quickly and can soon return to higher elevations on the same trip. However, because their bodies are obviously sensitive to altitude, they must spend time acclimatizing more thoroughly as the elevation increases.

High altitude cerebral edema (HACE) is caused by the leakage of fluid through blood vessels in the brain at high altitude (above 10,000 feet). The fluid can accumulate in brain tissue and cause swelling inside the cranium, interfering with normal brain functions. Early symptoms of HACE include headaches, lethargy and loss of coordination. Thinking processes become confused and muscular coordination can be problematic or fail. The only remedy for victims of HACE is to quickly descend to lower elevation.

## 8.4 Common Infectious Disorders – Intestinal, Influenza and Other Respiratory Disorders

Digestive tract upsets are common on many camping trips. Intestinal problems are generally caused by ingestion of microorganisms from contaminated water, food or contact with animal or human feces. As has been discussed in previous chapters, the best way to prevent waterborne infection is through water purification. All drinking, cooking and washing activities should be carried out with plenty of potable water. If you are traveling or camping outside of the US, you should be aware that tap water in many countries is not reliably potable. Also beware of ice in your drinks, the ice may be made from untreated water. In some countries even bottled water may be suspect due to poor initial water treatment, germs introduced from the outside of the bottle or from refilling of so-called treated water bottles with local, untreated water. Never accept a water bottle that does not have a good seal on the cap because it may contain untreated water disguised in a recycled bottle.

Giardiasis is a common intestinal disease caused by contamination of the water supply by animal waste containing a protozoan cyst. The cyst, Giardia Lambia, is found in many waters of the western US and it can be easily removed by filtration. After you have been exposed to the cyst, symptoms do not usually present themselves until one to three weeks later. Symptoms include severe diarrhea, cramps, gas and vomiting. The symptoms can be moderated using antidiarrheal drugs such as Imodium A/D and treated by prescription drugs such as quinacrine, metronidazole or tinidazole.

Food and dirty hands are easy routes for intestinal infection by many other microorganisms that disrupt the digestive tract. Most intestinal disorders caused by microorganisms result in diarrhea. Cautious food handling and preparation can reduce your health risks significantly. Recommended practices include washing food with antibacterial soap/detergent before eating or cooking and peeling fruits and vegetables. Avoid eating any raw foods such as fresh fruits, vegetables, seafood and meat. Eat well-cooked foods and drink boiled or treated water and bottled beverages. It is generally risky to eat food from street vendors in foreign lands because food handling and preparation practices are questionable and there is generally no refrigeration available for food storage. Eating in well-established restaurants is generally safe.

One of the best ways to avoid contamination by human or animal feces when you are on a camping trip is to wash your hands often with antibacterial soap. You can also use hand cleaners and moist disinfectant towelettes when water is scarce. It is surprising how frequently people can cross-contaminate their food or water with dirty hands. It is common for your hands to come in contact with mouse, deer or other animal feces during the course of a day's hike, especially if you use them for balance or scrambling up steep routes.

Diarrhea is the most common symptom associated with intestinal infections. The general treatment for diarrhea is to control the symptoms through the use of antidiarrheal drugs. If the diarrhea persists for more than a day, the body can lose a good deal of fluid and become depleted of electrolytes. In this case, the First Aid response should include replacement of electrolytes by mixing the appropriate salts into drinking water. Electrolyte replacement packets containing these salts are available at most pharmacies and should be carried in your group First Aid kit for emergency use. If these packets are not available, then drinking soup with salt in it can help rebalance electrolytes. "Lite salt" containing some potassium chloride is preferable to ordinary sodium chloride when used for this purpose.

Although simple upsets of the natural flora in the intestines are the most common causes of diarrhea, the condition can also result from more serious diseases. Food poisoning, dysentery, typhoid fever and cholera can all lead to severe and extended bouts of diarrhea, usually accompanied by vomiting and other symptoms. When you are planning any extended camping trip, especially to foreign countries, it is best to consult with your physician and/or a medical service specializing in foreign travel for up-to-date medical information. These sources can inform you about diseases and health conditions that you may encounter in your country of interest, get you any required vaccinations and documentation and supply you with the drugs that you may need to avoid being stricken. Such precautions are not necessary if you are embarking on a multiday outing in the US, Canada or much of Mexico or Europe, where good medical treatment is relatively close at hand. Items that you should include in your First Aid kit to combat common intestinal disruptions are provided in Tables 6 and 7.

Table 6. First Aid kit for an individual on a day hike

| |
|---|
| 2 Moleskin foam sheets for blisters (or equivalent liquid bandages) |
| 10 Band-Aids (or equivalent), one inch wide |
| 10 Butterfly bandages (or equivalent) |
| 1 Elastic bandage, three inches wide |
| 1 Adhesive tape roll, two inches wide |
| 4 Sterile gauze pads, four inches x four inches |
| 1 Antiseptic ointment tube (one-half ounce) |
| 1 Sunscreen ointment tube (two ounces, SPF 30) |
| 1 Lip balm, preferably tube (SPF 30) |
| 5 Antiseptic alcohol wipes for cleaning hands and wounds |
| 10 Antacid tablets (Tums or Rolaids, calcium preferred) |
| 10 Aspirin or ibuprofen (Advil) tablets |
| 10 Sodium naproxen tablets (Aleve or Motrin) |
| 12 cough drops |
| 1 tube or bottle of insect repellant |
| 3-day supply of any prescription drugs that you take for existing conditions |
| 2-day supply of antidiarrhea tablets (or equivalent) |

Influenza (flu) is a viral infection of the respiratory tract. The typical flu has a one to two-day incubation period and usually lasts for four to six days. The disease is spread by coughing, sneezing and close contact with another infected person. Early symptoms include headache, muscular pain, chills, weakness and general sluggishness. A dry cough, fever, stuffy nose, sore throat and sneezing can also occur. Diarrhea may accompany the flu symptoms but there are usually few signs of intestinal distress.

There is no specific treatment for flu but treatment of symptoms include aspirin every four hours for pain and discomfort, a decongestant for nasal stuffiness and sleeping aids if needed. Flu patients are generally advised to rest in a warm place, eat a light diet with plenty of fluids such as juices and soup and get plenty of sleep. If a fever persists and coughing results in pus-filled or bloody phlegm, this may indicate the onset of an infection of the respiratory system which may require antibiotic treatment.

Bronchitis is the infection of the bronchi and trachea, the passages to the lungs. The infection frequently occurs during or after a cold, but unlike the cold itself, it is a bacterial infection. Bronchitis can also develop in the absence of a cold. Signs of infection include a persistent cough that creates thick, green or yellow phlegm after a day or so. Weakness is an associated symptom but there are few other outward indications of illness. Treatment requires the administration of antibiotics and rest. Left untreated, bronchitis can lead to pneumonia.

Pneumonia is generally a bacterial infection of the lungs although milder forms of viral pneumonia also occur. It is a serious illness that can develop when the body has been weakened by fatigue, infections such as bronchitis, or other diseases. The infection causes the buildup of fluids in the alveoli, interfering with the transfer of oxygen and carbon dioxide from the air to and from the bloodstream. Symptoms include the development of a fever of 102 °F or higher and increased respiration rate and pulse. Coughing develops after a day or two, producing mucus and colored phlegm. Breathing can become labored and painful. Left untreated, pneumonia can be fatal as toxins from the infection and a lack of oxygen overcome the victim.

Treatment of pneumonia consists of providing oxygen to the patient to improve oxygen transfer to the blood and administration of antibiotics. If the patient is at high altitude, he should be removed to a lower elevation as soon as possible to improve lung performance. The patient should receive medical attention rapidly so that an effective antibiotic treatment can begin. Campers planning a trip to a remote area should consult a physician and consider carrying general-purpose antibiotics with them for use in this type of emergency.

Table 7. First Aid kit for four people on a multiday hike

| |
|---|
| 8 Moleskin foam sheets for blisters (or equivalent liquid bandages) |
| 40 Band-Aids (or equivalent), one inch wide |
| 30 Butterfly bandages (or equivalent) |
| 2 Elastic bandages, three inches wide |
| 3 Adhesive tape rolls, two inches wide |
| 8 Sterile gauze pads, four inches x four inches |
| 1 Sterile gauze roll, two inches wide |
| 2 Facial tissue packs |
| 1 Antiseptic ointment tube (one-half ounce) |
| 1 Eyewash liquid bottle (Visine or equivalent, one ounce) |
| 1 Sunscreen ointment tube (eight ounces, SPF 30) |
| 1 Lip balm, preferably tube (SPF 30) |
| 20 Antiseptic alcohol wipes for cleaning hands and wounds |
| 10 Alka-Seltzer packets |
| 30 Antacid tablets (Tums or Rolaids, calcium preferred) |
| 50 Aspirin or ibuprofen (Advil) tablets |
| 50 Sodium naproxen tablets (Aleve or Motrin) |
| 24 cough drops |
| 8 Oral rehydration salt packets (for one liter solution) |
| 1 each of tweezers, medium sewing needle, thread, cigarette lighter, penknife |
| 1 First Aid or field medicine manual |
| 1 hydrocortisone tube (one ounce) |
| 1 tube or bottle of insect repellant |
| 1 snake bite kit |
| 1 broad spectrum antibiotic |
| Flagl for intestinal infections (or equivalent) |
| Prescription drugs for each individual as needed to treat existing conditions for the planned number or days of travel plus five extra days |
| 24 person-day supply of antidiarrhea tablets (Imodium A/D or equivalent) |

## 8.5    First Aid Supplies

Tables 6 and 7 list supplies that are recommended to furnish First Aid kits for two types of trips. In the first case, the day hike kit (Table 6 and Figure 8-4a) contains items commonly needed for a one-day hike from which you expect to return to the trailhead or home after several hours. The multiday hike (Table 7 and Figure 8-4b) is designed for people who will be out for several nights and therefore may encounter more situations requiring First Aid or they may be required to treat injuries over a longer period of time.

(a)

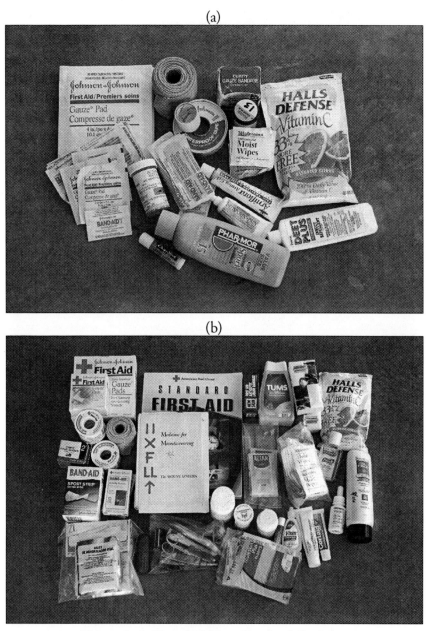

(b)

Figure 8-4. First Aid kits: a) a day hiker's kit
b) a multiday group kit

# CHAPTER 9

# RESPECTING AND ENJOYING NATURE

Hikers and campers make quite a few changes in their pattern of everyday living when they are outdoors. For one thing, life is simpler without the help of modern conveniences that we rely on at home. There is no electricity, no potable water flowing from faucets, no food stores nearby, and most of our belongings are still at home. Most outdoor enthusiasts agree that the simplicity of the outdoors is one of the strongest reasons to leave civilization behind.

To enjoy our stay in nature we need to modify our lifestyle and enjoy the natural environment and wildlife around us. We can do this by simplifying, adapting and observing. We can simplify our approach to camping and backpacking by making meals that are simpler and more compatible with the types of food we can carry and prepare outdoors. We can adapt our daily schedule and expectations to suit the natural rhythms of nature, rising at sunrise and retiring shortly after sunset so that we don't need long periods of artificial lighting. We can view natural events such as storms and encounters with wildlife as a source of entertainment and as a way of adapting to nature (Figure 9-1).

In this chapter, we will promote an approach to hiking and camping that will help us adapt to the environment rather than having to fight against it. With a little preparation and some patience, we can enjoy our time in the outdoors by slowing down our pace and observing our surroundings to gain a better appreciation of nature and its fellow inhabitants.

Figure 9-1. Remember your outdoor experience with photographs

## 9.1    ADAPTING TO THE ENVIRONMENT

As human beings we are used to following strict schedules based on work, mealtimes, meetings, children's events or favorite television programs. Many of these events are tied to the clock and do not bear any relationship to natural patterns in the environment. Only our eating and sleeping schedules vaguely resemble a natural rhythm — our biological clock. For most people, work schedules occupy our daylight hours and sleep time occurs at night. In the hectic everyday lives of most people in industrialized nations, the clock, schedule and necessity determine how and when we do things. We have grown dependent on utilities, transportation systems, entertainment and stores to provide us with the flexibility to maintain our lifestyles.

When we are outdoors, it is worth adapting to the natural patterns and rhythms of the environment because life is different. One of the most important reasons why we should do so is because we are basically diurnal creatures who depend on natural light for many outdoor activities. We rely on light to travel to and from our camp, therefore it is safer to travel over relatively unknown ground during the day to avoid potential hazards that may befall us after dark. It is safe to remain close to camp after dark to stay warm, sleep and avoid contact with nocturnal animals. But there are many things to do around camp in the evening that rely on light, such as cooking, cleaning and general entertainment. To accommodate these activities, we can build a campfire to provide temporary light or we can provide artificial light. Our reliance on artificial light requires us to carry electric, kerosene or gas-powered lamps and flashlights with us, as well as extra batteries or fuel to power them.

During the summer months, daylight is available for more than half of the day, and up to 24 hours if you are above the Arctic Circle in the Northern Hemisphere. For much of North America and Europe we can count on between 14 and 18 hours of daylight and relatively short nights in the summer. This allows us to complete most of the day's activities in daylight with only the occasional need for artificial lighting at night. But in winter the opposite is true and daylight may only be available for eight hours or less. At that time, particularly when we are winter camping, nearly all of our evening activities require the use of some form of artificial lighting.

As a result of our dependence on light for so many activities, it is advantageous for us to adjust our waking and sleeping hours to match the natural cycle of daylight rather than a clock schedule. Working in harmony with the natural cycle we can simplify our camping experience, minimize our use of artificial light and improve our camping efficiency and enjoyment. If we start breakfast soon after sunrise and get to bed after sundown, we can minimize the need to fumble around in the dark (Figure 9-2).

Weather conditions place limits on how and when we can carry out some outdoor activities. If a serious storm is approaching, it is wise to set up camp a little early to avoid the inconvenience of getting your clothes and gear soaked at the expense of gaining another mile of travel. Try to be flexible about your schedule and work around the weather. It may be a little inconvenient, but in most cases, you can still accomplish most of the goals of your trip. Plan for weather delays and you will not be upset when they occur. After all, we cannot control the weather, so we have to live with it.

Weather patterns that are predictable can be incorporated into your planned activities. In most parts of North America the sun powers the daily buildup of heat on the ground surface in the spring and summer, which provides the energy for afternoon and evening thunderstorms. Being familiar with the daily cycle allows you to travel, explore or enjoy nature during the morning and early afternoon before the storms occur. For example, mountain climbers and hikers in the western states start and finish their day trips early, before afternoon rain and thunderstorms set in. Similarly in the eastern US, it is common to begin a summer hike early in the cool of the day and avoid heavy exercise in the hot humid afternoon.

Even large-scale weather systems can be accommodated in your trip plans. In the central states low-pressure systems that migrate from west to east for two to three days at a time are common in the spring and

Figure 9-2. This could be the perfect campsite

early summer. If you recognize the storm pattern, you can estimate how many days of good weather you will have on your trip and then plan your activities accordingly. If you are going on a long backpacking trip and you expect to encounter a storm, bring heavy weather gear along to keep you dry while you are hiking. Otherwise, plan to hike around and explore your natural surroundings on days when the weather is good and be content to spend time around camp when the rain sets in. There will always be times when individual storm events that you were unable to anticipate interrupt your activities. But you can take them in stride if you have packed the right gear and are psychologically prepared to change your goals to suit the weather.

When you are out on a multiday camping trip, you should expect things to go wrong to a certain extent. After all, your fellow campers, the weather and Mother Nature do not conform to your perfect camping plan. You will inevitably forget clothing or equipment, someone in the group will lose something important, the weather may change for the worse, or a marmot may get into your food bag. However, despite the setbacks, you will discover that the more camping you and your friends do, the fewer really significant problems will happen. This is partly because with practice you will learn from your mistakes and either avoid them entirely or at least be prepared for them next time. As you camp more often, you will realize that many incidents that seemed very important the first time around become only minor inconveniences later.

When hiking and camping with other people, expect some delays to happen and learn to roll with the punches. Someone will sleep late, temporarily misplace an item they need for the day, or just seem maddeningly slow. These things happen, no matter how well you have planned the trip. As long as everyone is making an effort to get going and keep moving, there is little you can do in the middle of a trip to change the way events are unfolding. If you are a Type A personality, you need to find a way to burn up pent-up energy and occupy yourself while you wait for the others to catch up. Or you just need to slow down. On the other hand, if you happen to be the person that is holding up your group, try to pick up the pace so as not to frustrate everyone else (Figure 9-3).

Figure 9-3. Everyone has their own way of enjoying the lunch break

Communication is the solution to many real or perceived conflicts between members of an outdoor group. Very often the offending party has no idea he or she is causing anyone angst. If there is a problem causing you to walk slowly, for example a blister, you are feeling sick or your pack is too heavy, say something to your fellow hikers instead of struggling so that they know what the trouble is. Maybe they can help. Ventilating some festering issues can be healthy for group morale but minor complaints should be accepted as par for the course.

When hiking or backpacking it is advantageous to be flexible about your route-finding practices. If you are on a man-made hiking trail or road and it is going in the same general direction that you want to travel, make use of the opportunity. After all, animals frequently use human trails and roads too because they provide easy routes of travel. In off-trail situations, keep an eye out for deer, elk, sheep or goat trails that go where you want to travel (Figure 9-4). Animals have had a long time to select efficient routes to their favorite destinations. You may as well take advantage of their expertise and follow the same trails as long as they help you get to where you are going safely.

When traveling cross-country between two points, follow the path of least resistance. In other words, use common sense to avoid obstacles and difficult routes. A mountain goat track may lead up and over a rock face or a deer trail may wade through thick brush because these are routes that the animals have established to navigate through their native habitat. You can always go around these obstacles when you have an easier alternative. There is no need to beat your legs to death on hidden branches or risk a fall from a rocky slope unless you find it personally challenging to do so.

Figure 9-4. A deer trail crossing a meadow in Grand County, Colorado

A similar, practical approach should be applied when you are selecting your campsite. Select the site for its functionality and congeniality. You want to minimize potential natural hazards by avoiding setting up camp directly under rocky cliffs, avalanche chutes and low-lying areas subject to flooding. As a general rule, do not camp within 200 feet of a stream, spring or open water for sanitation reasons. Avoid camping right on an animal trail and blocking animals from coming down to their favorite watering hole for a drink or you may be surprised during the night. Also avoid areas where there are active signs of rodent activity such as marmot settlements, mouse holes and prairie dog colonies. This will prevent the camp from being invaded by hunger-crazed rodents that can chew through tents, pack straps, boots and food bags in no time and keep you awake with their sporadic chewing and scratching sounds at night.

Finally, slow down the pace and enjoy yourself. After all, finding peace and quiet is presumably why you came on the hiking or camping trip in the first place. Allow enough time to do the things that you want to do without feeling rushed and plan on delays and diversions. Follow the solar cycle, not a clock and day-timer.

## 9.2    SIMPLIFYING YOUR APPROACH TO THE OUTDOORS

Simplifying the way you do things outdoors can make a hiking and camping trip easier and more enjoyable. You need not give up everything you do at home, but you might have to eliminate some extra steps. You can start by cutting back on the gear that you bring with you. This will save you time, weight and frustration in the field. Durable equipment that is in good condition and functions without assembly is preferred. Any equipment that goes outdoors with you should be in good repair, not prone to failure or require significant maintenance while in the field. For instance, a camp stove that plugs up with soot, requires frequent cleaning or requires lots of extra time on maintenance can delay meals and prove to be a liability. Crampons or snowshoes that do not fit properly or which have lots of loose straps should be adjusted and the fitting problems resolved before you leave home. A backpack that is too small and requires you to tie lots of bundles or bags onto it in order to carry all your clothing and equipment should be replaced with a bag that is large enough to handle the job. Cords and strings for lashing your gear onto your backpack should be replaced with pack straps for speed and convenience. A safety harness that almost fits but keeps coming loose should be upgraded to a safer one of the proper size. Anything critical that "sort of works" should be repaired or replaced.

Try to choose durable, practical equipment that requires no extra tools for common repairs and maintenance. When this is not possible, take equipment that can be repaired with simple tools and then carry those tools with you on long trips. Keep the extra parts or tools together in one stuff sack or store them with the gear they fit. In general, it is a good idea to keep all equipment that you need for a specific activity together in one container or stuff sack for convenience.

When packing for a trip, it is generally not a good idea to bring along any new and untested equipment unless you have a backup for it. There is nothing more frustrating than finding out that a part is missing or that something does not work when you are in the field. Also, do not take along items of value, such as expensive watches or jewelry, in case they are lost, stolen or damaged.

The clothing that you take on a trip should meet the same criteria as your equipment. It should be practical, durable and meet your needs. Only carry enough changes of clothes as you really need, especially when backpacking. You might be able to wash some clothes as you travel, but in general, you will probably not be changing your clothing as frequently as you do at home.

Bring only essential items on your camping trip. It is easy to eliminate items that you don't really need when you are packing for the trip. If you are planning on backpacking, get all of your gear together ahead of time and see whether (1) it all fits into your backpack and (2) you can lift the pack up and carry it comfortably on your back for several days. Usually sheer bulk and weight cause you to limit what you really need to take with you. If you are going to be car camping, you will typically have less severe constraints on what you bring but it is still worthwhile to sort through and eliminate unnecessary equipment.

Your camping experience can be greatly enhanced if you have been careful to plan out your meals and food preparation needs in advance. Whether you travel by car, raft, canoe or on foot, simple meals greatly reduce the amount of food and cooking utensils carried and the time spent on food preparation. If you are car camping, rafting or canoeing, you are in a position to carry more supplies and cooking gear than if you are backpacking or hiking. Bringing a cooler lets you preserve fresh foods for a week or so, which allows you to cook many of the dishes that you would cook on the stovetop at home. If you carry a Dutch oven, you can even do some small-scale baking. But remember that cooking in camp and cleaning up afterwards takes more practice and timing than at home where extra stovetop burners, a microwave and sink are readily available.

The best way to confirm that you have packed all the right ingredients for each meal is to step through your proposed sequence of meals before you go. Plan on cooking practical meals on your trip. Remember that it may be raining and windy or you may be tired when you are ready to cook for a hungry group of campers. What seems easy in a modern kitchen will escalate outdoors. Do not try to be a gourmet cook unless you really want to spend the time and are willing to tolerate uncertain results.

Bring foods with you that you like to eat, are easily prepared and can be cooked in a single pot or pan if possible. While most food tastes better outdoors after a long hike, a camping trip is no place to experiment with a new, untried recipe. Results will vary! Most campers are content with macaroni and cheese, pasta, soups, casseroles, burgers, hotdogs, eggs and cereal (Figure 9-5a). Without refrigeration, fresh meats will spoil in a day, so plan for that when you select your foods.

Weight is a major concern if you are out backpacking. If your trip is expected to last several days you will probably need to include a few freeze-dried meals to your diet to reduce how much weight you have to carry (Figure 9-5b). But do not feel restricted to only freeze-dried meals, there are a variety of other dried foods available in supermarkets that work quite well on backpacking trips. For instance, dry packaged soups manufactured by Lipton, Campbell, Knorr and others are very tasty and easy to prepare. So are many brands of precooked rice and pasta dishes packaged in Styrofoam or foil containers, which only require reheating or the addition of hot water. Small tins of chili, beef stew, meat sauces and various other canned meals are possible choices if they are not too heavy to carry. We have found that some of the best sources of protein per packaged weight are chunks of cooked chicken, tuna and other meats packed in foil packets with minimal packing water or oil. Remember that any packaging materials that you carry in must also be carried out.

(a)

(b)

Figure 9-5. Camping foods: a) simple dinner food b) freeze-dried dinners

Prepare your gear, clothing and food (as much as possible) a day or two ahead of the trip. Lay it out to be sure you are not forgetting something (Figure 9-6). List the meals and their contents to make sure that you have included the right combination of ingredients, portions and condiments. After the trip, clean, repair and replace your gear and clothing in preparation for the next trip. Store your gear together in large plastic storage tubs or boxes in the same room if possible to keep it organized and to avoid getting some items separated or lost. This will make it easier to get ready for the next trip.

Figure 9-6. Camping gear spread out before a trip

## 9.3    OBSERVING NATURE AND PURSUING HOBBIES

There is always a lot going on around you when you are outdoors. Yet much of your surroundings may go unnoticed unless you pay attention and take some time to observe nature. Only then can you learn to enjoy it. Enjoyment of the outdoors is not just about breathing fresh air, viewing scenic vistas and leaving urban noise and hassles behind you. Enjoyment is derived from developing a familiarity and appreciation for these surroundings.

To begin to enjoy nature, you need to slow down, sit quietly and observe. If you have lost the ability to be quiet and observant or if you have simply forgotten what it is like, don't despair, these qualities will come back to you and be very fruitful with a little practice. Switch off the headset, stop thinking about work or next week's commitments, and look, listen and smell what is around you. First you may notice that objects are moving around you, such as clouds, birds, animals or water. Next you may become aware of several sounds — a bubbling stream, screeching hawk, or the scratching of a rodent. Rustling noises are indications of the surreptitious movements of hidden creatures engaged in digging up seeds and roots, creating paths through the grass, or feeding on vegetation as you are sitting quietly nearby.

Plants and animals surround you wherever you go. Vegetation varies from place to place based on climate, elevation and season. Every plant, from the smallest flower to the tallest tree, plays a valuable role in the ecosystem and is there for your enjoyment. Since vegetation influences the nature and variety of animal life that dwell in a given area, you can admire the plants and flowers for their own natural beauty or you can appreciate the animal life they support. There are so many ways to enjoy the vegetation outdoors. You can paint colorful landscapes, watch birds, photograph your favorite wildflowers, collect plants in plant presses and save them for reference or use them to create artwork. Sometimes, just identifying the plants and birds around you with a guidebook can be lots of fun and increases your familiarity with your surroundings (Figure 9-7).

Learning to observe animal behavior and identify wild animals can be another great source of entertainment in the outdoors. There is nothing more thrilling than finding a bird's nest with eggs or chicks in it, or to see a deer or mountain lion for the first time. As hikers and campers, it is fun to know who our wild neighbors are. After all, they are the full-time residents and we are just visitors. If we are quiet and respectful of their home environment, we can get to know something about them, their habits and way of life. We also have a responsibility not to harm them or destroy their habitats during our visit.

Figure 9-7. This Gray Jay is spying on the camp

Animals can be identified by their appearance, behavior, tracks and droppings. Animal sightings tend to be fleeting because they usually see us first and quickly move away into cover for their own safety. With practice, we can learn to identify some of the more common animals by memorizing their key features and characteristic movements, even if we only get a quick glimpse of them. Animal tracks and scat left along the trail are useful indicators of native wildlife and there are several guidebooks available to help you develop your identification skills. Scat is particularly diagnostic of large mammals because it allows you to not only identify the animal in question but it also tells you what the animal has been eating.

Besides plant and animal identification, there are many hobbies that are compatible with the outdoors. Where else can you observe the stars without city lights, look up at the clouds and sky, and study geology and landforms without the obstructions and influence of human activity? Nature provides the setting and opportunity. All you need is the imagination and interest to enjoy your surroundings.

---

### WISCONSIN PLANT COLLECTING

When we were growing up in Wisconsin as budding young scientists, my brother and I identified and collected plants as one of our hobbies. When we had trouble identifying a plant we would go to the small town of Woodstock nearby to see a man well known for his knowledge of forest plants and flowers. If we had a flower or root from an unknown plant he would nearly always be able to identify it for us. He would look it over, smell the flower and pinch and smell the root. Then he would pronounce his verdict, find a picture of the plant in one of his many identification books and teach us more about the plant, how to identify it in the future and tell us which animals eat it or which insects pollinate it. He knew a lot. But what else could we expect from a retired schoolteacher who had also taught himself Welsh, did cube roots in his head, sculpted and made arrowheads?

---

## 9.4   SHARING THE TRAIL AND OPEN SPACE

When you are out enjoying your favorite outdoor activity, you need to learn and observe proper etiquette. Good manners allow all outdoorsmen to enjoy the environment. You also need to respect the full-time residents of the outdoors — the vegetation and wildlife that live there. Remember that you don't individually own the land that you pass through but share it with other beings. As visitors, you should treat the environment and its inhabitants as you would if you were a guest in someone's house. You should also treat other hikers and campers as equals and neighbors, not like someone you compete with in heavy traffic.

On the trail there are some simple rules of the road that you should follow to foster harmony with other hikers and the environment:

1) People on mountain bikes should yield to hikers and horseback riders. The main reason for this is that mountain bikes have a mechanical advantage that hikers do not have. Also if you are riding a bike, you are more likely to lose control of your bike and crash into a pedestrian than vice versa. Our experience on trails is that only one in four bikers actually yields. Usually bikers just go crashing along and pedestrians scramble out of the way for their own safety, especially when bikers are coasting downhill at full speed. Bikers should also yield to horses because the sound of clanking bicycles may scare some horses and cause them to panic (Figure 9-8).

Figure 9-8. A mountain biker meets hikers on the trail

In our opinion, mountain bikes and hikers are not compatible on most narrow, one-lane hiking trails. On such trails, bikes should be restricted to limited hours or not be allowed at all. On the other hand, bikes and pedestrians can easily share roadways and multiple-lane trails. Most mountain bikers seem more interested in speed and daring than scenery, therefore they could easily be redirected into mountain bike parks or courses specifically designed for mountain bike enthusiasts.

This would also limit the considerable trail erosion inflicted by knobby bike tires.

2) Uphill traffic has right of way on a trail or road, unless otherwise indicated. This rule came about years ago as a result of horse-drawn wagons. The logic behind it is that it is much harder for a horse and wagon going uphill to get started again after stopping, than for those going downhill. The same is true when you are hiking.

3) If someone comes up behind you and is going faster than you, you should step aside in a convenient spot and let them pass you. Everyone has a different pace and speed, so don't feel bad if someone overtakes you. If you are the one who comes up behind a slower hiker, announce yourself when you are still a few paces away so that you do not startle the other hiker. Then be patient and wait for them to let you pass. If necessary, ask them if you can pass and then do so along a wide stretch in the trail, or when they step aside.

4) Do not block the trail. If you need to stop to rest or fix your pack, step off the trail so that others can pass. Some common examples of poor etiquette that we have observed on the trail are: a) people stopped dead in the middle of the trail, blocking the way and forcing others behind them to stop in order to get past; b) people sitting down on the side of the trail forcing others to step over their legs so that they can get around them on steep hillsides; c) people allowing their dogs to lie down on the trail, tails a-wagging and blocking traffic; and finally, d) people hiking with unruly children who see nothing wrong with obstructing the trail and creating a general ruckus. Although it seems obvious to passers-by, most people who block the trail either don't realize that they are inconveniencing others or they just don't care.

5) If you are hiking with a dog, carry a "poop" bag with you. Dog waste left on the trail is rude and unsanitary. If you are not willing to take responsibility for your animal, don't take it on the trail with you.

6) Dogs taken on hikes should be on a leash (Figure 9-9). There may be some exceptions but even dogs that are normally well

behaved at home can run amok when you let them loose outdoors. Dogs should not be allowed to chase wildlife under any circumstances. This will quickly clear the area of all birds and animals and take away other hikers' enjoyment of their trail hike. It is not the dog's fault, but the owner should please be considerate of other hikers.

Figure 9-9. Dogs can share the trail too if properly handled

7) Do not follow another hiker too closely so that you crowd him or make him nervous. As a rough guide, keep at least two paces of distance between yourself and the hiker in front of you so that if he falls, he does not take you with him, and vice versa (Figure 9-10).

8) When hiking on a steep, rocky trail with switchbacks, be careful that you do not accidentally kick loose rocks down the hillside onto someone below you. Similarly, if you are following another hiking party, keep an eye out for rocks rolling down from above. If need be, wait until the people above you have moved on and the way is safe. If you dislodge a rock, even a small one that falls down the hillside, warn anyone below you by shouting loudly

"Rock! Rock!" At least then people below you will be aware of the falling rock and may be able to dodge it.

Figure 9-10. Spread out and enjoy your hike

9) If you encounter someone on the trail that looks like they are lost or need help, stop and see what you can do to help. If they are misplaced, you can help them get reoriented. If they have an equipment problem, maybe you can help with a repair. Sometimes sharing some water and a chocolate bar with someone in trouble can give them a boost. If they are injured, provide First Aid and, if need be, help them back to the trailhead. We once helped somebody find a lost contact lens on the trail!

10) When hiking, minimize disturbance to the environment by staying on established trails, packing out your wastes, and trying not to disrupt the local flora and fauna.

When you are camping there are also a number of simple rules and manners that should be observed if you want to be harmonious with your natural surroundings. These are listed below. Many are common sense courtesies like not getting too close to another person's camp and trying not to interfere with their outdoor enjoyment. Others involve protecting the environment and keeping a campsite clean and safe. All the rules that we have suggested are intended to reduce your impact on fellow campers, resident wildlife and the environment.

1) If you are in a public campground try not to reduce the enjoyment of other campers by making a messy camp, hogging too much space or monopolizing shared resources such as washing or cooking facilities, restrooms and water supply. Do not play music so loudly that you disturb other campers no matter how good you feel or how much you crave attention.

2) Do not contaminate a campsite or local water supply with waste or food (even odors) because you can ruin the next camper's enjoyment of the area.

3) Leave a campsite as clean or cleaner than it was when you arrived. This means do not dig or tear the place up with car or bicycle tires, do not leave any trash lying around, and try to restore any damage that you have created.

4) Do not build a campfire directly under any part of a tree. You are likely to damage some tree branches and may start a forest fire. Do not make an excessively large campfire because you are more likely to lose control of it.

5) If a campsite already has an established fire ring, do not build a new one. Use the existing fire ring even if you have to remove someone else's trash from it first. Do not leave trash or tin cans in the fire ring when you leave the campsite. Finally, do not try to burn plastic in the fire because it will melt and you will have to remove it when you leave (Figure 9-11).

6) When camping in an area that someone else has already found, do not set up your camp right next to their camp. It is better to find another site a few hundred yards away if possible so that you don't invade their space. If there aren't any other reasonable camp sites nearby and it is getting late, it is best to ask the campers if it is OK to camp nearby. They will almost always say yes, and you can establish a neighborly relationship. In commercial or USFS campsites, try to space yourself a reasonable distance away from others, unless there is no other

choice. Remember that people go camping to enjoy nature and get away from others. If they wanted to be close to other people, they would have stayed in the city.

7) If camping with children or pets, do not let them wander around and bother the neighbors. Tie up your dog on a long leash unless it is extremely well trained. Do not create a situation where a nearby camper has to come over to tell you to tie up your dog or discipline your kids. Also, do not let your dog chase wildlife under any circumstances. In many states dogs can be shot for chasing wildlife and owners can be fined.

There are many other courtesies that you can observe when in the outdoors, but most of them are extensions of the same courtesies that we should practice in our everyday lives. In general, you should conduct yourself in such a way as to avoid inconveniencing others or making them feel uncomfortable. When in doubt about the effect you have on someone else, you can always ask them. Communication resolves most unspoken issues. Displaying courtesy in the outdoors will also help you make your outing more enjoyable.

Figure 9-11. Nothing can beat the warm glow of a campfire at the end of the day

# GLOSSARY AND ACRONYMS

| | |
|---|---|
| Aerobic | Exercise that enhances your breathing rate and improves cardiovascular ability. |
| Albedo | The fraction of incident radiation that is reflected from the surface of a material. |
| Altimeter | An instrument that measures elevation above mean sea level. |
| Alto | A prefix used to denote clouds that develop at high elevations in the atmosphere. |
| Alveoli | Microscopic membrane sacks in our lungs where exchange of atmospheric oxygen to the blood and carbon dioxide from the blood takes place. |
| AMS | Acute mountain sickness. The general term for a number of health effects caused by a rapid increase in elevation and the lower air pressure and decreased oxygen content associated with air at high altitude. Includes the effects of HAPE and HACE. |
| Apparent temperature effect | See heat index. |
| Avalanche chutes | Mountain gullies, clear of mature trees that avalanche frequently in winter. |
| Average boiling time | A measure of stove performance based on how quickly the stove can heat a given volume of water to boiling point. |

| | |
|---|---|
| Azimuth ring | See bezel ring. |
| Azimuth | A term indicating direction measured from 0 to 360 degrees clockwise from true north, and where both 0 and 360 degrees represent north. |
| Back bearing | The opposite direction from the azimuth, or the azimuth plus or minus 180 degrees. |
| Back stay | A narrow, vertical strip of leather that covers the rear seam of a boot upper and serves to seal and protect it. |
| Backpacking | The form of travel where you hike to your campsite carrying all of your equipment and supplies with you in a backpack. |
| Barometric pressure | The pressure of the atmosphere at a given location usually measured in inches or millimeters of mercury. |
| Bearing ring | See bezel ring. |
| Bezel ring | The circular dial around the perimeter of the magnetic needle housing of a compass, which is marked clockwise from 0 to 360 degrees, and where both 0 and 360 degrees represent north. Also called azimuth ring or bearing ring. |
| BLM | US Bureau of Land Management. |
| Bronchitis | A bacterial infection of the bronchi and trachea, the passages to the lungs. |
| BTU | British Thermal Units. A direct measure of the heat generated by burning fuel. |

| | |
|---|---|
| Cirrus clouds | Thin, wispy clouds formed from fine ice crystals at high altitudes in the atmosphere (above 20,000 feet). |
| Climate | Long term (seasonal, multiyear) changes in atmospheric conditions, typically associated with large-scale changes in solar radiation affecting the earth. |
| COG | Center of gravity. |
| Cold front | The boundary between a warm air mass and a cold air mass along which cold air displaces warm air. |
| Compass bearing | The uncorrected bearing read from a compass measured from zero degrees at magnetic north. Usually expressed as a direction. Also called magnetic bearing. |
| Compass | An instrument that measures the direction of magnetic north on the earth's surface. |
| Conditioning | Physical exercise that improves the function of our muscles, lungs and circulatory system. |
| Contour interval | The difference in elevation or spacing between adjacent contour lines on a contour map. |
| Coriolis effect | The Coriolis effect is due to the earth's rotation which causes air to flow clockwise around areas of high pressure and counter clockwise around areas of low pressure in the Northern Hemisphere. The circulation is reversed in the Southern Hemisphere. |

| | |
|---|---|
| Cornices | Steep-sided snowdrifts deposited on the leeward side of ridges in mountainous terrain, often forming substantial cliff overhangs. |
| Counters | Additional leather or rubberized patches added to a boot to strengthen the heel and toe of the upper and protect them against abrasion. |
| CPR | Cardiopulmonary resuscitation. |
| CTL | Central trend line of travel, the general direction in which you walk. |
| Cumulus clouds | Fluffy clouds with rounded tops and somewhat flattened bottoms containing water droplets that develop in the atmosphere at low to high elevations (below 6,500 feet and above 20,000 feet). |
| Dead reckoning | The practice of navigation that uses only bearing and distance information without visual cues. |
| Declination | The difference between true north and magnetic north on a map, measured in degrees. |
| Depth hoar | Poorly connected snow crystals formed by the melting and recrystallization of a layer of snow deep within the snow pack. |
| Diastolic blood pressure | The blood pressure in your arteries during the relaxation of the heart. The lower number given for blood pressure measurement, as in 120/80. |

| | |
|---|---|
| Double-boots | Winter boots comprised of a flexible, warm inner boot placed inside a more rigid, heavyweight outer boot. |
| EMP | Estimated maximum pulse calculated as 220 beats per minute minus your age. |
| Equator | Parallel of zero degrees latitude. A great circle of the earth that is everywhere equidistant from the poles and divides the earth's surface into the Northern and Southern Hemispheres. |
| Equinox | The time of year when the sun is directly over the equator and day and night are everywhere of equal length. |
| Exoskeleton tent | A type of external frame tent in which the poles are clipped to the tent body rather than being inserted in sleeves. |
| Fill-power | A rating system describing the insulating power of down clothing based on the volume per ounce of down filling. |
| Filter life | The volume of water that a water purification filter can treat before it must be replaced. |
| First Aid | The immediate care given to a person who has been injured or has been suddenly taken ill. |
| Foot placement | The orientation of the foot as it moves through each step. |
| Footbed | A removable insert placed on the insole plate inside a boot to provide cushioning and arch support and to center the foot in the boot. |

| | |
|---|---|
| Frostbite | A medical condition caused by acute exposure of body tissue to extreme cold, resulting in freezing of parts of the body, usually extremities such as fingers and toes or exposed skin on cheeks, noses and ears. |
| Full-grain leather | The hard, smooth outer layer of cattle leather usually used in the manufacture of hiking boot uppers. |
| Gaiters | Waterproof, cloth sleeves worn to cover your pant legs from calf to boot so that you can prevent snow and debris from entering the top of your boots. |
| Giardia Lambia | The protozoan cyst that causes Giardiasis. |
| Giardiasis | A common intestinal disease caused by ingestion of drinking water contaminated by animal waste containing the protozoan cyst, Giardia Lambia. |
| GPS | Global Positioning System. A network of navigational satellites that orbit the earth at designated locations. Each satellite contains a very accurate clock and radio transmitter broadcasting its coordinates with a specific and unique frequency. |
| Gusset | The material used to attach the tongue of a boot to the upper. |

| | |
|---|---|
| HACE | High altitude cerebral edema. A medical condition caused by the leakage of fluid through blood vessels in the brain at high altitude. The fluid can accumulate in brain tissue and cause swelling inside the cranium, interfering with normal brain functions. A severe form of acute mountain sickness. |
| HAPE | High altitude pulmonary edema. A medical condition characterized by the accumulation of fluid in the alveoli of the lungs, reducing the surface area available for gas exchange. A severe form of acute mountain sickness. |
| Heat exhaustion | A medical condition in which the body overheats because of excessive physical exertion and its cooling processes are unable to keep up with the heat load. |
| Heat index | A measure of the apparent temperature of humid air on a warm day. Also called apparent temperature effect. |
| Heat stroke | A medical condition in which the body's cooling system appears to shut down, overwhelmed by the heat load placed upon it. |
| High-pressure area | A small, localized air mass with high barometric pressure relative to its surroundings and characterized by outward air flow. |
| Hiking | Traveling to a destination on foot for an extended distance. |

| | |
|---|---|
| Hypothermia | A medical condition caused by excessive heat loss from the body due to exposure to cold air or water, which renders the body unable to maintain its core temperature above 95 degrees Fahrenheit. |
| Influenza | A common viral infection of the respiratory tract. Also called flu. |
| Insole | The layer of a boot or plate that is usually placed on top of the midsole. |
| Knapsack | A simple backpack consisting of a cloth or leather bag with shoulder straps sewn onto them and no frame. |
| Lap-felled seams | Seams, usually of tents, that are double-folded and double-stitched to provide extra strength. |
| Last | The shape of foot or footform used by manufacturers to build a boot. |
| Latitude | The angular distance north or south from the equator measured through 90 degrees. A parallel of latitude is a line parallel to the equator. |
| Layering | The practice of wearing several thin layers of outdoor clothing rather than one thick layer so as to adjust the clothing as weather and conditions change throughout the day. |
| LEP | Lower exercise pulse, the recommended lower limit for your pulse to achieve aerobic exercise, equal to 60 percent of the EMP. |

| | |
|---|---|
| Longitude | Measurement east or west from the Prime Meridian. A meridian of longitude is a line passing entirely around the globe and through the poles as a great circle. |
| Lost Point | The location designating where you first realized that you were lost. |
| Low-pressure area | A small, localized air mass with low barometric pressure relative to its surroundings and characterized by inward air flow. |
| Magnetic bearing | See compass bearing. |
| Magnetic north | The direction a compass indicates as toward the north magnetic pole. |
| Map view | The view of a landscape from above as on a map. |
| Maximum heart rate | The highest rate at which your heart will beat at a specific age. |
| Meteorology | The scientific study of atmospheric phenomena. |
| Midsole | The platform of a boot onto which the insole and the upper are built. |
| msl | Mean sea level. |
| Nimbo | A prefix used to denote clouds that are rain-bearing. |
| Nimbus clouds | Rain clouds. A variety of dark, gray clouds that are thick with moisture, rain-forming and associated with thunderstorms. |

| | |
|---|---|
| NPS | US National Park Service. |
| NWS | US National Weather Service. |
| Outsole | The bottommost layer or heel of a boot that utilizes either a ridge pattern containing lugs or a soft malleable material to provide traction. |
| Pace | The rate of making steps or strides. |
| Partial pressure of oxygen | The fraction of atmospheric pressure contributed by oxygen in the air at a given elevation. |
| Pedometer | An instrument that measures distance by counting the number of steps that you take. |
| Pneumonia | A severe bacterial infection of the lungs, although milder forms of viral pneumonia also occur. |
| Prime Meridian | Meridian of zero degrees longitude, which passes through Greenwich, United Kingdom. |
| Pronation | A common tendency of the heel to roll inward while you are walking. |
| Pump rate | The number of pump strokes required by a water purification unit to filter one liter of water. |
| Quadrangle map | A type of USGS topographic map representing an area measuring 7.5 x 7.5 or 15 x 15 minutes of latitude and longitude, respectively. |

| | |
|---|---|
| Rand | A rubberized seal placed around the welt in many boots to seal the seam and waterproof the boot. |
| Relative humidity | The percent water saturation of air relative to 100 percent saturation. |
| Rest Step | Technique used by mountaineers and hikers to allow leg muscles to rest briefly during each upward step by locking the knee back temporarily to rest before taking the next step. |
| Rucksack | Alternate name for knapsack. |
| Scree collar | The padded top portion of the upper of a boot designed to soften any rubbing that occurs against the skin and keep dirt and debris out of the boot. |
| Shank | A metal or synthetic plate attached along a portion of the length of the midsole of a boot to stiffen the sole. |
| Sole | A general term used to describe the bottom portion of a boot consisting of three components: the insole, midsole and outsole. |
| Solstice | The time of year when the sun reaches its farthest point north or south of the equator. |
| Speed | The body's rate of movement along the central trend line. |
| Spirit ring | A depression in the fuel tank of a camping stove in which a small amount of fuel is burned to pressurize the tank by external heating. |

Split leather        The soft, pliable inner layer of cattle leather commonly used in the manufacture of lightweight boots and shoes.

Stationary front     The boundary between a warm air mass and a cold air mass along which limited mixing occurs.

Stratus clouds       Layer clouds characterized by flat tops and bottoms, which form at low to mid-elevations in the atmosphere (above 6,500 feet and below 20,000 feet).

Stride diagram       The graphical representation of foot placement as you walk.

Stride               The length of the individual steps we make while walking.

Sugar snow           See depth hoar.

Systolic blood pressure     The blood pressure in your arteries during the contraction of the heart. The upper number given for blood pressure measurement, as in 120/80.

Tongue               A long strip of leather used for closure of a boot.

Topographic map      A scaled map in which elevations on the ground surface are represented by contour lines representing lines of constant elevation on the landscape.

Tramp step           Walking with the foot pushed or tramped down onto the ground, an extension of flat-footed walking.

| | |
|---|---|
| Tropic of Cancer | Parallel of 23.5 degrees north latitude. |
| Tropic of Capricorn | Parallel of 23.5 degrees south latitude. |
| True bearing | The bearing read from a compass measured from zero degrees at true north and adjusted for magnetic declination. |
| True north | The direction to the North Pole. |
| UEP | Upper exercise pulse, the recommended upper limit for your pulse during exercise, equal to 80 percent of the EMP. |
| UIAA | Union Internationale des Associations d'Alpinisme. The principal international association of mountaineering organizations. |
| Upper | The upper portion of a boot above the sole which encloses the foot and provides support. |
| USFS | US Forest Service. |
| USGS | US Geological Survey. |
| UTM | Universal Transverse Mercator. An alternate coordinate system to latitude and longitude, expressed in meters. |
| Vestibule | The covered porch or canopy formed by draping a portion of the rain fly over one or more entrances to a tent. |
| Walking flat-footed | Method of walking that minimizes the heel-to-toe action of the foot so that nearly all of the foot is placed on and removed from the ground simultaneously. |

| | |
|---|---|
| Walking Indian style | Walking with efficient, low-wobble strides with near-parallel foot placement. |
| Warm front | The boundary between a warm air mass and a cold air mass along which warm air displaces cold air. |
| Waypoints | Points along your travel path, often recorded to track your course. |
| Weather | Relatively short-term (hourly, daily, weekly) changes in atmospheric conditions. |
| Welt | The seal by which the upper of a boot is glued or stitched onto the midsole. |
| Wet-fitting | The method of soaking boots in water and wearing them on a long hike to break them in. |
| Wind chill | A measure of how cold the air feels on bare skin when there is a breeze blowing. |
| Wind slabs | Layers of drifting snow deposited by wind on leeward slopes in mountainous terrain. |
| Wobble | The side-to-side and rotational movement that our body makes with each stride as we walk. |

# SELECTED MANUFACTURERS AND INFORMATION SOURCES

## INFORMATION SOURCES FOR HIKERS AND CAMPERS

BUREAU OF LAND MANAGEMENT (BLM)
US Bureau of Land Management
Office of Public Affairs
1849 C Street NW, Room 406-LS
Washington DC 20240
202-452-5125
www.blm.gov
This Web site describes the programs, lands and activities administered by BLM. It links to all of the offices and lands in each of the western states where BLM has public lands. These include national monuments, national conservation areas, range lands, national scenic and historic trails, wild and scenic rivers and wilderness areas.

BUREAU OF RECLAMATION (USBR)
Bureau of Reclamation
1849 C Street NW
Washington DC 20240-0001
202-513-0501
www.usbr.com
The agency manages lands related to water projects in 17 western states, including dams, power plants, canals and reservoirs (such as Lake Powell). Many of the sites are available for public recreation. The site is a factual source for USBR contacts and activities but is not oriented to provide recreation information.

## NATIONAL PARK SERVICE (NPS)

National Park Service
1846 C Street NW
Washington DC 20240
202-208-6843
www.nps.gov (PARKNET)

The Web site provides information on all national parks, monuments, seashores, lakeshores, heritage areas, historic sites, historic trails, preserves, recreation areas and wild rivers administered by NPS. The site lists contact information, activities, history, fees, access restrictions, trails, roads, events, maps, campgrounds and other information about nearly all of the NPS properties.

## NATIONAL WEATHER SERVICE (NWS)

NOAA/National Weather Service
1325 East West Highway
Silver Springs MD 20910
No national number. Look for regional office number in your telephone book under Commerce Department, NOAA.
www.nws.noaa.gov

This agency is a division of the National Oceanic and Atmospheric Administration (NOAA) of the Department of Commerce. The Web site is a convenient source for weather and climate information nationally and for US territories. It has local and regional weather forecasts, national maps, satellite and radar views and other information.

## RECREATION WEB SITE

No address or telephone given
www.recreation.gov

This is a government Web site that serves as a central link to a large number of government managed recreation areas, including those managed by all of the federal agencies and bureaus. It allows you to search the Internet by state and recreational activity for a list of public lands where you can do that activity. The Web site is linked with nearly all state public land management agencies as well. So it is a very good starting point for searching the Web for information about sites near you.

## US DEPARTMENT OF INTERIOR (DOI)
1849 C Street NW
Washington DC 20240
202-208-3100
www.doi.gov
This is the Web site for the entire Department of Interior. It contains links to all of the bureaus within DOI, including the Bureau of Indian Affairs (BIA), Bureau of Land Management (BLM), Bureau of Recreation (USBR), Minerals Management Service (MMS), Office of Surface Mining (OSM), National Park Service (NPS), US Fish and Wildlife Service (FWS), and US Geological Survey (USGS).

## US FISH AND WILDLIFE SERVICE (FWS)
No national information address is available. Call the telephone number below or visit the Web site to find the regional office nearest you.
800-344-WILD
www.fws.gov
The Web site lists activities and programs managed by this bureau of DOI. It includes general information about the National Wildlife Refuge System, and wetlands managed by FWS. There is a national map showing the locations of all lands in the FWS system. Addresses, activities, contact information and maps area are given for regional and field offices, fish hatcheries, wetlands, and refuges.

## US FOREST SERVICE (USFS)
USDA Forest Service
1400 Independence Avenue SW
Washington DC 20250-0003
202-205-8333
www.fs.fed.us
The Forest Service is part of the US Department of Agriculture and manages national forests and grasslands. The Web site provides a wide range of information, including locations of properties, activities, contact information, wildlife population and behavior data, fire ban and avalanche information, publications and maps. Web pages are available for all individual sites and there are links to related state forest service Web sites.

US GEOLOGICAL SURVEY (USGS)
US Geological Survey
National Center
12201 Sunrise Valley Drive
Reston VA 20192
888-ASK-USGS for Earth Science Information Center
www.usgs.gov
topomaps.usgs.gov for topographic map information
The bureau does not manage public lands itself but it is the agency that provides mapping, geological, geographical, and hydrological information for public and private lands throughout the United States and other parts of the world. The USGS produces a large range of earth science publications and topographic and thematic maps for most regions of the earth.

# SELECTED LIST OF OUTDOOR EQUIPMENT MANUFACTURERS

ADIDAS AMERICA, 5055 N. Greeley Ave., Portland, OR 97217, 971-234-2300, www.adidas.com, Boots, outdoor clothing.

ALPINA SPORTS CORP., PO Box 24, Hanover, NH 03755, 603-448-3101, www.alpinasports.com, Trekking poles.

ARC'TERYX, 170 Harbour Ave., North Vancouver, BC, Canada V7J 2E6, 800-985-6681, www.arcteryx.com, Packs.

ASOLO USA, INC., 190 Hanover Street, Lebanon, NH 03766, 603-448-8827, www.asolo.com, Boots.

BIBLER/BLACK DIAMOND EQUIPMENT LTD., 2084 E. 3900 S., Salt Lake City, UT 84124, 801-278-5533, www.biblertents.com, Tents.

BIG AGNES, INC., 735 Oak Street, Steamboat Springs, CO 80477. 877-554-8975, www.bigagnes.com, Sleeping bags, sleeping pads, tents.

BOREAL, SW Partners Inc. distributor, PO Box 7116, Capistrano Beach, CA 92624, 949-493-3464, www.borealusa.com, Boots.

BRUNTON USA, 620 E. Monroe Ave., Riverton, WY 82501, 307-856-6559, www.brunton.com, Compasses, GPS equipment.

CAMP TRAILS/JOHNSON OUTDOORS, INC., 555 Main Street, Racine, WI 53403, 800-572-8822, www.camptrails.com, Outdoor gear and clothing, packs, sleeping bags, tents.

CARIBOU MOUNTAINEERING, INC., 400 Commerce Rd., Alice, TX 78332, 800-824-4153, www.caribou.com, Packs, sleeping bags.

CASCADE DESIGNS, INC., 4000 First Ave. S., Seattle, WA 98134, 800-531-9531, www.cascadedesigns.com, Packs, sleeping bags, sleeping pads.

COGHLAN'S LTD., 121 Irene Street, Winnipeg R3T 4C7, Canada, 204-284-9550, www.coghlans.com, Full range of camping supplies.

COLEMAN CO., 3600 N. Hydraulic, Wichita, KS 67219, 800-835-3278, www.coleman.com, Camping stoves, packs, sleeping bags.

DANA DESIGN, 19215 Vashon Highway, Vashon, WA, 98070, 888-357-3262, www.danadesign.com, Packs.

DANNER SHOE CORP., Outlet Store, 12722 NE Airport Way, Portland, OR 97230, 800-345-0430, www.danner.com, Boots.

DECKERS OUTDOOR CORP./TEVA, 495A S. Fairview Ave., Goleta, CA 93117, www.deckers.com, Teva sandals.

DELORME, Two DeLorme Drive, PO Box 298, Yarmouth, ME 04096, 800-561-5105, www.delorme.com, GPS units, maps, software.

DUNHAM/NEWBALANCE, NB Web Express, 1537 Fencorp Drive, Fenton, MO 63026, 800-595-9138, www.nbwebexpress.com, Boots.

EASTERN MOUNTAIN SPORTS/EMS, One Vose Farm Rd., Peterborough, NH 03458, 888-463-6367, www.ems.com, Full line of outdoor gear and clothing.

EUREKA!/JOHNSON OUTDOORS INC., See CAMP TRAILS/ JOHNSON OUTDOORS, INC.

FEATHERED FRIENDS, 1119 Mercer Street, Seattle, WA 98109, 206-292-6292, www.featheredfriends.com, Sleeping bags.

GARMIN INTERNATIONAL, INC., 1200 E. 151st Street, Olathe, KS 66062, 913-397-8200, www.garmin.com, GPS equipment.

GENERAL ECOLOGY, INC., 151 Sheree Blvd., Exton, PA 19341, 800-441-8166, www.generalecology.com, Water filters.

GOLITE, PO Box 20190, Boulder, CO 80303, 888-546-5483, www.golite.com, Outdoor clothing, tents.

GRANITE GEAR, PO Box 278, Two Harbours, MN 55616, 218-834-6157, www.granitegear.com, Backpacks, accessories.

GREGORY MOUNTAIN PRODUCTS, 27969 Jefferson Ave., Temecula, CA 92590, 800-477-3420, www.gregorypacks.com, Packs.

HI-TEC SPORTS USA, INC., 4801 Stoddard Rd., Modesto, CA 95356, 800-521-1698, www.hi-tec.com, Boots.

INTEGRAL DESIGNS, INC., 5516 Third Street SE, Calgary, Alberta, Canada T2H1J9, 403-640-1445, www.integraldesigns.com, Sleeping bags, tents.

JANSPORT, PO Box 1817, Appleton, WI 54912-1817, 800-426-9227, www.jansport.com, Packs.

KATADYN, See PUR.

KELTY, INC., 6235 Lookout Rd., Boulder, CO 80301, 800-423-2320, www.kelty.com, Packs, sleeping bags, tents.

L.L. BEAN, Freeport, ME 04033-0001, 800-441-5713, www.llbean.com, Full range of outdoor gear and clothing.

LEKI-SPORT USA, 356 Sonwil Drive, Buffalo, NY 14225, 716-683-1022 Ext 10, www.leki.com, Trekking poles.

LOWA BOOTS LLC, Peter Sachs, 86 Viaduct Rd., Stamford, CT 06907, 203-353-0311, www.lowaboots.com, Boots.

LOWE ALPINE, 2325 W. Midway Blvd., Broomfield, CO 80020, 303-465-0522, www.lowealpine.com, Outdoor clothing, packs.

MADDEN MOUNTAINEERING, Russi Mountain Works, 6654 Gunpark Dr., Suite 101, Boulder, CO 80301, 720-214-2194, www.maddenusa.com, Packs.

MAGELLAN/THALES NAVIGATION, INC., No US address, 800-707-9971, www.magellangps.com, GPS equipment.

MARMOT MOUNTAIN LTD., 2321 Circadian Way, Santa Rosa, CA 95407, 800-882-2490, www.marmot.com, Outdoor clothing, sleeping bags, tents.

MERRELL FOOTWEAR, PO Box 4249, Burlington, VT 05406, 800-789-8586, www.merrellboot.com, Boots.

MONTBELL AMERICA, 2800 Wilderness Place, Boulder, CO 80301, 866-546-6824, www.montbell.com, Outdoor clothing, packs, sleeping bags, tents.

MONTRAIL, 1003 Sixth Ave. S., Seattle, WA 98134, 800-647-0224, www.montrail.com, Boots.

MOONSTONE MOUNTAIN EQUIPMENT, 1700 Westlake Ave. N., Seattle, WA 98109, 800-390-3312, www.moonstone.com, Sleeping bags.

MOSS, INC., 4000 First Ave. S, Seattle, WA 98134, 800-531-9531, www.msrcorp.com, Tents.

MOUNTAIN HARDWARE, 4911 Central Ave., Richmond, CA 94804, 800-330-6800, www.mountainhardware.com, Outdoor clothing, packs, technical gear, tents.

MOUNTAIN SAFETY RESEARCH/MSR, 3800 First Ave. S., Seattle, WA 98134, 800-531-9531, www.msrcorp.com, Camping stoves, technical gear, tents, water filters.

MOUNTAINSMITH, INC., 18301 W. Colfax. Bldg. P, Golden, CO 80401, 800-551-5889, www.mountainsmith.com, Packs, sleeping bags.

NIKE, INC./A.C.G., One Bowerman Drive, Beaverton, OR 97005-6453, 800-344-6453, www.nike.com, Boots, sportswear.

THE NORTH FACE, INC., 2013 Farallon Drive, San Leandro, CA 94577, 800-447-2333, www.thenorthface.com, Outdoor clothing, packs, sleeping bags, tents.

OPTIMUS USA/BRUNTON USA, 620 E. Monroe Ave., Riverton, WY 82501. 307-856-6559, www.optimususa.com, Camping stoves.

OSPREY PACKS, 115 W. Progress Circle, Cortez, CO 81321, 970-564-5900, www.ospreypacks.com, Packs.

OUTDOOR RESEARCH, 2203 First Ave. S., Seattle, WA 98134-1428, 888-467-4327, www.orgear.com, Gaiters, clothing, mitts, accessories.

PACIFIC OUTDOOR EQUIPMENT, 521 E. Peach, Unit 4, Bozeman, MT 59715, 406-586-5258, www.pacoutdoor.com, Sleeping pads.

PATAGONIA, PO Box 8900, Bozeman, MT 59715, 800-638-6464, www.patagonia.com, Outdoor clothing.

PRIMUS AB, Suunto USA is the North American distributor, No US address, 760-931-6788, www.suuntousa.com, Camping stoves.

PUR/KATADYN, 2229 Edgewood Ave. S., Minneapolis, MN 55426, 800-787-5463, www.purwaterfilter.com, Water filters.

RAICHLE, No US address, www.raichle.com or www.mammot.ch/Raichle, Boots.

RECREATIONAL EQUIPMENT INC./REI, Sumner, WA 98352-0001, 800-426-4840, www.rei.com, Full line of outdoor gear and clothing.

THE ROCKPORT COMPANY LLC, Rockport Customer Services, 60 N. Ronks Rd., Ronks, PA 17572, 866-290-6431, www.rockport.com, Boots.

SALOMON NORTH AMERICA, INC., 400 E. Main St., Georgetown, MA 01833, 800-225-6850, www.salomonsports.com, Boots.

SIERRA DESIGNS, 1255 Powell Street, Emeryville, CA 94608, 800-635-0461, www.sierradesigns.com, Sleeping bags, tents.

SILVA PRODUCTION, No US address, 800-572-8822, www.silvacompass.com, Compasses.

STEPHENSONS-WARMLITE, 22 Hook Rd., Gilford, NH 03246-6745, 603-293-8526, www.warmlite.com, Sleeping bags, sleeping pads, packs, tents.

SUPERFEET WORLDWIDE LLC, 1419 Whitehorn Street, Ferndale, WA 98248-8923, 800-634-6618, www.superfeet.com, Footbeds.

SUUNTO USA, 2151 Las Palmas Drive, Suite F, Carlsbad, CA 92009, 800-543-9124, www.suuntousa.com, Compasses.

SWEETWATER, INC., See CASCADE DESIGNS, INC.

TECNICA USA, 19 Commerce Ave., West Lebanon, NH 03784, 800-258-3897, www.tecnicausa.com, Boots.

TEVA SANDALS, See DECKERS OUTDOOR CORP.

THERM-A-REST, See CASCADE DESIGNS, INC.

THE TIMBERLAND COMPANY, 200 Domain Drive, Stratham, NH 03885, 800-445-5545, www.timberland.com, Outdoor clothing, boots.

TRAILS ILLUSTRATED, A division of National Geographic Society, 1145 17th Street NW, Washington, DC 20036-4688, 800-962-1643, www.trailsillustrated.com, maps, software.

VASQUE, 314 Main Street, Red Wing, MN 55066, 800-224-4453, www.vasque.com, Boots.

WESTERN MOUNTAIN SPORTS, 1025 S. Fifth Street, San Jose, CA 95112, 408-287-8944, www.westernmountaineering.com, Sleeping bags.

ZAMBERLAN MOUNTAINSPORT, REI distributor, No US address or telephone number, www.zamberlan.com, Boots.

# REFERENCES AND ADDITIONAL READING

American Red Cross, *Standard First Aid and Personal Safety*. New York, NY, Doubleday and Company Inc., 1993.

Armstrong, Betsey R., and Knox Williams, *The Avalanche Book*. Golden, CO, Fulcrum Publishing, 1992.

Axcell, Claudia, et al., *Simple Foods for the Pack: The Sierra Club Guide to Delicious Natural Foods for the Trail*. Sierra Club, 1986.

Ferguson, Michael, *GPS: Land Navigation*. Boise, ID, Glassford Publishing, 1999.

Graydon D, and K. Hanson, *Mountaineering: The Freedom of the Hills*. Seattle, WA, The Mountaineers, 1997.

Herzog, M., *Annapurna: Conquest of the First 8,000 Meter Peak*. London, The Reprint Society, 1952.

Kellstrom, Bjorn, *Be Expert With Map & Compass: The Complete Orienteering Handbook*. US Geological Survey & Orienteering Services, Macmillan, 1994.

LaChapelle, E.R., *ABC of Avalanche Safety*, Seattle, WA, 2d edition, The Mountaineers, 1985.

McHugh, Gretchen, *The Hungry Hiker's Book of Good Cooking*. New York, NY, Alfred A. Knopf, 1982.

Meuninck, Jim, *Edible Wild Plants & Useful Herbs: The Basic Essentials*. 1988.

Plowman, S.A., and D.L. Smith, *Exercise Physiology for Health, Fitness and Performance*. San Francisco, CA, Benjamin Cummings Press, 1998.

Prater, Gene (Dave Felkley, editor), *Snowshoeing*. Seattle, WA, The Mountaineers, 4th edition, 1997.

Prater, Yvonne, and Ruth Dyar Mendenhall, *Gorp, Glop & Glue Stew: Favorite Foods from 165 Outdoor Experts*. Seattle, WA, The Mountaineers, 1982.

Raleigh, Duane, *Knots & Ropes for Climbers*. Mechanicsburg, PA, Stackpole Books, 1998.

Selters, Andy, *Glacier Travel and Crevasse Rescue*. Seattle, WA, The Mountaineers, 2nd edition, 1999.

US Army, *US Army Survival Manual, FM21-76*. New York, NY, Dorset Press, 2002.

Wilkerson, James A. (editor), *Medicine for Mountaineering and Other Wilderness Activities*, Seattle, WA, The Mountaineers, 4th edition, 1992.

Wilkerson, James, A., Cameron C. Bangs, and John S. Hayward (editors), *Hypothermia, Frostbite, and Other Cold Injuries: Prevention, Recognition, and Prehospital Treatment*. Seattle, WA, The Mountaineers, 1986.

Williams, Jack, *The Weather Book*. Vintage Books, 1992.

# Index

CPR. *See* Cardiopulmonary Resuscitation

Crampons 87, 92, 229

CTL. *See* Central Trend Line of Travel

Cuts 201–203, 205

# D

Dead Reckoning 154, 169–170, 248

Declination. *See* Magnetic Declination

Depth Hoar 193, 248, 256

Diarrhea 214–216

Dogs 5, 197, 229, 238–239, 242

Double-Boots 94–95, 98–99

Down 21–23, 28–30, 35, 37, 40–42, 55, 58–63, 69–71, 79, 84, 88, 97, 99, 101, 103, 106, 108–109, 111, 114, 118, 122, 123–125, 129, 138–141, 151–154, 163, 172–173, 175, 179, 185, 188, 195, 206–208, 210, 221, 226, 228–229, 234, 238, 239, 249, 251, 256

# E

Elevation 13, 17–18, 21, 28, 46, 49, 138–143, 150, 151, 158, 163, 179, 211–213, 217, 234, 245, 247, 254, 256

Elevation Gain 13, 18, 21, 46, 138, 139

Emergencies 18, 20, 24, 67, 111, 162, 164, 171, 202, 215, 217

EMP. *See* Estimated Maximum Pulse

Equator 153, 156, 173–174, 249, 252, 255

Equinox 249

Equipment
checklist 7, 68
maintenance 66, 229
organization 2, 75, 202
storage 42, 53, 56–57, 70, 85, 106, 117, 156, 175, 215, 233

Estimated Maximum Pulse 49–50, 249, 252, 257

Etiquette 236, 238

Exercise 2, 6, 41–42, 44, 46–52, 198, 205–206, 224, 245, 247, 252, 257, 272

Exoskeleton Tent 120, 249

# F

Fatty Acids 42–43

Fill-Power 124, 125, 249

Filter Life 66, 128–130, 249

Fire ix, 18, 24, 53, 59, 62–64, 67–70, 99, 129, 132, 241, 261

First Aid 3, 18, 24, 69–70, 201–204, 207, 215–216, 218, 218–220, 240, 249, 271

First Aid Kit 18, 24, 69–70, 215–216, 218, 220

Flashlight 18–20, 66–70

Flood 190–192

Foam Pad. *See* Sleeping Pad

Food
storage 57, 70, 215
types 221

Foot Placement 28, 30–32, 34, 249, 256, 258

Frostbite 205, 209–211, 250, 272

Fuel
butane 129–130, 132
gas mixtures 132
kerosene 67, 70, 129–130, 133, 223
propane 129–130, 132
white gas 129–132, 211

# G

Giardiasis 214, 250

Giardia Lambia 65, 214, 250

Global Positioning System 151–157, 162, 250, 263–265, 271

Glucose 42–43

Glycogen 42–43

Goal 2, 5–8, 27, 35, 47, 105, 136–137

GPS. *See* Global Positioning System

GPS Receiver 152–156

Guidebook 234

## About the Authors

**Fred Baker** grew up in rural, southwest Wisconsin and spent much of his youth exploring the rivers, forests, caves and hills of the Midwest. Early travels in western North America and Europe confirmed his desire to work in and explore the outdoors, leading to an educational focus on geology and water resources throughout his university years in Wisconsin and Colorado. During this period, he was strongly influenced by the writings of Aldo Leopold, John Muir, and other nature and adventure writers. Given a choice between a research position at an eastern university and living in mountainous Colorado, he moved west to live near the wild mountains and forests that stirred his imagination. He completed his education with graduate degrees in civil engineering and hydrogeology. Dr. Baker pursued his career in environmental consulting in the states of Washington, California and Colorado, his present-day home. He has camped, backpacked, canoed, climbed and explored wild lands on four continents. He led an unsupported expedition across the Juneau Icefield in Alaska in 1985. He has also climbed numerous mountains in Europe and the Americas, and recently climbed Mt. Kilimanjaro in Africa.

**Hannah Pavlik** grew up on the Caribbean island of Trinidad where she first experienced nature on hikes in the jungles, mountains and seashores of her homeland. She traveled to the USA to pursue her university education and professional career as a geoscientist. Dr. Pavlik completed her education at the University of Colorado in geochemistry and shortly afterwards began a career in environmental consulting. Her scientific research and consulting have taken her to many wild and untrampled places throughout the western United States and Canada, where she has worked on projects to protect and restore our natural resources from the effects of mining and industrial pollution. Over the years she has waded through swamps, blazed trails through tropical vegetation, backpacked in mountain ranges in North and South America and explored wild and mountainous terrain on three continents in the pursuit of outdoor recreation and wildlife viewing.

CPSIA information can be obtained at www.ICGtesting.com
Printed in the USA
LVOW091701231111

256313LV00001B/133/A

9 781425 908676

JAN 2 4 2012